Reading and Writing Nature

Guy Rotella

READING & WRITING
NATURE

*The Poetry of
Robert Frost,
Wallace Stevens,
Marianne Moore,
and Elizabeth Bishop*

Northeastern University Press

BOSTON

Northeastern University Press

Copyright 1991 by Guy Rotella

Library of Congress Cataloging-in-Publication Data

Rotella, Guy L.
    Reading and writing nature.
    Includes bibliographical references and index.
    1. American poetry—20th century—History and
criticism.   2. Nature in literature.   3. Frost, Robert, 1874–
1963—Criticism and interpretation.   4. Stevens, Wallace,
1879–1955—Criticism and interpretation.   5. Moore,
Marianne, 1887–1972—Criticism and interpretation.
    6. Bishop, Elizabeth, 1911–1979—Criticism and
interpretation.   I. Title.
PS310.N3R68   1990   811'.520936   90-7576
ISBN 1-55553-086-9 (alk. paper)

Designed by Ann Twombly

This book was composed in Meridian by The Composing Room of
Michigan, Inc., Grand Rapids, Michigan. Printed and bound by
McNaughton & Gunn, Inc., in Saline, Michigan. The paper is Glatfelter,
Offset, an acid-free sheet.

MANUFACTURED IN THE UNITED STATES OF AMERICA
95 94 93 92 91   5 4 3 2 1

for Mary Jane

CONTENTS

PREFACE

IT HAS BEEN SAID that critics "make . . . fiction[s] to school the urgency of reading; no more." And, I suppose, no less. Here, my "fiction" is that Robert Frost, Wallace Stevens, Marianne Moore, and Elizabeth Bishop continue and contest the American tradition of turning to nature in order to pose epistemological and esthetic questions about how and how much we know and about the power of art and artists to discover or create meaning and form. The tradition is a familiar one: it begins with confidence that nature is a book inscribed by God for men and women to read; it "ends" with the suspicion that nature's many texts are written by ourselves on a blank page or a palimpsest. The initial confidence was always uneasy; the recent suspicion is sometimes a source of delight. What began as a search for the meaning of God now questions the meaning of meaning.

The first chapter is introductory and defines the context in which the chapters on individual poets are carried out. It traces aspects of American nature poetry from its Puritan beginnings through the practice of Emerson and Dickinson. This is in no way complete. For instance, I ignore the examples of Poe and Whitman, in the same way that by focusing on Frost, Stevens, Moore, and Bishop I ignore Eliot, Pound, H.D., and Williams (to give only a few and more or less canonical examples). My interest is in poets who have "mixed" attitudes toward the transcendent as truth or illusion, and toward nature as text or inscription—especially as those attitudes motivate a nature poetry that explores issues of knowledge and considers the potential and limitations of poetry to discover truth or to invent it. John Hollander has described such poets as evading "the consequences of visionary seriousness." That sounds like condemnation. It might be praise.

For the Puritans, the existence of a transcendent God was not in doubt, but God's transcendent presence was an absence by definition. Transcendence assured God's permanence and authority; it guaranteed that absolutes are absolute indeed. Puritan theology and polity required unbridgeable distance. But Puritan selves also desired a God sufficiently immanent that he might be believed in and loved as well as obeyed. Perhaps nature could provide for closer contact. Understood as the creation of God's originating Logos, nature was God's "work," his second book, a companion to the Bible. Nature could therefore be read for signs of God's presence and of his providential truth. This was attractive, especially given the Puritans' position in the natural landscape of "the new world garden." But there were dangers in turning to nature as a source of truth. If God became wholly immanent, both nature and human beings would seem to be divine; authority—in all its senses—would become relative, merely a matter of power, accident, or negotiation. Furthermore, both nature and humanity had fallen. No longer a garden, nature was at least in part the locus of evil, a "howling wilderness." The book of nature was obscured and defaced. Its readers were disabled and prone to errors of interpretation.

The Puritan "solution" to those conflicting needs and assumptions was a very delicate balance. Nature might be read for evidence of God's presence and truth, but only in ways sharply restricted to an elect readership and to a prior interpretative scheme encoded in the Bible, the method of type and antitype. Much, perhaps too much, has been written about the process by which that delicate balance slipped, about the ways in which authoritative and authoritarian typology shifted toward subjective, self-reliant tropology as the priority of Word to world was reversed and American consciousness proceeded from puritanism to transcendentalism and beyond. I discuss those issues again, I hope with the precision born of a sharp focus and with the nuance inherited from several generations of preliminary and revisionist scholarship.

Without claiming a single line or center, I trace the development of nature poetry from Anne Bradstreet and Edward Taylor, through the theology of Jonathan Edwards, to Emerson and Dickinson. In very general terms, Emerson believed in the ability of individuals to discover transcendent truths in nature, while Dickinson wrote a poetry of doubt. But eventually, by alternate routes (in his case by means of a radical epistemology of personal vision that he later began to doubt; in her case by means of a rigorously empirical and conservative Trinitarian typology that she practiced without the required benefit of "adjusted sight"), Emerson and Dickinson reached a shared "conclusion": both sought the truth in nature but suspected that the world we read is the world we write, that "knowledge" is an artifact that is humanly inscribed and humanly or otherwise erased.

The introduction also discusses the role of nature in American national life, including the tensions generated by its multiple conceptions as garden, wilderness, and rural "middle landscape," and by its becoming the national religion at the very moment when national achievement exacted its destruction. The introduction concludes by examining changes in American attitudes toward poetry and the poet from the time of the Puritans to the early twentieth century. For the Puritans, poetry was at worst a sensual snare, at best a didactic craft, and in any case peripheral and dependent. By the mid-nineteenth century, the poet had become a seer, poetry was a central mode of cognition with special access to absolute truths, and both poetry and poets had unprecedented social influence and value. By the early twentieth century, poetry was peripheral once more, a genteel irrelevance. Those developments are also part of the context in which Frost, Stevens, Moore, and Bishop began their work.

In discussing Emily Dickinson in the introduction, I shift my emphasis from intellectual and literary history to the poetry itself. This is also the method of the chapters on individual poets. Although contextual issues remain in play, the "argument" of those chapters is somewhat muted. There are several reasons for this. Frost, Stevens, Moore, and Bishop all resist conclusions, and I have wanted to honor that resistance. Theirs is a poetry of interrogation and exploration, not of resolution. Furthermore, beyond the general similarities that relate them to the issues taken up in the introduction, each of the four poets has diverse intellectual and esthetic assumptions. Recalling Frost's remark that he was "afraid of too much structure," and Bishop's claim that "the poet's concern is not consistency," I have tried to take each poet on his or her own terms. Thus, each chapter is independent of the others and uses critical strategies and vocabularies derived from the poet's work.

Nonetheless, the chapters are connected by a single context and perspective. Frost, Stevens, Moore, and Bishop all turn to nature in order to pose epistemological and esthetic questions. Each suspects that all readings of transcendence, whether based on the Word or the natural world, are humanly inscribed, and that poetry and the poet are therefore radically limited in their capacity to know and create. Yet each also continues the effort to discover or make meaningful patterns of order. Furthermore, each poet engages in that effort while simultaneously challenging the authority of every system of knowledge and of every work of art—including his or her own. All four poets affirm that the attempt to find or invent meaning is a vital and definitive human act (they are, at least to that degree, essentialists), yet each insists that the results of such attempts are at worst destructive frauds and at best conditional or "fictive" consolations, not redemptive truths. Each believes that if we are to live felicitous lives we require the provisional satisfactions that art and other cultural acts and structures provide, yet each remains subversively alert to the exclusion and oppression that occur when the provisional is taken as absolute and authoritative and is reified by power. Those and other similarities directly relate each poet to matters taken up in the introduction, and to one another.

The chapters on individual poets, then, are tailored to particular careers, but common considerations appear in all of them, although in varying degrees. For example, I explore each poet's intellectual and religious background and ascribe to each a particular mode of "natural supernaturalism" as one way of suggesting how traditional structures of transcendence survive and are challenged in his or her work—then I track those survivals and challenges through each poet's career. I discuss the tendency of each poet to employ and subvert traditional poetic forms. And I consider the proclivity of each to think of opposites as complementary rather than mutually exclusive terms. Perhaps the most important of these common considerations is the always implicit, sometimes explicit attempt to define each poet's place between a variously complete challenge to the formalist and logocentric tendencies of high modernism on the one hand, and a variously incomplete anticipation of post-modernist assumptions and devices on the other. This is especially apparent in discussions of analogy, of the ways in which each poet negotiates the competing claims of metaphorical and metonymic modes of representation—for Frost, Stevens, Moore, and Bishop all work in the space between reading and writing nature, between metaphysics and a poetry of earth.

A project of this sort incurs innumerable obligations. My most specific debts to scholars are acknowledged in the Notes; there are surely many others. I want to thank my teachers, especially Peter Fiore, Vianney Devlin, Leonard Casper, John Mahoney, Anne Ferry, and the late Samuel French Morse. Thanks, too, to my students, to Edward Doctoroff of Widener Library, and to my editor, Deborah Kops. To M. X. Lesser and Jon Lanham, cheers, with gratitude for the conversations—and the beers.

ACKNOWLEDGMENTS

The quotation from "Essay on Poetics" is from *Collected Poems 1951–1971* by A. R. Ammons. Copyright © 1972 by A. R. Ammons. Used by permission of W. W. Norton & Company, Inc.

Quotations from the poems of Emily Dickinson are reprinted by permission of the publishers and Trustees of Amherst College from *The Poems of Emily Dickinson*, edited by Thomas H. Johnson, Cambridge, Mass.: The Belknap Press of Harvard University Press, copyright 1951 © 1955, 1979, 1983 by the President and Fellows of Harvard College. Quotations from *The Complete Poems of Emily Dickinson*, edited by Thomas H. Johnson, copyright 1929, 1935 by Martha Dickinson Bianchi; © renewed 1957, 1963 by Mary L. Hampson. Reprinted by permission of Little, Brown and Company.

Quotations from *The Poetry of Robert Frost* edited by Edward Connery Lathem. Copyright 1916, 1923, 1930, 1934, 1939, 1947, © 1969. Copyright 1942, 1944, 1951, © 1958, 1962 by Robert Frost. Copyright © 1967, 1970, 1975 by Lesley Frost Ballantine. Reprinted by permission of Henry Holt and Company, Inc. Quotations from *Selected Prose of Robert Frost* edited by Hyde Cox and Edward Connery Latham. Copyright 1939, 1954, © 1966, 1967 by Holt, Rinehart and Winston, Inc. Copyright 1946, © 1959 by Robert Frost. Copyright © 1956 by the Estate of Robert Frost. Quotations from *Selected Letters of Robert Frost* edited by Lawrance Thompson. Copyright © 1964 by Lawrance Thompson and Holt, Rinehart and Winston, Inc. Quotations from *The Letters of Robert Frost to Louis Untermeyer*. Copyright © 1963 by Louis Untermeyer and Holt, Rinehart and Winston, Inc. All reprinted by permission of Henry Holt and Company, Inc.

Quotations from *The Collected Poems of Wallace Stevens*, *Opus Posthumous* and *The Necessary Angel* by Wallace Stevens and from *The Letters of Wallace Stevens*. Reprinted by permission of Alfred A. Knopf, Inc.

Quotations from the poetry of Marianne Moore are reprinted by permission of Macmillan Publishing Company from *Selected Poems* by Marianne Moore, copyright 1935 by Marianne Moore, renewed 1963 by Marianne Moore and T. S. Eliot, and from *Collected Poems* by Marianne Moore, copyright 1944, and renewed 1972, by Marianne Moore. Quotations from the poetry of Marianne Moore are reprinted by permission of Faber and Faber, Ltd. The quotation from "Tell Me, Tell Me" in *The Complete Poems of Marianne Moore*, copyright © 1960 by Marianne Moore and originally published in *The New Yorker*, reprinted by permission of Viking Penguin, a division of Penguin Books USA, Inc. Quotations from *The Complete Prose of Marianne Moore*, copyright © 1959, 1960, 1961, 1962, 1963, 1964, 1965, 1986 by Clive E. Driver, Literary Executor of the Estate of Marianne C. Moore, reprinted by permission of Viking Penguin, a division of Penguin Books USA, Inc. The quotation of "A Fool, A Foul Thing, A Distressful Lunatic" and the use of unpublished material by Marianne Moore are with the permission of Marianne Craig Moore, Literary Executor for the Estate of Marianne Moore. All rights reserved.

Quotations from *The Complete Poems, 1927–1979* by Elizabeth Bishop. Copyright © 1979, 1983 by Alice Helen Methfessel. Reprinted by permission of Farrar, Straus and Giroux, Inc. Quotations from *The Collected Prose* by Elizabeth Bishop. Copyright © 1984 by Alice Methfessel. Reprinted by permission of Farrar, Straus and Giroux, Inc. Quotations from the unpublished letters of Elizabeth Bishop are reprinted by permission of her Estate, copyright © 1989 by Alice Helen Methfessel.

Reading and Writing Nature

CHAPTER ONE

EVASIONS OF AS

IN HIS POEM "Essay on Poetics," A. R. Ammons describes reality as "abob with centers." One bobbing center of American poetry is its practitioners' persistent habit of writing about nature in order to engage epistemological and esthetic questions—questions about what, how, and how certainly we know, and questions about the power of poetry to discover meaning or to impose it. Despite the conventional wisdom, that habit endures in the works of many modern and postmodern American poets.

The American practice of writing nature poetry with epistemological and esthetic implications begins with the Puritans. For them the world is a cosmos, an orderly system whose meaning is guaranteed by God. The significance we come upon in nature has been placed there for us to discover. In finding it out we attain to knowledge of absolute truth (potentially, at least, given our fallen natures and a fallen world). For the Puritans, the word "invent" means "to discover." During the next several centuries, however, the Puritan confidence in God's guarantee erodes. By the nineteenth and twentieth centuries, faith in the correspondence between knowledge of the here and now and of an absolute beyond it is everywhere challenged and often lost. In the twentieth century, confidence that the metaphysical under-writes the physical is frequently replaced by a sense of the world as having no metaphysical dimension at all, as a place where meaning is "unspon-sored, free." For modern and postmodern writers, then, the word "invent" is less likely to have its old sense of "to discover," and more likely to have one or another of its two more common current senses: to create or con-struct by original thought or ingenuity; or, to contrive something false or fictitious, to fabricate, feign, or make up.

The loss of metaphysical confidence can be a happy or an unhappy occasion. Both current senses of "invent" locate the source of meaning in men and women, but with different emphases. The first definition is confident, even celebratory: liberated from the tyranny of the absolute, we become creators ourselves, free to make multiple truths. The second definition is marked by fear: without the guarantee of an absolute, our creations may be mere contrivances, ungrounded impositions of will or desire. Modern and postmodern American poets react to these matters in a variety of ways, anxious or otherwise. In doing so they continue to turn to nature to address their epistemological and esthetic questions. In this sense some of our finest twentieth-century poets, among them Robert Frost, Wallace Stevens, Marianne Moore, and Elizabeth Bishop, are nature poets (for whom "nature" ranges from wilderness to rural "middle landscapes," suburban yards, urban parks, and even the more fully framed "representations" of zoos or paintings or books).

The broad outlines of the epistemological and esthetic concerns of those poets appear in a passage from Wallace Stevens's "An Ordinary Evening in New Haven," a passage expressing confidence in the creative power of the human imagination when it is freed from constraining absolutes, and doubt about the significance of human constructions in a world from which absolutes have been withdrawn:

> A more severe,
>
> More harassing master would extemporize
> Subtler, more urgent proof that the theory
> Of poetry is the theory of life,
>
> As it is, in the intricate evasions of as,
> In things seen and unseen, created from nothingness,
> The heavens, the hells, the worlds, the longed-for lands.[1]

As he often did, Stevens posits a more-than-human human figure attaining proportions of mythic mastery in a godless world. That figure is a kind of "supreme poet," who would prove that poetry and life are one, who would, like God, create "things seen and unseen" ex nihilo, "from nothingness." Such creations would be exuberantly plural, producing an endless sequence of spontaneously generated constructions, "the heavens, the hells, the worlds, the longed-for lands." Still, however godlike those constructions might be, they would not be God's. Their extemporized plurality insures that they will be neither permanent, essential, nor absolute. Furthermore, their "creator" is less a living figure than a figment: a creation, a *proposed* creation, not a fact.

Those competing ideas and attitudes pivot on the issue of language. If the world is God's word, then it might be known. That belief has underwritten

Western science and art for centuries. The world contains, concealed, a mysterious but more or less knowable truth, or Logos, that it is our task and reward to reveal. But if the ground of God's word is removed, then the world is words, our words, and the same groundlessness that frees us to make our own meanings may make those meanings groundless. Thus Stevens's emphasis on the master's analogical, figurative means of proving and creating: "the intricate evasions of as."

On the one hand, the "as" by which the artist makes his figures is an escapist evasion, a contrivance concealing difference in assertions of similitude, a fabrication devising the false or fictitious. On the other hand, the "as" is what the mastering artist might evade, reaching essence through creation, a "place" where, in the words of the same poem, "as and is are one." Yet the only guarantee for that "invented" equation would be the artist's guarantee (and an imagined artist's, at that). So, while "evasions of as" might liberate us from delusively authoritative (and authoritarian) singular systems into the pluralistic free play of human system making, they might also snare us in a maze of competing systems, with no grounds for choice, commitment, or belief, where knowledge is only a fiction among fictions.

Of course, Stevens's words are themselves an intricate evasion, subtle in their urgency and resistance, jittery stuff for all their equable syntax. Stevens does not choose between, resolve, or even quite frame the polarities mentioned. Aware of other issues and other compensations, he presents them conditionally, sketching the contours of modern and postmodern versions of an old American mode: How do we know what we know? Is poetry most true or most feigning? Do we find or falsify, discover or invent? Hyatt Waggoner puts it this way: "From the beginning, the most representative American poets have anticipated the characteristic that more than anything else distinguishes the American poetry of our own day from that of the past and of other societies: in it *nothing* is known, nothing given, everything is discovered or created, or else remains in doubt."[2] From that position, American poets, modern and postmodern ones from this urban century, as well as Puritans, transcendentalists, and "realists," have turned to nature to begin.

God's Back Parts

At a critical moment in the book of Exodus, after the episode of the Golden Calf and the "breaking" of the first set of commandments, the transcendent God of Israel (whose manifestations of immanence usually take the form of visible radiance) speaks to Moses "face to face, as a man speaketh unto his friend." The anthropomorphic quality of God's immanence here is emphasized in the reassertion of his transcendence that follows. Speaking to Moses "face to face," God tells him, "Thou canst not see my face: for there shall no man see mee, and live. . . . I will put thee in a clift of the rocke, and will cover thee with my hand, and thou shalt see my backe parts: but my face shall not be seen." From this remove, Moses will mediate between God and his chosen people. Their distance from God is now immense, for God punishes the Israelites' breaking of covenant by withdrawing his presence, refusing to go up to Canaan with them: "I will not goe up in the midst of thee: for thou art a stiffenecked people, lest I consume thee in the way." But God's withdrawal is not complete. Moses will still see him, and God promises the people an angel in his stead. Furthermore, God's absence is also an act of kindness, an accommodation calculated to spare the Israelites the apocalyptic consequences of both his righteous anger and his transcendent glory.

The New England Puritans conceived of themselves as God's newly chosen people, and of their theocratic leaders and elect individuals as so many Moseses. For them the existence of the transcendent God is an unquestionable given. *That* knowledge is unshakeably certain. Matters of immanence are less assured. As a result of the primal breaking of covenant, the Fall, God's anthropomorphic presence is gone from the world. That presence was crucially renewed in the saving incarnation of Christ, and its return is guaranteed in the promise of the Second Coming, but for now God is invisible; his people, like the Israelites before them, are profoundly distant from him. Still, and again like the Israelites, they are not wholly abandoned. Their accommodating God has inscribed himself in the Bible and in his second book, the creation. Because the people are fallen, the signs are hard to read and can be vanishingly faint: the transparency of the Bible is somewhat lost to them, leaving their reading of it open to error; as for the creation, not only is nature's transparency lost to men and women, nature itself is fallen and therefore obscured, its legibility reduced. Nonetheless, the Puritans preserve relative confidence in the power of *regenerate* souls to read God's word and world aright. If they cannot see God "face to face," they can see his "backe parts" (now understood more figuratively than literally or anthropomorphically). Of course, interpretation is hardly secure. Human knowledge is radically limited, and it is impossible for any individual to attain reliable knowledge of election, the prerequisite for confident reading.

These apparent contradictions give rise to the standard version of Puritan attitudes toward nature and poetry. Since nature is God's creation, it has potential value as a repository of his truth. However, access to that truth is blocked by epistemological obstacles: nature's fallen condition and humanity's weakened faculties. Fallen nature is suspect, associated with evil, sin, and temptation. Its appeal is to the senses, which are subject to error in their fallen state, and which distract us from higher things. According to the standard view, then, Puritan respect for nature as God's handiwork and as a source of knowledge was overcome by *contemptus mundi*. As to poetry, the Puritans supposedly distrusted it with an anti-esthetic iconoclasm born of the commandment against graven images and part of the general Protestant reaction against what they considered to be Roman Catholic idolatry—a confusion of sign with substance that threatened to dilute or dissolve transcendence, and that smacked of a presumptuously prideful claim to share in the act of creation reserved to God. What poetry the Puritans produced despite their iconoclasm they supposedly wrote while begrudging its artistry. Thus, as with their churches, they stripped poetry to a plain style best suited to the expression of religious truth, placing all their emphasis on doctrine and admiring verse only because of its didactic utility for inculcating dogma.

That view is a caricature. Recent scholarship, particularly the work of Robert Daly, Mason Lowance, and Michael Clark,[3] shows that the Puritans did not so much despise poetry as insist that it be reconciled with truth. Having moderated their iconoclasm by a finely drawn distinction between the proscribed worshipping of images for their own sake and the approved making of images for God's greater glory, they believed that the fancifulness and error to which art is subject could be controlled and that art could act in the service of truth. This belief was upheld by fundamental Puritan conceptions of nature and of the artist, conceptions that, at least in principle, resolved the tensions implied above.

In Daly's convincing argument, the Puritans were neither Gnostics nor Manichaeans. Their universe was unitary. While they posited a radical gap between the transcendent God and his immanent creation, they perceived the relation of spirit to matter as hierarchical rather than dualistic. Nature is fallen, but it is not the product of an evil creator nor itself evil. Although the gap between nature and its creator remains, God is reflected in his creation: nature's beauty, for instance, mirrors God's infinitely greater beauty. Nature *is* different from spirit, but only in degree, not in kind. The muted intensity of nature's reflection of the divine is the result of the Fall, and a sorrowful fact. But when viewed in the light of accommodation, muted intensity is a gift. It preserves us from destruction by the infinite glory of God's fully revealed face and grants us glimpses of his back parts, glimpses as awesomely intense as our fallen faculties can bear. Thus, the Puritans maintain their sense of God as radically transcendent without losing touch with signs of his presence in created nature.

In this view, natural facts are real, and they have meanings that point to the absolute realm beyond them. Those meanings are not the result of human fancy or creativity. Humans do not make meaning; they perceive it. In keeping with the Puritan notion of nature as God's book, meaning is already present there, inscribed by God. The task of the regenerate soul is to observe that meaning. If the regenerate soul is a poet, he or she has the additional task of conveying that meaning to others. For the Puritans, the poet is not an individual genius who creates meaning, but God's instrument, who participates not in God's creative word (his Logos) but in his accommodated word, his use of nature and scripture to manifest and explain his presence at a degree of intensity in keeping with human frailty. Seen in this way, poetry is an extension of the sanctioned traditions of meditation, with their practice of the verbal development of observed truths. This gives poetry its value in the Puritan economy of thought.

Puritan confidence that God has invested nature with instituted meanings is doubly warranted: by the incarnation, which bridged the gap between invisible and visible worlds by making spirit flesh, and by the revealed word of scripture, which repeatedly asserts the correspondence of the visible and the invisible. Scripture also provides an interpretative key to reading God's hieroglyphic marks in nature, and an exemplary deployment of esthetic forms and figures that the poet can imitate in transmitting the meaning of those marks to others. Thus, while the Puritans do practice *contemptus mundi*, insist on a plain style, fear graven images, and suspect their own claims of election, they also retain faith in nature's partial legibility, in the power of the elect and of the elect poet to read evidence of God's truth in nature, and in the power of poetry to convey that truth by means of sensuous images and appeals.[4] For the Puritans, then, "invention" is a matter of discovering the meaning placed in the world by God. The poet's discovery is controlled by scripture and is held in common with all of the elect. The poet's special task is to convey that discovery with an artfulness that serves its truth and that does not succumb to the temptation of "ornament."

The sort of poetry such views can support is limited. The poet is free to turn to nature in search of knowledge, but the range of his or her freedom is narrowly bound by the insistence that nature is a drama scripted by God and that the interpretative key to the drama's meaning is already present in the revealed codes of the Bible. The poet, to repeat, is a craftsmanlike conveyer of observed truths already inscribed in the world, not an imaginative perceiver or maker with a share in the creation of those truths. Furthermore, for the Puritans, the polysemous reading of natural facts available to Catholic interpretative traditions and to the artists who followed them is reduced to single and predictable correspondences. Charles Feidelson provides a prose example in his discussion of a passage from John Winthrop's journal. Winthrop records one of those unusual events that the Puritans defined as "remarkable providences," special manifestations in the natural world of God's ever-present purposes. During an elder's sermon to the synod at Cambridge, a snake appeared behind the pulpit, where it was killed. Winthrop's application of the biblical codes is swift and sure. The event may be singular, but its meaning is single, simple, and clear beyond doubt to the regenerate sensibility. "This being so remarkable, and nothing falling out but by divine providence, it is out of doubt, the Lord discovered somewhat of his mind in it. The serpent is the devil; the synod, the representatives of the churches of Christ in New England. The devil had formerly and lately attempted their disturbance and dissolution; but their faith in the seed of the woman overcame him and crushed his head." Similar interpretations occur again and again in Puritan writing, and what Feidelson calls their "queer leap from fact as fact to fact as meaning" can seem comically mechanical. Nonetheless, as Feidelson goes on to say, the Puritan habit of welding objective experience to the assured meaningfulness of the Bible maintained the possibility of both epistemological attention to nature *and* the making of poems. It also provided the ground from which a richer, more troubled American art would spring.[5]

The epistemological and esthetic range of Puritan nature poetry is illustrated in Anne Bradstreet's "Contemplations." She begins by describing the brightly colored trees of a New England fall:

> Their leaves and fruits seem'd painted, but was true
> Of green, of red, of yellow, mixed hue,
> Rapt were my sences at this delectable view.

Bradstreet's Puritan suspicion of sensory snares ("seem'd painted") is overcome by her genuine delight in natural beauty. However, the ultimate source of her rapture proves to be less nature itself than the meaning nature signifies. She trusts her response to the "delectable view" primarily because the sensuous appeals of nature provide fallen men and women with present knowledge of their transcendent God.

> If so much excellence abide below;
> How excellent is he that dwells on high?
> Whose power and beauty by his works we know.
> Sure he is goodness, wisdom, glory, light,
> That hath this underworld so richly dight.

Nature's value is as a sign of God's virtues. However richly attired the "underworld" may be, it remains a poor second to the "overworld." Cold winters and dark nights make it painfully clear that the present world is no paradise; it is a "Fond fool" who "takes this earth . . . for heav'ns bower." Still, Bradstreet lovingly describes other natural delights: an ancient oak, the sun, insect and bird song, frisky fish, a river's swelling course to the sea. But each natural fact is quickly displaced by the abstraction it suggests, the abstraction it exists in order to suggest. For instance, the river's rush to dissolve in the engulfing sea signals the soul's urgent desire to merge with God. Less pleasantly, the strength and age of oak and sun indicate human weakness and impermanence. Still, there are other measures of brevity; the long-lived oak and the sun also point to the ultimate superiority of the human over the natural, that is, the superiority of spirit to matter:

> . . . they shall darken, perish, fade, and dye,
> And when unmade, so ever shall they lye,
> But man was made for endless immortality.[6]

Bradstreet does not deny the pleasures of the flesh and the world, but she insists that those pleasures are to be enjoyed less for their own sake than for their meaning: spiritual pleasures, unchangeable and unmarred by pain, are infinitely superior to physical ones. God's back parts, glimpsed in nature as both presence (beauty and strength) and absence (change and death), hint at the eternal glory of the promised vision of his face. That accommodated and accommodating fact is nature's essential worth.

Given this view, Bradstreet's sense of the poet's role is predictably circumscribed. Her task is to "resound" her "maker's praise," and to do so while humbly denying her skill: "But Ah, and Ah, again, my imbecility!" Signs of God's truth are inscribed in nature. Within her limits the poet can confidently read them there (thus her song is a re-sounding). But her poetry can convey only a diminished version of his grandeur. Nature and poetry give pleasure. Those pleasures are good; they provide comfort and knowledge. But nature, poetry, and pleasure are corrupted if they become ends in themselves. Their purpose, and justification, is in pointing beyond.

Bradstreet's poem is as doctrinally correct as Winthrop's exegesis. Still, her reading of natural events extends beyond "remarkable providences" and is less tightly tied to biblically sanctioned codes than his is. Winthrop's seducing serpent-Satan and snake-crushing heel have specific scriptural analogues. Bradstreet's interpretation of nature's text is less anchored, more individual and inventive. Here is the enemy within, the threat at the heart of Puritan epistemological and esthetic thinking, a danger the Puritans were deeply aware of and struggled to control. Protestant purifications of too proudly "creative" Catholic exegetical and artistic practices ran the risk of making God's character and his providential behavior utterly inaccessible to human knowledge. Art could help bridge the gap, but the reformers were sure that the unbridled exercise of human creativity would reduce God to all too human dimensions, dooming humanity to prideful error and to the damning worship of idolatrous substitutes for transcendent divinity. The Puritan solution to this dilemma was the famous device of type and antitype.

Typology had been part of Roman Catholic practice and was variously restricted or free to move toward creative allegorizing, but until the Reformation it was only one in a battery of available epistemological and esthetic weapons. For the Puritans, typology, its range tightly bracketed, would be the entire arsenal. The enormous value of typology to Puritan thought is that the types and antitypes exist in history, the revealed history of scripture. Unlike humanly invented tropes, their reality and meaning are sanctioned by God; their proper analogical relationships are already clarified by the divinely inspired authors of scripture: Moses is type, Christ is antitype; Canaan is type, millennial paradise is antitype; and so on. In theory, then, typology is a closed system, secure from idolatrous innovation. It describes and explains an already completed relationship between the Old Testament and the New. In practice things are not so precise. The Old and New Testaments are related by the method of Hebrew prophecy as well as by typology. With its emphasis on future fulfillment, prophecy modifies the assumption that all types have already been consummated in their antitypes and extends such consummation into the future.

The sense of typology as a closed system was further modified by the special character of the Puritans' experience. Their thorough grounding in Biblical imagery and story joined with the facts of their history to make a typological reading of the Puritan present all but inevitable. Their oppression and exile seemed a new Israelite captivity, embarkation for America a new Exodus, the difficult journey a new wandering in the wilderness, arrival and settlement a new entry into (New) Canaan. The psychological, spiritual, and theocratic values of this extension of typological practice were generally too great for the Puritans to resist it. Some Puritan thinkers did insist that the typological dispensation had been completed and abolished by the incarnation, death, and resurrection of Jesus Christ; most maintained that Puritan historical experiences were divinely composed parallels to the experiences of the Hebrews. Puritan history was to be understood and explicated in terms of biblically actual types. This would be done by extending into the present biblically sanctioned analogical methods, methods through which one literal reality explains the significance of another and lodges it in a divinely revealed and developing continuum, the thrust of which is toward fulfillment.[7]

The momentum of this expanded application of typological practice often encouraged Puritan poets to discover typological significance not only in general Puritan history but also in their personal lives and in their interactions with the variously hellish and Edenic natural reality of the new world.[8] In theory, idolatrously allegorical interpretations were avoided by the strict limitation of typological practice to those historical, domestic, or natural events known as "remarkable providences" and as amenable to scriptural explanation as Winthrop's snake. In practice, the pressures of faith often caused poets and other commentators to exceed those limits. In any case, in nature poetry, as elsewhere, the challenge was the same: to retain typology's value as a sanctioned method for discovering and setting forth evidence of God's presence and purpose in this world without succumbing to the temptation of mistaking fanciful human inventions *for* such discoveries. Especially for poets, the danger is that analogizing will slip over into figures beyond the biblical, historical, and factual—into figures invented by human ingenuity and signifying what human fancy dictates rather than what God has inscribed.

Most Puritan poets managed to hold the line, but they sometimes did so more by the correctness of their doctrine than by limiting themselves entirely to instituted figures. As a minister, Edward Taylor was relentlessly orthodox, and he usually employed divinely ordained types in the imagery of his poems. Yet Taylor could be remarkably baroque in his inventive elaboration of those types: in "The Reflexion," for instance, a rose (a type of Christ) is depicted as carving meat at table.[9] Furthermore, like Bradstreet and other Puritan poets, Taylor sought "typical" analogues of divine truth in ordinary experience. He was confident that God had invested all his creation with meaning, confident enough to clarify the action of grace by comparing it with beer.[10] In a few of his poems, Taylor expanded typological practice by extending it to facts and events in nature, again developing his own figures for discovering God's truth.

"Upon a Spider Catching a Fly" describes the behavior of a spider as it responds to the appearance in its web of a wasp and a fly. The wasp is treated with almost tender deference, since the spider respects its capacity to destroy the web. The fly is easy prey and is quickly dispatched. Taylor renders the details with a naturalist's precision, but when he applies them, in an elaborate analogy for humanity's relationship to God, he retrospectively alters the facts to fit his doctrinal purposes. Nature and empiricism have a place in the Puritan epistemological hierarchy, but it is a relatively low place. In Taylor's analogy the spider is a devil with multiple stratagems for ensnaring souls, especially souls that sin has made as weak as flies. The wasp is God, whose power frees us from the devil's snares by breaking the cords of his web. In a final, violently metaphysical twist, the soul is transformed from an insect into a bird, and God from a web-wrecking wasp into the maker and keeper of a cage in which the captive bird is content to sing (God's grace having taught the soul to find freedom in limitation, contentment in bending its will to God's).[11]

Karl Keller describes Taylor as a fairly conventional typologist, whose enthusiastic and inventive "stretching" of types nevertheless "assisted him in probing the nature of reality," allowing him to discover the continuity of individual human and natural experience with divine experience. Taylor's "consciousness of self and his recognition of the fantastic variety of correspondences of self with Nature" makes him "a first, small version of Emerson." He finds in nature a divinity that unifies it and gives it meaning. The world thus "takes on glory to him, has a place for him in its order, and gives the specific realities of his life a spiritual dimension." Keller concludes that Taylor's method of discovering the spiritual dimension in ordinary experience and in nature extends typology to the point where it portends transcendentalist epistemology and esthetics.[12]

Axis of Vision, Axis of Things

Excavating the Puritan past to uncover sources of romantic symbolism has been an obsessive pursuit of American literary scholarship. Driven by what Lawrence Buell calls "the myth of Puritan antecedence,"[13] that pursuit has often involved what now seem dubious metaphors of national character, continuity, development, and destiny, as well as an all too narrowly canonical sense of what qualifies as American literature. Nonetheless, the primary insights of Perry Miller, Charles Feidelson, and others into the connections between Puritan typological procedures and transcendentalist symbolic practice remain illuminating.[14] If they no longer light up all of American literary and cultural history, and must now be understood in less uniform and inclusive terms than they once were, those insights are still essential to a discussion of what might be called epistemological nature poetry. Whether or not we concur with Keller in adding Edward Taylor to the list of Puritan antecedents of transcendentalist thought, the transformation of typology into romantic troping affects the writing of American poets who emphasize epistemological issues and turn to nature to explore those issues and their esthetic implications.

Literary archaeologists tracing the transformation of typology into tropology often focus on the work of Jonathan Edwards, particularly that portion of his work that concerns issues of analogy. In spite of his fundamental conservatism, Edwards continued into the eighteenth century the effort implied by the contractual emphasis of seventeenth-century New England covenant theology, that is, the attempt to modify the utterly arbitrary God of Calvinism in such a way as to exonerate both reason and nature as sources of truth.[15] David Lawrence has recently offered an emphatic reformulation of that essential fact. "Edwards' main literary task," Lawrence writes, "was to construct a figurative scheme in which a God whose natural form is naturalistic force is transformed into a God whose spiritual and human form is love."[16] Again, Edwards's eighteenth-century errand recapitulates a seventeenth-century one: the attempt to develop an epistemology that would retain the sense of God as a radically transcendent being, while still providing sufficient contact with his presence to make practical life—and even belief itself—possible. Edwards's approach to that task again involved the use of types. At times, he tested the limits of typological application to

see how much stretching the types could sustain without becoming idol-
atrous. In this sense, Lawrence is right to describe Edwards's project as the
construction of a "figurative scheme." But insofar as the phrase implies a
conscious and deliberately metaphorical re-creation of God in terms more
nearly fitting humanity's image (an essentially romantic model), it may be
an exaggeration. For Edwards, as for his Puritan forebears, the issue of
whether the figures' inventions are discoveries or impositions remained
crucial. This is the source of Edwards's importance here. And although his
influence is more obviously epistemological than esthetic, even in that he
prefigures a long line of American writers who were, in Buell's deft phrase,
more interested in perfecting their epistemology than their plots or pentam-
eters.[17]

A common (if narrow) concern of Edwards scholarship has been deter-
mining the extent to which he holds to or deviates from the Puritan ty-
pological line and, therefore, the extent to which his thinking anticipates
transcendentalism. The arguments have been many; the conclusions, var-
ied. The issue is unresolved. However, the terms of the argument are signifi-
cant. The test case for Edwards's view of such matters has typically been his
Images or Shadows of Divine Things, a collection of brief passages in which the
analogical principles of typology are extended to natural phenomena. Perry
Miller published his edition of Edwards's manuscript in 1948; his introduc-
tion begins with a distinction between types and tropes. Arguments about
the relationship of Puritan typology to transcendentalist symbolism turn on
that distinction.

Where the type depends on historical and horizontal development (from
the Old Testament to the New, from scriptural to Puritan history), the trope
depends on an essentially neo-Platonic metaphysics that is neither historical
nor horizontal. The conception of the physical world as a symbol of the
spiritual world above or beyond it encourages vertical figurative readings of
experience and nature that are not grounded in the literalness of scriptural
or historical fact (that is, transcendentalist symbols). Such readings—which
could be extremely inventive, yet might still be reined in by doctrinal
truth—had characterized the so-called allegorical emphases of medieval
Catholicism. They were rejected by the Reformation because of their pride-
ful creativity and because, in their lack of firm footing on the rock of in-
stituted scriptural reality, they were liable to subjectivity and error. Thus the
Puritans denigrated the trope and privileged the type. Nonetheless, the de-
sire to preserve some contact with God and to retain reason and nature as
sources of knowledge caused Puritan poets and exegetes to expand ty-
pological practice to include not only their own general history but also their
personal experiences in domestic and natural spheres. Those expansions ran
the risk of slipping from typology back into tropology. Thus, conservative

modes of exegesis, which insisted on an absolute limitation of typological practice to the Old and New Testaments, and liberal modes of exegesis, which favored an extension of the types to Puritan, personal, and natural history, were "constantly at war during the late seventeenth and early eighteenth centuries."[18]

In his introduction to *Images or Shadows of Divine Things*, Miller argues that Edwards believed liberal exegesis had strayed too far in the direction of tropology and had tumbled over into idolatrous luxuriance. According to this view, Edwards stood toward the liberal typologists of his day (who were too nearly tropologists) as the Protestant reformers had stood toward the medieval scholastics. His goal—part of his larger attempt to restore Calvinist orthodoxy to New England in a kind of second Reformation—was chastisement of the tropes and clarification of the types.[19] Mason Lowance, in the revisionist discussion of *Images or Shadows* in his *The Language of Canaan*, offers a more nuanced version. He agrees with Miller that Edwards was a conventional typologist, and that he recognized the danger of too-liberal exegesis, but Lowance is convinced that Edwards's effort and achievement in *Images or Shadows* is not the reestablishment of conservative typology, but the reconciliation of the opposed modes. According to Lowance, Edwards effected this reconciliation by transforming the types so that nature was added to scripture as a source of revelation. While Edwards endorsed the extremely traditional positions of Reformation Calvinism when it came to human "sinfulness and God's restorative grace," in his epistemological writings "the concern with God's accommodation of the divine idea through a natural revelation" is strong enough that he may sometimes "be viewed as supportive of . . . liberal typology."

Lowance charts the varieties of Edwards's typology from the conservatism of *A History of the Work of Redemption*, through the intermediate stage of the "Miscellaneous Notebooks," to the relative liberalism of *Images or Shadows*. In the "Miscellaneous Notebooks" Edwards goes beyond "the historical scheme established between the two testaments," which he used in *A History*, and "embraces the correspondences between external representations and the spiritual ideas they shadow forth." His deliberate application of "the nomenclature of orthodox typology" to "allegorical correspondence" "opened the floodgates for the interpretation of the universe in terms of types . . . and antitypes." Edwards further extends this application in *Images or Shadows*, where he uses "the framework of typological exegesis" to interpret impressions he received from nature. "The nomenclature of orthodox typology is employed throughout, but the intention of the 'exegete' is clearly to expand the boundaries of scriptural typology."[20]

Miller also notes this development, but he sees Edwards's use of the typological framework as an attempt to clarify the types and to bring New

England exegetical practice back from tropology. For Lowance, Edwards's expanded application of the types has quite different consequences. By establishing in *Images or Shadows* a system of analogy "through which natural objects have spiritual counterparts in the allegorical fashion" (so that a silkworm is a figure of Christ), Edwards leaves "little room for the . . . historical relation between the type and its antitype" on which conventional typology depends. He gains thereby a "method of reading nature that should supplement scripture." He does so by returning to a "medieval habit of mind by which the physical universe was believed to represent the spiritual in a Platonic or neo-Platonic fashion." In other words, in his "repeated insistence that the natural universe was not only a type of Christ . . . but might also be a direct reflection" of him, Edwards comes near to practicing tropology while chastising it.[21]

Whether we accept Miller's or Lowance's conclusions about Edwards's expansion of typology in *Images or Shadows*, the issues and problems Edwards faces there remain largely the ones that confronted his Puritan predecessors. His epistemological difficulty is still to discover the actual presence of God in nature without imposing that presence in terms suiting his own will and desire. To solve that problem, Edwards applied the ancient tools of typology, but also every contemporary intellectual instrument available to him. One of those instruments, the new epistemology of empirical science, actually intensified Edwards's desire to accommodate nature to scripture. Empiricism encouraged close attention to the natural world and seemed to promise the discovery of new and convincing evidence that would confirm the truths of God's presence and purpose already known from scripture and by means of faith and grace. Similarly, Edwards made use of Lockean psychology and philology, brilliantly reimagining them so as to fuse abstract ideas (God's power, say) with individual emotions (a personal response to a thunderstorm, for instance).[22] In a sense, those applications sprung a trap. In *Without God, Without Creed*, James Turner shows the degree to which religion made unbelief possible, therefore contributing to its own decline, precisely by making common cause with alien standards of truth. Because the theologians were so thoroughly confident of God's existence, they were certain that nature, science, and reason would inevitably discover further evidence of that existence. The attractions of empirical evidence for supplementing faith were so great that the implicit weakening of transcendence (the tendency to equate God with his creation) seemed a negligible price to pay for the potential gains in conviction. Eventually, though, empiricism would come to make faith, scripture, and even God himself seem unnecessary.[23]

Edwards was more aware of this danger than most theologians of his day, and he fought back mightily, retaining Calvinist notions of transcendence

bing spirit." He did so by joining the old Puritan interest in finding a way to hold communion with nature to the new attention to nature urged by empirical thought. Thus he combatted the dry chill of Calvinism *and* of Boston rationalism, finding in nature "a dynamic world, filled with the presence of God, quickened with divine life, pervaded with joy and ecstasy." He hoped he did so without falling into the snare of tropological mysticism, an error he resisted by maintaining the priority of scripture and by insisting that human depravity is as clearly inscribed in nature as is God's glory.

Whether or not Edwards kept this difficult balance is arguable. In either case, "implicit in the texture, if not in the logic, of his thought" are ideas that lead to conclusions the reverse of his own. Miller puts it this way: "If God is diffused through nature, and the substance of man is the substance of God, then it may follow that man is divine, that nature is the garment of the Over-Soul, that man must be self-reliant, and that when he goes into the woods the currents of Being will indeed circulate through him." Edwards would have damned such conclusions, but, for less rigorous minds than his, Edwards's strategies for holding immanence and transcendence in balance could seem to lead inevitably to those results. As Miller says, all that prevented such deductions "was the orthodox theology, supposedly derived from the word of God, which taught that God and nature are not one, that man is corrupt and his self-reliance is reliance on evil. But take away the theology, remove this overlying stone of dogma from the well-springs of Puritan conviction, and both nature and man become divine."[24] Whether we agree with Miller that Edwards was the last figure with sufficient intellectual and spiritual force to keep the stone in place, or with Lowance in seeing Edwards as loosening the stone Emerson would lift away, Edwards provides the connection between Puritan and transcendentalist epistemologies. As did the Puritans before him, Edwards turned to nature to consider what, how, and how certainly we know. Emerson would turn there, too, rewriting the questions as well as the answers and redefining their esthetic implications.

It is a short step from Edwards to Emerson, but several planks would have to be set in place before the step could be taken. Perhaps this is the wrong analogy; we are as likely to be dealing here with punctuated as with gradual evolution. Edwards's influence on Emerson was not particularly direct. It would be conveyed by way of the Scottish Enlightenment philosophers, and then transformed by German and English idealists, especially Coleridge, before Emerson could receive it. By then, a number of other developments had occurred. Orthodox theology *had* been taken away, at least for the transcendentalists. They would repeat Edwards's resistance to Boston rationalism, but in radically altered terms, setting intuition against empiricism and its materialist epistemological, social, and political values. In doing so, the transcendentalists would jettison other conventions as well. For them, traditional theology was a dead, or dying, issue. Jesus was just another man, although a most remarkable one; evil was no longer a palpable, terrifying, or even chastening presence, but the mere absence of good or a failure of vision; history, which along with scripture had provided the guarantee of access to truth on which conservative typology rested, was now an obscuring obstacle to the direct cognition of truth; the Bible was just another book.

The priority of the Word to the world, on which Calvinist theology and its rigorous or tenuous control over natural revelation had depended, was turned upside down. In their varying degrees, the Puritans and Edwards had welcomed "natural theology" insofar as it supported scripture. Emerson, in an unanticipated development of Edwards's view that if "scripture types were to persevere, they must be accommodated in the light of natural revelation,"[25] made natural revelation the test of scriptural validity. Emerson followed Edwards in using the attention to nature demanded by empirical science as a means of resisting the deadening materialism to which science and its theological and technological applications supposedly led. But what Emerson did in the name of spirit was precisely what Calvinist spiritualism had most feared. In its full-blown form Emerson's transcendentalism reduced the distance between the transcendent God and his human and natural creations to the vanishing point. There spirit and matter were joined, humans and nature were one with the divine, and God was again seen face to face. Of course, there are even more Emersons than Edwardses. Still, in one of those Emersons the long American opposition of spirit and matter was momentarily resolved.

This is not the place to tell again the story of transcendentalism and its American and European relations. Still, a few reminders are in order. The epistemological problem, the problem of knowledge, had become central to Western thought with Descartes's division of reality into knowing subject and known object. This partition divided not only reality but the act of knowing as well, since in Cartesian terms knowing becomes a relation between subject and object. Thus, as Feidelson puts it, the question arises as to whether "there can be any integral act of knowledge at all." A number of responses were attempted in the seventeenth, eighteenth, and nineteenth centuries. They can be subsumed under three headings. Materialism gave priority to the object and made the perceiving subject a more or less passive receptor of sense impressions. Idealism gave priority to mind and made the perceiving self an active participant in producing the sensory object. In literary terms, materialism would lead to realism and naturalism; idealism, to romanticism. The third response to the problem of knowledge was symbolism. Unlike materialism and idealism, symbolism attempted to solve the problem by getting outside the dualism that defined it. As a new starting point, symbolism is "both philosophical and literary." It "is designed to recapture the unity of a world artificially divided." Symbolism is typically a modernist stance, yet, as Feidelson makes clear, it affects major aspects of nineteenth-century American literary thought and practice. In essence, symbolism assumes the existence of "concrete facts" "into which both mind and matter enter as relative terms." In the versions of this fusing of mind and matter that accept language as integral rather than as external to reality, words and their syntax become "vehicles for the conception of objects," and all three terms, language, conceiving mind, and conceived objects, are "felt as aspects of a single process of meaning." Although Emerson and transcendentalism are typically idealist in orientation, at times the Emerson who transformed Edwards was a symbolist. In this, his position is somewhat different from romantic egoism and adumbrates certain strains of modernism.[26]

Before we proceed to the symbolist Emerson, another matter needs remarking. M. H. Abrams has pointed out the romantic tendency to collapse the three primary terms or elements of traditional Christian thought (God, human souls, and nature) into the two terms of post-Cartesian philosophy—mind and nature, or subject and object. In the Christian formulation, God is origin, omnipotent controller, and final goal of the other two elements, humanity and nature. The romantic revision of this view, in the de- and re-mythologizing conservative revolution Abrams characterizes as "natural supernaturalism," tends to eliminate God. But it does so in a way that assimilates rather than deletes him. In extreme secular renditions of this essentially idealist formulation, the prepotency of God is taken over by mind or spirit, which now performs "the initiative and functions" that were once "the prerogative of deity." The goal of this secularized Christianity is to return regenerate humanity to a renewed world in which a lost primal unity (as reflected in mind-body and mind-nature dualities) will be restored, and in a higher, more richly integrated form.[27] Emerson shares this goal. But in Emerson, as in other nineteenth-century radicals who remain theists, the romantic revision is incomplete, so that God is still a transcendent reality *beyond* the world, and is known *in* the world in those moments of intuition when the divinity immanent within the self fuses with the divinity immanent within nature, moments that have a dimension in language when words fuse with things. Such moments are fundamentally theological ones in which time intersects with the eternal. In Emerson's terms, a fact intuitively perceived is "an Epiphany of God."[28]

This view of facts is tied to another nineteenth-century synthesis of previously separate categories, the esthetic but fundamentally theological ones of nature as beautiful and sublime. The traditional conception was that

God's original creation, a place of utter harmony where humanity was perfectly content, was in all ways smooth and regular (the word "Eden" is Sumerian for "flatland"). After the Fall, God's wrath altered nature, producing such unpleasant and irregular features as mountains, seas, storms, and the more difficult seasons. In the simplest view of the matter, the remnants of unfallen nature—beauty—showed God's continuing love, while fallen nature was the abode of evil. In esthetics, this led to the celebration of those aspects of nature compatible with notions of harmony and order, the avoidance of those discontenting ones associated with chaos, and the encouragement in life as well as in art of the cultivation or conversion of the latter into the former. But, in a gradual and complicated process, the supposedly chaotic aspects of nature came to take on a more nuanced theological and esthetic character. Underlying this change was the concept of the sublime. In its usual eighteenth-century form "the sublime" still considered wild nature to be frightening and painful but nonetheless found value in it. Vast scenery and impressive meteorological effects still evoked terror, but because they were suggestive of the infinite, and thus of deity, they also came to evoke awe and even admiration. At first, they did so in ways largely compatible with the inscrutable and omnipotent God of Calvin, and of Winthrop, Bradstreet, Taylor, and Edwards. However, by the early nineteenth century this revaluation had proceeded considerably further. Assisted but not limited by Kant's transference of qualities from objects themselves to the sensibilities perceiving them, by the general shift in the analogy of perception from mirror to lamp, and by the rise of empirical science, human confidence in its ability to recognize the God within the self in his manifestations in nature grew stronger. Eventually, for many artists and thinkers the beautiful and the sublime were fused. Encouraged by optimistic notions of inevitable progress and human perfectibility, and by such views as Hegel's that Christianity was merely a stage in the human advance toward truth, they thought of awe less as a function of fear and inferiority than as part and parcel of a response to beauty, which was now reconceived to include sublimity and grandeur.[29] As Emerson says, "There is no object so foul that intense light will not make it beautiful."[30] Thus, as all creeds came to be seen as being in touch with the one Logos, all of nature could be identified with God, either pantheistically, or, more commonly, in the mystical sense in which nature becomes not the sign but the symbol of God. The creation was whole and original once more, a restoration with significant implications for American nationalism as well as for epistemology.

Insofar as the symbolist Emerson can be isolated from his other selves, he is the Emerson of *Nature*. There the divine immanence the Puritans had sometimes sought, always feared, and usually resisted is asserted as fact. Nature becomes a "recognized avenue to the center of being."[31] Emerson's

Nature maps the route, and its epistemology is, or tries to be, not so much idealist as symbolist. One of Emerson's fundamental transformations of Edwards is his inversion of the priority of Word and world, of scripture and nature. *Nature* gives Emerson's justification for this. If God is a *living* God, then he *is*, not was.[32] Our knowledge of him should be equally present. But the "age is retrospective." Instead of seeing God ourselves we take him secondhand, in the dead forms of scripture. Furthermore, in accepting his transcendence we ignore his immanence: "foregoing generations beheld God . . . face to face; we, through their eyes. Why," Emerson goes on to ask, "should not we also enjoy an original relation to the universe? Why should not we have a poetry and philosophy of insight and not of tradition, and a religion by revelation to us, and not the history of theirs?" The rhetorical implication is that we should, and can. We can because nature is present to us, and nature is God's symbol.

All this is said on the first page of *Nature*. The rest is method. God is accessible to every person in an immediate and continuous revelation. Nature is the medium of that revelation—all of nature, which in its "endless variety" makes a "unique," that is, a single, impression (54, 10). Revelation occurs—God is beheld face to face—when nature and sensibility (object and subject) merge, healing the split between self and world and joining self and world with God, or, rather, discovering the union that is already there. This is the fundamental significance of the famous, much lampooned transparent eyeball passage. Seeing *is* seeing into, seeing through. Therefore, immediate, intuitive, personal experience is each and all. Both scriptural reports of God's historical presence (which controlled Calvinist thought) and logic (which dominated rationalist theology) are now seen as legitimate only in the degree to which they fit experience, not the other way around. For Emerson, experience authenticates itself.

This is just where Emerson seems radically subjective in precisely idealist terms. It is where he is most fully a symbolist. For the Emerson of *Nature*, the truest knowledge is not the product of will; it is not something "we imagine or wish or 'make up,'" a romantic projection of sensibility. Neither is it the result of simply reading nature as a sign. Signs, as Hyatt Waggoner says, *pace* the semioticians, have no importance in themselves, nor are they in any essential sense related to what they signify. We look at them only to see where they are pointing. This is how the Puritans tended to view nature, as a sort of cosmic public service. But Emerson is neither a spiritualist in the Puritan sense, nor a materialist in scientific, Deist, or even Unitarian ones. Nor is he always an idealist in the romantic sense. In *Nature*, Emerson is a symbolist for whom knowledge inheres in the ecstatic intersection and merging of self and other, mind (or spirit) and nature.[33]

Of course, Emerson is enough of an idealist to include in *Nature* a chapter called "Idealism" and to say in it that "[t]he sensual man conforms thoughts to things; the poet conforms things to his thoughts" (65). Yet Emerson's goal in *Nature* is to correct idealist as well as materialist epistemologies. When the idealist mood is upon him he is quick to correct himself: "Yet it is certain that the power to produce this delight, does not reside in nature, but in man, or in a harmony of both" (14). Admittedly, the example limps some. Throughout *Nature*, though, there are stronger statements of the symbolist position. "The beauty of nature reforms itself in the mind, and not for barren contemplation, but for new creation" (29). "This relation between the mind and matter . . . stands in the will of God" (43)."Reason" perceives "the analogy that marries Matter and Mind" (46). Idealism has its value; it accounts better for nature's effects on us than materialism does. "Yet, if it only deny the existence of matter, it does not satisy the demands of the spirit. It leaves God out of me" (78). Finally, both the materialist and the idealist views leave nature a wreck. "The ruin or the blank, that we see when we look at nature, is in our own eye. The axis of vision is not coincident with the axis of things, and so they appear not transparent but opake. The reason why the world lacks unity, and lies broken and in heaps, is, because man is disunited with himself" (91). When we *are* whole, the axis of vision and the axis of things coincide; we see the world as it is, a transparent symbol of God in which we, ourselves transparent symbols of God, participate in full.

Emerson is less a coherent philosopher than a religious and literary thinker. His ideas about art and language, his esthetics, are based on his symbolist outlook. God's creation of the world is an artistic act in progress (Emerson's God has the usual romantic preference for process over product). Because we are created in God's image, when we appreciate the "fitness" of God's artistry in nature the artist in us is responding to the original Artist: "man has access to the entire mind of the Creator, is himself the creator in the finite" (80). Thus what we perceive in nature is actually there: "perception is not whimsical, but fatal."[34] Here is the source of Emerson's faith in intuition, and of the doctrine of self-reliance. It distinguishes Emerson's from the idealist view and connects him with his Puritan forebears—with an essential difference. The Puritans limited the aspects of nature in which God's handiwork might still be seen, and they distrusted the ability of even putatively regenerate souls to read even those aspects correctly. They saw self-reliance as sinful, and they subjected individual interpretations of nature to the dictates of scripture and of institutionalized doctrine. For Emerson, none of that is needed. The fall into sin never took place, only the fall into consciousness. And *that*, each individual could redeem without divine or institutional intervention. The world, all of the world, is, and always has been, God's continuous act of creation. Each individual can renew the self and confidently discover God both there and in the world. Those beliefs have important implications for Emerson's ideas about poetry and the poet—by way of his theory of language.

Emerson's own summation is not to be outdone: "1. Words are signs of natural facts. 2. Particular natural facts are symbols of particular spiritual facts. 3. Nature is the symbol of spirit."[35] Underlying those precepts is the sense that there is "a necessity in spirit to manifest itself in material forms." Facts, "day and night, river and storm, beast and bird, acid and alkali, preexist in necessary ideas in the mind of God, and are what they are by virtue of preceding affections, in the world of spirit. A Fact is the end or last issue of spirit. The visible creation is the terminus or the circumference of the invisible world" (43–44). This restores the creative Logos to a *living* expression. Human expression, the language of "the creator in the finite," is potentially in touch with this Logos. It is rarely actually so. This is where Emerson's notion of the fall into consciousness comes into play. Once, words were fused with things, and all speech was poetry. But our language has lost most of this original quality. Nonetheless, in the famous phrase from "The Poet," "all language is fossil poetry," and we can still hear remnants of the primal unity of word and thing in language. Even our most abstract moral and intellectual usages have roots in "some material appearance. *Right* originally means *straight; wrong* means *twisted. Spirit* primarily means *wind; transgression,* the *crossing of a line; supercilious,* the *raising of an eyebrow"* (32–33). Furthermore, "It is not words only that are emblematic; it is things which are emblematic. Every natural fact is a symbol of some spiritual fact" (33). "Nature is the symbol of spirit." Thus, to say it again, words rightly used put us in touch with nature and with God. Such use is rare: "The corruption of man is followed by the corruption of language" (37–38). But each individual can attain redemption by undoing corruption and again using words so as to know nature and God: "wise men pierce this rotten diction and fasten words again to visible things" (39) (a notion that reverberates in American theories of poetic diction). It is never entirely clear whether Emerson sees the poetic use of language as providing knowledge of God or as the sign that such knowledge has been attained. In either case, though, the use of "picturesque language" is "a commanding certificate that who employs it, is a man in alliance with truth and God" (39). Those who progress toward using language as poetry may come by degrees "to know the primitive sense of the permanent objects of nature, so that the world shall be to us as an open book, and every form significant of its hidden life and final cause" (44–45).

Emerson's conceptions of poetry and the poet continue and radically alter Puritan views. For instance, he shares the Puritan emphasis on the *individual's* relation with God by making everyone potentially his or her own regenerate poet (a term that Emerson does not limit to persons who write poems). Yet it is precisely by extending that potential to everyone that Emerson rejects essential Puritan beliefs in sin and damnation, just as he rejects any need for institutional mediation. Those denials evince an anti-Puritan, typically democratic desire to offer everyone access to salvation (and to art and culture). Emerson also differs from the Puritans in his sense of the poet as seer. The Puritan poet is special only in commanding the craftsmanship to convey descriptively the truth that is equally available to every elect soul. Emerson shares the Puritan emphasis on the poet's responsibility to report the truth and to inculcate its moral and ethical (if not dogmatic) application, but he is nearer the romantics in his notions of the poet as possessing special insight and of the poetic act as realization. Even so, with a kind of Puritan abstemiousness, Emerson refuses the larger egoism of the romantics' elevation of the poet to culture hero. He insists that the poet's heightened sensibility is simply a more developed form of what is latent in everyone. Emerson also shares the Puritan distrust of ornament and even of artistry itself, rejecting the neoclassical stress on completion, regularity, and refinement in favor of spontaneous and organic creation. He does so, though, not because artistry bespeaks idolatry, but because it betrays enslavement to tradition, institution, and history and implies a lack of sincerity, *the* romantic test of artistic truth. Finally, what Emerson shares most importantly with the Puritans is his faith that God's truth is *in* nature to be discovered by regenerate selves. This most fundamental point of contact is also the point of sharpest difference. What is revolutionary in Emerson as he turns to nature to know his God is confidence that neither humanity nor nature is fallen, that God is continuous with his entire creation, that God is revealed to us in nature, that the trivial rightly envisioned is sublime, and that our perceiving, poetic selves have a role in revelation when we find out the oneness of words with things.

Emerson's inability to realize his symbolist epistemology and esthetics in actual poems is notorious. In "Days," as in "The Sphinx," which is clumsier, he came close. It is necessary to see through his apparent intention to realize just how close. The "hypocritic Days," the "Daughters of Time," offer the poet a choice of gifts ranging from "bread" to "kingdoms, stars, and sky that holds them all."

> I, in my pleached garden, watched the pomp,
> Forgot my morning wishes, hastily
> Took a few herbs and apples, and the Day
> Turned and departed silent. I, too late,
> Under her solemn fillet saw the scorn.[36]

Retrospectively, the poet judges his choice a poor one and allows himself to be instructed, of all things, so as to see his selection of the humble "herbs and apples" as a missed chance at the glories of transcendence. This is fallen consciousness at work. The symbolist Emerson sees it otherwise. As F. O. Matthiessen says, the objects of his choice do not "share in the ugliness of wrong. His instinctive taking of the few herbs and apples is the fitting expression of his spontaneous trust in the amplitude to man's needs of his immediate surroundings."[37] In the words of *Nature*, "How does Nature deify us with a few and cheap elements! Give me health and a day, and I will make the pomp of emperors ridiculous" (21–22). Seen in this light, the poet of "Days" rejects the ancient, dissembling, and pompously imperious judgment by which he seems to be cowed. Whatever his second thoughts, by choosing intuitively and self-reliantly, he justified a symbolist way of knowing in which every fact, when rightly perceived, "holds them all," is valuable in itself, and is an epitome of God.

Suspected Instruments

Emerson was a genius by his own definition: "true genius," he said, "seeks to defend us from itself."[38] Emerson joined his age in consecrating sincerity, yet he could admit to being "always insincere, as always knowing there are other moods."[39] The frank dissonance of his renditions of "other moods," as in "Days," where self-reliance is so easily challenged, caused Henry James, Sr., in apparent exasperation, to address him as a "man without a handle."[40] All of this is by way of saying what any reader of Emerson already knows. In representing Emerson as a symbolist I have presented him very selectively, perhaps to the point of misrepresenting him. I have done so in order to emphasize the Emerson who found in symbolism a theory of knowledge and a method of living and writing in which the axis of vision (idealism, mind, spirit) and the axis of things (materialism, matter, nature) could coincide, so that each became what it was meant to be, transparent, and one with God. This is the Emerson who went self-reliantly to nature to redeem the self and to discover God; the Emerson who believed words could be one with objects; in short, the Emerson for whom this world is a cosmos revealing sure and certain knowledge of God to men and women. The actual Emerson, evading "foolish consistency," and maybe some other kinds as well, is a good deal more, and less. The monist is paired with a dualist. In his own version of Coleridge's distinction of fancy from imagination, Emerson notes that we lead two lives, one of the understanding, the other of reason, or the soul. "The worst feature of this double consciousness is, that the two lives, of the understanding and of the soul, which we lead, really show very little relation to each other; never meet and measure each other: one prevails now, all buzz and din; and the other prevails then, all infinitude and paradise; and, with the progress of life, the two discover no greater disposition to reconcile themselves."[41] Often, then, the symbolist center could not hold; the axes of vision and things failed to coincide. One dominated the other; either the materialist "sensual man" or the idealist poet had the upper hand.

It is a common charge that Emerson's symbolism was more often an idealism that devalued or canceled the reality of nature, skipping over or annihilating it on its way to God. This is the Emerson for whom "infinitude and paradise" prevail. Perhaps this prevalence is the inevitable result of his beliefs. For instance, Emerson's theory of language insists that every achieved work of art must become the ultimate scripture. Thoreau's *Walden* can bear witness to the homily's value as inspiration. But Emerson's emphasis on the present, on presence, and on process insists that no writing, no scripture could *be* ultimate (thus the typically prospective cast of his descriptions of the desiderated poet and poem, and his nearly constant sense of a gap between what is and what might be[42]). Beset by the difficulties of an eternally open-ended process, the goal of which is by definition unattainable, Emerson was sometimes tempted to take shortcuts that would lead to his objective instantaneously and without mediation. In *Nature*, the devaluation of physical reality is usually minor, and of a sort in keeping with symbolist vision, as in this pregnant sentence: "All the facts in natural history taken by themselves, have no value, but are barren like a single sex. But marry it to human history, and it is full of life" (35). Nonetheless, the idealist tendency occasionally looms there: "this beauty of Nature which is seen and felt as beauty, is the least part. The shows of day, the dewy morning, the rainbow, mountains, orchards in blossom, stars, moonlight, shadows in still water . . . become shows merely, and mock us with their unreality" (24). Even here, though, the lingering catalogue is in touch with life. Later in *Nature*, Emerson can wonder "whether nature outwardly exists" (59); quickly declare the question irrelevant: "what difference does it make, whether Orion is up there in heaven, or some god paints the image on the firmament of the soul?" (59–60); and bluntly state the idealist view that the poet animates nature "like a creator" (68), so that "the solid seeming block of matter . . . [is] pervaded and dissolved by a thought" (69).

Emerson usually avoided or qualified such extreme idealist statements in *Nature*. In much of his writing he did not. His tendency to consider the actual world as maya, as a veil of illusion, could overwhelm his faith in particulars. Like so much in Emerson, this idealist tendency also has roots in his theory of language. When the second and third propositions of that theory are stressed at the expense of the first, the process of thought is likely to take priority over language and natural objects as the preferred route to the divine mind. To narrow the area of discussion, this can lead to an "escapist" view of art. Matthiessen notes Emerson's fidelity to Bacon's description of poetry as the "best definition": "Poetry, not finding the actual world exactly conformed to its idea of good and fair, seeks to accommodate the shows of things to the desires of the mind, and to create an ideal world better than the world of experience." Emerson never quite subscribed to this scientific-minded reduction of poetry to mere wish fulfillment, but his adherence to Bacon's formula did encourage him to ignore those "harsh or ugly" aspects of experience that would not conform to his optimistic vision. Combined with his virtually congenital preference for harmonious reconciliation over conflict or paradox; it could cause him to brush nature impatiently aside in his urgency to reach the absolute source of truth. One consequence is stylistic. Matthiessen recounts a journal passage in which Emerson, who had made racy colloquialism a trophy of symbolist alignment with truth, records distress that his "fine thought" about books finding their own level in the world by a sort of specific gravity was "spoiled" by his earthy memory of potatoes floating or sinking in the tub at home.[43]

In poetry Emerson's idealism produced the glib abstractions of "The Rhodora" and the dismissive nullification of common facts in "Each and All." It also led to the more impressive "Uriel" and to what is perhaps the clearest articulation of Emerson's idealism, the finely crafted "Brahma." There, the oppositional categories that give life its human shape, and the natural particulars that compose those categories, are submerged in cosmic oneness. Slayer and slain, sunlight and shadow, shame and fame, gods vanished and present, heaven and hell themselves are mere illusions, dissolved in the ineffable unity of a god beyond even good and evil. In such a vision natural objects have no role but to be erased.

At this point the structure of the argument requires a materialist Emerson as the other term of the idealist / materialist pair into which his symbolism sometimes collapsed. The formula is too neat for the facts. There is no materialist Emerson. There *is* an Emerson far more grounded in intractable reality than either symbolist or idealist definitions would suggest, an Emerson for whom the "buzz and din" of life more nearly prevails. In the essay "Experience," he writes, "It is very unhappy, but too late to be helped, the discovery we have made, that we exist. That discovery is called the Fall of Man." The passage is famous, and much quoted. Roy Harvey Pearce points out that the ensuing sentence is rarely included: "Ever afterwards, we suspect our instruments."[44] That suspicion—of eye, mind, language, or art—is the source of an Emerson more chastened, rationalistic, and melioristic than the intuitive perceiver of God in or beyond nature. Hyatt Waggoner's summary is definitive. The thought that all experience is illusion was a threat to Emerson's symbolist and idealist faith. More threatening still, his ability to experience nature daily as an ecstatic, revelatory epiphany—the rock on which his faith was built—grew less and less as he grew older, especially after the death of his son Waldo in 1842.

[I]f the illuminations did not come, then what? How could he go on being a Transcendentalist?

Gradually, almost imperceptibly, he modified his thinking in the direction of the sort of theistic evolutionary humanism we find in *The Conduct of Life* and in the late poem "The Adirondacks." Nature, which once had impressed him chiefly as an opportunity for illumination [or as something easily vaulted over on the way to the One], now was redefined as "limitation," another word for "fate." The Over-Soul was now an emergent deity, and natural evil, which he had once called merely "privative"—that is, the absence of good, not ultimately Real in itself—was now the starting point of his thinking, as it is in "Fate." Opposing fate there was now thought, with its untested powers of creativeness, instead of illumination.[45]

This falling off of vision is, in part, yet another result of Emerson's ideas about language. One implication of his three propositions is that the "mind validates analogizing language, and analogizing language validates the mind." Good. But language itself is double, "a system of signs *and* symbols of spirit." Briefly, the upshot *can* be that the "unity of mind and nature— symbolized by language—can be apprehended only in language, where it ceases to be a unity." Language writes us and becomes fate. Our symbols and correspondences are merely impositions.[46] Sometimes this chastened realization is seen as a failure and used to "prove" the absurdity of Emerson's earlier alogical views. It has also been seen positively: for instance, as lending Emerson a tragic dignity as he comes to terms with the reality principle and accepts his limitations. More recently it has been used to "rescue" him from his early logocentrism by making him out a forerunner of poststructuralism who abandoned metaphysics and began to see language as an endless metonymic chain of displacements and deferrals, an argument partly justified by Emerson's disjunctive and "polyphonic" style.[47] Other approaches also see his loss of vision as a gain in power. Waggoner's suggestion that Emerson's "theistic evolutionary humanism" foreshadows James's pragmatism and Dewey's instrumentalism speaks to this point, as does David Van Leer's case that in certain of the essays Emerson begins by making strong statements that he then deliberately undercuts in order to indicate new epistemological limits.[48]

For defining Emerson's influence on later poetry, an especially fruitful response to his more constricted circumference is R. A. Yoder's in *Emerson and the Orphic Poet in America*. According to Yoder, Emerson's original view of the poet was as an Orpheus-like prophet who, having received revelation of eternal truth, uses poetic power for reshaping the world to fit that truth. In the poems of the 1840s and 1850s, however, Emerson's Orphic figure "lost first his supernatural connection, then his giant proportions and prophetic insight, so that he eventually descended . . . to a middle region where poetry is a limited power and the poet a man of common size or less." Yoder's conclusion is that Emerson's poetry followed and completed the arc of his prose. "Its tendency is away from revelation and transcendence and toward solution by immanent equilibriums," so that "a once sacred marriage" of imagination and reality is converted "into a series of pragmatic reconciliations" in which each is "delicately adjusted to the other."[49]

So, three Emersons: symbolist, idealist, and pragmatic reconciler. A nearly unslayable myth of American literary history has been that of Emerson's almost pangenic paternity. Alicia Ostriker has exposed the gender bias of this view, with its sources in Emerson's own giveaway vocabulary of ejaculation and "spermatic . . . man-making words."[50] Even so, it is tempting to see Whitman's merging of vision with things and things with vision as an outcome of Emerson's symbolist hopes, and Poe's desperate obliteration of all "individuals and particulars" en route to "Supernal Beauty" as an extremity of Emerson's idealism; Yoder lists Dickinson, Frost, and Stevens among the offspring of Emerson the pragmatic reconciler. Mutlu Konuk Blasing's genealogy is wiser. It enriches the gene pool, finding in Emerson, Whitman, Poe, and Dickinson three fathers and a mother for the modern and postmodern poets who follow. But, as Blasing points out, dynastic myths are insufficient to account for the webs of literary relationships.[51] In any case, the various strains in Emerson had some splendid results—in *Nature*, in the great essays and addresses, and in a few first-rate poems. Those same strains could also leave him in "a very poor plight," like the *Pequod* "sorely strained" between the weight on one flank of a right whale's head and on the other of a parmacetti's, a circumstance Ishmael likens to hoisting in Locke on one side and Kant on the other. Emerson's unit of composition remained the sentence, and, in Feidelson's telling phrase, he remained an "artist in the medium of theory."[52] It was left for others to fully exploit the literary potential implicit in the epistemological and esthetic plight of symbolism as it struggled to balance the nineteenth century's antagonistic inclinations toward materialism and idealism—Melville in fiction, Dickinson in poetry.

In *Nature and Culture* Barbara Novak illustrates the "ecumenical spirit of reconciliation" by which landscape painters managed to contain the "explosive bundle of contradictions" that characterized the nineteenth century: science and art, empiricism and idealism, analysis and synthesis, technology and nature. Following Emerson, the painters dissolved contradictions in a "spiritual light." In doing so they combined two supposedly antithetical esthetic principles: the attainment of general effect (privileged by idealist Western esthetics from the beginning through the eighteenth century and beyond) and the cultivation of detail (demanded by both empirical and symbolic reevaluations of particulars).[53] This meant, for instance, that in painting plants landscape artists could borrow both Asa Gray's wealth of botanical facts and Louis Agassiz's "amplified idealism," his confidence that facts are the thoughts of God.

Gray and Agassiz represent the poles of American reactions to Darwinism. More generally, they represent opposed responses to the vexed relationship of empiricism and idealism. In matters of speciation, as elsewhere, religious, scientific, and secular forces in America had worked out an almost instinctual, loosely held but utterly essential synthesis of empiricism and idealism, detail and overall effect, being and becoming, mensurable fixity and organic process. This synthesis was essential not least because of the profound connection of nature to American nationalism, about which, more later. The new science threatened that synthesis. Although he was surely an empiricist, Agassiz was in tune with pre-Darwinian science and continued in the tradition of accommodating discovery to design by which scientific revelations were "enlisted as . . . proof of providential creation." Gray, while he tried hard to accommodate Darwinism to design, kept his emphasis on the facts and on the search for an empirically demonstrable general system that would confirm those facts. As Novak says, the enormous popularity of Agassiz indicates the typical American view.[54] But if the people chose Agassiz, while the painters practiced reconciliation, other artists took other routes. Emily Dickinson's poetry exposes precisely those conflicts between particular and general, scientific empiricism and religious or philosophical idealism, that so many nineteenth-century artists muted or submerged.

Emily Dickinson was raised in a Trinitarian household and in Trinitarian schools in and around Trinitarian Amherst. This at a time when materialism, science, technology, and—a little later—the Civil War, urbanization, and immigration were transforming the country, changing it in ways that made Trinitarianism seem as extinct as the dinosaurs whose bones were unearthed in her own Connecticut Valley. Dickinson famously resisted the Trinitarian conversion experience—in which individuals surrendered autonomy to a loving, comforting, and ultimately reedeeming God, receiving in return for that surrender an adjusted vision that permitted them to accept suffering and death and to see clearly in nature signs of God's character and purpose that corresponded to the revealed truths of scripture. Dickinson kept her autonomy. She often found the God manifested in nature to be a patriarchal monster. With a vision adjusted only by her own experience, she discovered in God's creation a relentless experiment in separation and death that made scripture seem a vast deception.[55] Yet throughout her work Dickinson's epistemological categories and methods remained those of Trinitarian thought. Her notions of typology and natural religion were nearer those of the Calvinist Edwards than they were to Emerson's. Nonetheless, Dickinson's intellectual and poetic applications of Trinitarian methods produced a radical challenge to both Calvinist and transcendentalist versions of nature as a safe route to God. Her "Certainties of Noon" are certainties of negation. Her skeptical "Acres of Perhaps" weaken the analogical foundations on which spiritualist and symbolist trust in nature and in God are based. The bulk of Dickinson's nature poetry—and there is a great deal of it—falls into one or another of those categories. That is not quite the whole of it. There is "Finite infinity," as well.

Cynthia Griffin Wolff writes that for Dickinson the word "noon," naming the moment of fullest light, is a darkly condensed chiasmus of negation, reading "no" from right to left as it does from left to right, and centered in the double zeroes that equate infinity with nothingness.[56] Edwards had believed that the experience of election partially restores fallen faculties. Emerson was sure that individuals could save themselves unaided, redeeming their own disfigured sight. Trinitarian faith also credited the conversion experience with a guaranteed adjustment of vision that cured spiritual blindness and made nature's meanings visible. The Trinitarian version of recovered sight approximates Edwards's: although conversion *is* personal, divine and institutional intervention are essential to it; mind remains separate from matter; and the extension of typological methods to natural theology continues to be subjugated to scriptural models and truths. The Trinitarians valued nature not so much as a sign of God's existence—that was never seriously in question—as for its capacity to give evidence of God's character and purposes. They joined Edwards in moving away from the Puritan emphasis on remarkable providences (with their potential for disruption) and toward the more secure and seemingly immutable general laws that scientific analysis discovered in nature. Dickinson, who had received an excellent education in the science of her day, acquiesced in nearly all of this: the scientist / naturalist's vision of nature could be trusted to reveal God's qualities and intentions. But she demurred on one crucial point.

Trinitarians expected converted souls to use empirical observation and rational argument in order to interpret nature. They were confident that their discoveries would align perfectly with scripture. Conversion provided the adjusted vision that enabled "aligned" discovery; thus, only regenerate faculties could be trusted to see. Dickinson refused (or simply did not experience) the self-surrender of conversion, yet she trusted her own unadjusted eyes and reason. In this radical self-reliance—there is none of Bradstreet's "imbecility" here—Dickinson can appear Emersonian (she seems hardly to have thought of original sin). But where Emerson's faith found coincident

axes, she found an ax. It cleaved the world of things from the vision prom-
ised by scripture. Like Emerson, Dickinson inverted the Calvinist priority of
Word to world, but where he could regard scripture as merely a book among
books, she believed in the God of her fathers with more conviction and
convention. She spent much of her career using the world (and *her* words)
to try his Word.

Dickinson's experiment with nature discovered darkness at noon. The
world was indeed inscribed with God's truth; the truth was a horror. Ed-
ward Hitchcock, the distinguished scientist-theologian who was president of
Amherst College, represents a more standard result. Dickinson had surely
heard and probably read Hitchcock's *Religious Lectures*, in which he describes
natural facts and processes in order to develop the scriptural and spiritual
truths they illustrate. The growth of wheat from seed, the springtime return
of flowers, foliage, and birds, the metamorphoses of insects, all these and
many others are emblems of the resurrection. Ice storms and rainbows are
signs of God's creative glory and his covenant promise. Sunrise signals de-
feat for the dark night of sin and death. And so on. God inscribes nature for
humanity's edification. Here, Hitchcock reads the brilliant leaves that mark
New England's autumn:

> The gay splendor of our forests, as autumn comes on, may seem to
> some inappropriate, when we consider that it is the precursor of
> decay and death. But when we remember that the plant still lives,
> and after a season of inaction will awake to new and more vigorous
> life, and that the apparent decay is only laying aside a summer robe,
> because unfit for winter, is it not appropriate that nature should
> hang out signals of joy, rather than of sorrow? Why should she not
> descend exultingly, and in her richest dress, into the grave, in hope
> of so early and so glorious a resurrection?

Subsequent pages make the analogy to Christian souls even more explicit.
Hitchcock also offers a *principle* of interpretation. Listing Christ's parables,
he concludes: "Now with such illustrious examples, is it not the part of
wisdom to attempt to seize upon passing events in nature . . . and make
them subservient to moral instruction?"[57] Hitchcock encouraged empirical
attention to nature, but his vocabulary of subservience and seizure indicates
how fully scripture and doctrine remained ascendant. Of course, in his
adjusted view of the matter, science's world and God's Word could only
coincide. Dickinson's empiricism was more complete. Where Hitchcock saw
corresponding promises of redemptive hope in the accommodating inscrip-
tions of the Bible and of nature, she beheld an abyss. Dickinson accepted
Hitchcock's principle. She then faithfully recorded the "moral instruction"
her researches unveiled. Often it seemed an everlasting no.

The Trinitarian and more general nineteenth-century emphasis on vision in matters of both spiritual and scientific knowledge underlies this epigram:

> "Faith" is a fine invention
> When Gentlemen can *see*—
> But *Microscopes* are prudent
> In an Emergency.[58]

Conventional advice about scientific support for endangered faith, and a joke. With its teasing quotation marks and italics, its light taunting of "Gentlemen" (perhaps Hitchcock and the Sage of Concord, or knowing patriarchs in general), with its dig at New Englandly prudence, its play on emergent (as against, say, fully metamorphosed) souls, and with its toying use of the word "invention" (microscopes enshrined as instruments of faith; faith reduced to a gadget), the poem takes on a wonderful wobble of tone, complemented by its tripping, then tripped rhythm and rhyme. Perhaps the obscure or enigmatic in Dickinson is itself a challenge to Hitchcock's explanatory clarities. In any case, Dickinson turned her microscopic and telescopic sights on nature. She spied clarities of her own.

Contemporary scientist-theologians discovered a sign in the sunset, a reiteration in nature of the scriptural promise that Christian death is a going home to God in calm expectation of the new day's resurrection. Here is Dickinson's view.

> How the old Mountains drip with Sunset
> How the Hemlocks burn—
> How the Dun Brake is draped in Cinder
> By the Wizard Sun—
>
> How the old Steeples hand the Scarlet
> Till the Ball is full—
> Have I the lip of the Flamingo
> That I dare to tell?
>
> Then, how the Fire ebbs like Billows—
> Touching all the Grass
> With a departing—Sapphire—feature—
> As a Duchess passed—
>
> How a small Dusk crawls on the Village
> Till the Houses blot
> And the odd Flambeau, no men carry
> Glimmer on the Street—
>
> How it is Night—in Nest and Kennel—
> And where was the Wood—
> Just a Dome of Abyss is Bowing
> Into Solitude—

> These are the Visions flitted Guido—
> Titian—never told—
> Domenichino dropped his pencil—
> Paralyzed with Gold— (#291)

There is no recreative or redemptive promise here. Nature drips with blood or liquid fire, is drained, goes up in flames, dies to embers, and goes out. The "old" modulates to the merely "odd." God's Noachian pact—destruction by fire, not flood, next time—is mocked when "Fire ebbs like Billows." And not only nature is put to death. The human spheres of society (the Village) and individuals (in Houses) are obliterated, too. In a wild mixture of Gothic effects, steeples pander to a vampiric knitter who bloats on blood and flame; darkness "crawls" on houses, is blotted up, blots out. What light is left is illusion's "Glimmer"; God's creative and covenanted divisions (earth from air, fire from water, natural from human, darkness from light) all collapse. Everything returns to the undifferentiated yet shaped "Abyss" of primal chaos.

Where Hitchcock found comforting doctrine, Dickinson found doctrine decreated, drained, expunged. Her blasphemy is bold. Touched, perhaps, with prophetic fire, her lip "inverted," like the flamingo's, she dares report what her eyes see. Her words erase and replace scripture; her voice displaces God's. She defies other artists, too. Baroque limners of sensuous saints were "Paralyzed" by the gold of church patronage or the illuminated capitals of scripture, or were merely blinded by the sun (or Son). They lacked the force to depict the "Visions" her words paint. Yet her Promethean power is circumscribed. The romantic reach for creative force falls short. It is not she who domes the abyss, and it bows not to her but to Nature, or God, or empty Solitude. It is all one.

Another commonplace Trinitarian emblem of God's saving care is the return of spring. Dickinson's seasons roll indifferently around. The ringing "New" of redemption's pledge is wrung to weary death.

> New feet within my garden go—
> New fingers stir the sod—
> A Troubadour upon the Elm
> Betrays the solitude.
>
> New children play upon the green—
> New Weary sleep below—
> And still the pensive Spring returns—
> And still the punctual snow! (#99)

Against the grave in the garden, the oxymoron of "New Weary," and that displaced exclamation, faith seems child's play. Other pastoral pacts are equally undone. Indian summer, for instance: "These are the days when skies resume / The old—old sophistries of June— / A blue and gold mistake" (#130). Another autumn poem deflates poetic and religious enthusiasms for nature's benignity with a puncturing comma: "Gone—Mr. Bryant's 'Golden Rod'— / And Mr. Thomson's 'sheaves.' / / Still, is the bustle in the Brook— / Sealed are the spicy valves—" (#131). So much for books in the running brooks. Enjoined to read God's character in nature, and to generalize about that character on the basis of natural phenomena, Dickinson delivers her lab report. It is empirically blunt.

> Apparently with no surprise
> To any happy Flower
> The Frost beheads it at its play—
> In accidental power—
> The blonde Assassin passes on—
> The Sun proceeds unmoved
> To measure off another Day
> For an Approving God. (#1624)

Of course, Dickinson did sometimes experience transport in nature, a transcendent intensity that lifted her beyond death and above space and time. In "I taste a liquor never brewed," she is "Inebriate of Air" and "Debauchee of Dew." She storms heaven with her own ecstatically intoxicated self. Yet even in that poem, the self is diminished, a "little Tippler," a little drunk. Usually when Dickinson practiced the Calvinist, transcendentalist, or Trinitarian faith that nature's script repeats scripture's, the inscription she read said "nothingness" and "death" and gave scripture the lie. She was not always so certain of "noon." Many of her nature poems are exercises of doubt, metaphysical doubt, and epistemological and esthetic doubt as well. Wolff notes that Dickinson found her frozen northern God in the word "no" huddled in the heart of "snow."[59] She must have read the "no" in "know" as well, where the homonym insists. Often knowledge offered her no ledge on which to build or stand. In many poems, the notion of discovery itself is challenged.

Emerson was sure that the poet's corrected vision discovers an "integrity of impression from manifold objects": every detail points to a single truth. Dickinson selects a detail; its meanings multiply.

> "Morning"—means "Milking"—to the Farmer—
> Dawn to the Teneriffe—
> Dice—to the Maid—
> Morning means just Risk—to the Lover—
> Just revelation—to the Beloved—
>
> Epicures—date a Breakfast—by it—
> Brides—an Apocalypse—

Worlds—a Flood—
Faint-going Lives—Their Lapse from Sighing—
Faith—The Experiment of Our Lord— (#300)

Word, occasion, experience, poetic convention, allegorical term, or spiritual symbol, "morning" means different things to different people (even an island has its definition). From the workaday round of the farmer and the gambles and gambols of lovers, to the chronologies of biblical historians and the hope of the dying for salvation, these variant readings of the world's code are presented without judgment, evaluation, or comment. There is no hierarchy of meaning. The farmer's morning is as real to him as is the expiring soul's to it. Where Hitchcock instructed his audience to make natural events "subservient to moral instruction," Dickinson gives a lexicographer's report, one that harbors suspicions about the role of language itself in constructing reality.

The most powerful way in which Dickinson anticipates twentieth-century poetry is in shifting epistemological questions from the meaning of God toward the meaning of meaning. While she usually enacts the problem in religious terms, her emphasis on language and ambiguity, on the gulfs between and among name, namer, and named, has a contemporary feel. It is tempting to exaggerate that dimension of Dickinson's work, to see her attacks on the analogies between world and Word, words and Word, and words and world as participating fully in modernist and postmodernist erasures of logocentrism, to see her poems as prototypes of Kenneth Burke's ironic "perspective of perspectives" or Mikhail Bakhtin's polyphonic dialogics. Too much stress on those positions, with their assumption of thoroughgoing relativism, underplays the impact of Dickinson's cultural context. Even so, there is a good deal of truth in Blasing's claim that the "subversive literal play of [Dickinson's] language points up the necessary deviation of the signifier from its referent and thus dismantles the rhetoric of the Logos, the identity of word and thing that analogy upholds."[60] As Buell points out, analyses of Dickinson's work from feminist and religiocentric perspectives alike find a deconstructive element there. Both critical viewpoints see her "as appropriating the terms of an orthodoxy identified as masculine to construct her own 'anti-allegory' . . . in which her sense of the gap between signifier and signified becomes the basis for decentered use of key words and images."[61]

At the same time, as Buell also sees, Dickinson's deconstructions are firmly lodged within the nineteenth-century practice of romantic irony, "a systematic breaking of the poetic illusion in order to call attention to it as artifice."[62] So understood, romantic irony both continues a more confident romanticism's rejection of neoclassical artifice *and* enunciates its own shaken or lost faith in romantic claims of idealist or symbolist unifications of vision and things. And Dickinson's skepticism is also part and parcel of the doubt that invariably accompanies intelligent belief, as well as an expression of her sometimes acute awareness that her own vision was unadjusted by conversion: she could mock her own certitude as well as others'. In any case, much of Dickinson's nature poetry deploys ambiguity in order to challenge Christian and romantic assertions of analogical or symbolic correspondence between nature and scripture, physics and metaphysics. At times, it considers the possibility that meaning is more constructed or contrived than it is discovered.

Edward Taylor knew his spider for Satan. Dickinson's arachnid is another matter.

> A Spider sewed at Night
> Without a Light
> Upon an Arc of White.
>
> If Ruff it was of Dame
> Or Shroud of Gnome
> Himself himself inform.
>
> Of Immortality
> His Strategy
> Was Physiognomy. (#1138)

Perhaps this spider is not Satan but God, weaving his "Physiognomy" into the fabric of the world to be a sign of his immortal presence and promise. If so, when we seek to know him, applying physiognomy—the (dubious) practice of judging character by observing the face—there is no way to distinguish the saintly ruff (or halo) from an elvish, devilish (and gnomic) shroud. God's informing act (a giving of information; a taking shape or becoming manifest) only informs himself. Or perhaps the spider is the human soul, sewing (sowing) in the dark in a blind act of faith that is the only strategy its ignorant condition provides for attaining immortality. Of course, this might mean that immortality is imagined or constructed rather than discovered or achieved. Possibilities ramify; clarity is denied. And this is the point. The Trinitarian version of the Calvinist practice of reading nature promised a single, clear, and comforting meaning. It is a practice and promise reflected in transcendentalism and throughout the New England "emblem" tradition—for instance, in Emerson's "The Rhodora" or Bryant's "To a Waterfowl," with their machinelike movement from observation to application. This is what Dickinson's poem denies. Where convention demanded singular clarity, she found manifold obscurities.[63]

Perhaps all that distinguishes Dickinson's from postmodernist modes of deconstruction here is her willingness to be skeptical of even her own skepticism and her continuing to operate within an at least potentially meta-physical dimension. In any case, poem after poem sets multiple, often dis-senting meanings against simple and consoling ones. Dickinson's strategies of ambiguity or multiplicity are strongest in her great quartet of death poems: "Safe in their Alabaster Chambers—" (#216), "I felt a Funeral, in my Brain" (#280), "I heard a Fly buzz—when I died—" (#465), and "Because I could not stop for Death—" (#712). None of these is quite a nature poem, yet each uses natural details to underline its ambiguous sense of the relationship between the scriptural promise of eternal life and the impersonal, insufficient, and contradictory evidence of experience. More pertinent to our concern with poets who turn to nature to address epistemo-logical and esthetic questions is "It Sifts from Leaden Sieves—." It, too, confronts physiognomy:

> It sifts from Leaden Sieves—
> It powders all the Wood.
> It fills with Alabaster Wool
> The Wrinkles of the Road—

> It makes an even Face
> Of Mountain, and of Plain—
> Unbroken Forehead from the East
> Unto the East again—

> It reaches to the Fence—
> It wraps it Rail by Rail
> Till it is lost in Fleeces—
> It deals Celestial Vail

> To Stump, and Stack—and Stem—
> A Summer's empty Room—
> Acres of Joints, where Harvest were,
> Recordless, but for them—

> It Ruffles Wrists of Posts
> As Ankles of a Queen—
> Then stills its Artisans—like Ghosts—
> Denying they have been— (#311)

In part, the poem is a literal description of a winter storm; even there ambiguity obtains. The sifting snow is domestic and gentle ("Sieves," "powders," "Wool," "wraps," "Fleeces"), but it comes down hard ("Lead-en," "powders," "Alabaster," "wraps" heard as "raps"), and it piles deep (taking the fence "Rail by Rail / Till it is lost," covering low stump, higher haystack, still higher stem). And the poem is more than description, or seems to be. It takes literally the Trinitarian exhortation to find God's face in nature. God's physiognomy *is* there in the falling snow, "an even Face," with an "Unbroken Forehead." But if this manifests God, what does it say about him? It might bespeak nothingness, "A blanker whiteness of benighted snow / With no expression, nothing to express," as Frost's "Desert Places" puts it, in a virtual redaction of this poem. An "even Face" with an "Unbroken Forehead" lacks the features that enable physiognomists to interpret character. Or it shows the character itself to be a blank.

On the other hand, the snow is an active force; creative and decreative in godlike ways, it "fills," "makes," "deals," and denies. Those disturbing actions create by erasing the details of this world, particularly the signs of humanity's presence and activity in it. In a sense, this is doctrinal. God's manifestation recalls our puny insignificance and the insignificance of our earthly concerns. Yet God's manifestation cruelly obliterates all that locates us in nature, the markers that lend landscape its human significance and shape: rutted roads, fence rails, "Stump, and Stack—and Stem—." There is a frightening enough reach in that penultimate dash. But things go further, until even the largest God-given distinctions are effaced, so that mountains are indistinguishable from plains and the compass points contract to a lone and directionless direction. This, too, is doctrinal: the manifold world is reduced to unity in the resurrection's eastering blaze of white. It is also terrifying. When the "Joints" of corn stubble left in the fields are covered up, the very notion of harvest seems threatened—and "harvest" is a potent word in the lexicon of salvation. But perhaps what we imagine to be God's face is just snow, and our reading of it just a way of talking. If so, then what?

There are other possibilities as well. God's is not the only physiognomy here. His face erases another face, ours, in a premature burial. Snow fills "Wrinkles" and covers up "Joints," both "Ankles" and "Wrists"—another horror, but also a joke. The end of the poem retrieves the "make-up" imagery latent in "powders" to produce a quite conventional picture of the snow as a cosmetician-dresser who conceals the wrinkles of old dame nature's face, sets handsome ruffles at her wrists, and thus saves her from humanity's disfiguring ravishments, giving her back as a virginal beauty. But is this a miraculous transformation or a conjurer's trick, and how frigidly barren is the result? In any case, as a good cosmetician would, this one leaves no trace. The miracle is wrought; the artistry denied. Once more, this has a doctrinal dimension. God made the world as a perfect expression of his truth, but our fallen faculties, the result of humanity's first denial, render it obscure to us. Yet the same passage also makes God out to be a trickster. He promises clear evidence of his artisanship—the presence of his spirit ("Ghosts") in the world's flesh—then gives only vague hints, and denies even those.

One implication of these "manifold impressions," of the poem's refusal of any neat fit between natural event and homiletic application, is that snow is snow and any reading of it is just that, a "reading." Whether we construe the snow as a murderous act of obliteration, as a miraculous transformation, or as a cosmetician's legerdemain, we are projecting our own fears and hopes, our own felt sense of mystery on the blank slate of the world. Thus poems, or sermons, do not discover meaning but invent and impose it. In the phrase "Celestial Vails," the word "Vails" puns topographically on "vales" and, significantly in a poem about faces, on "veils." It echoes biblical "availeths" and "availeth nots," and hints at domestic "valances" and at scientific "valences" of force. Its own multiple meanings—profit, acquisition, a yielding because of fear or respect, a lowering or descent—all have resonance here; all are obsolete. The poem does not so much conclude as evanesce. Its whispering exit is the life-denying annihilation of "Certainties of Noon." Or the inevitable sigh of "Acres of Perhaps." Or just an imitation of the storm, blowing itself out to stilly calm. There is fun and fear in this diminuendo to speechlessness. It provides a comment on Dickinson's poetic strategy for dealing with the apparent gap between the axis of vision and the axis of things, between God's Word and the world.

In her poems of negation, Dickinson discovered in nature facts that contradict scripture's promises. Her response as a poet was to report the truth. She did so boldly, replacing scripture's Word with her words, God's voice with her voice. She became herself the frolicking architect of snow, the creator and destroyer of worlds. She was not content with the victory. In the poems of doubt, Dickinson tests not only God's meaning but the meaning of meaning as well. This is an important aspect of "It Sifts from Leaden Sieves—." There she resists the efforts of nature and God to render the world "Recordless." The word is fraught with a writer's anxiety. Her strategy of resistance is to become a creator and destroyer herself, multiplying the range of possible meanings in a dizzying array. This works, but at a cost. It gives us the world as either a marginless palimpsest or a blank page. It undoes the tyranny of authoritative or authoritarian significance. But it either places us in a boundless field of meanings with no way to choose among them, or it gives us a world emptied of meaning, as even, unbroken, and snowy white as a blank page. There, we can write, but willfully, wishfully, with no hope of certainty, permanence, or conclusion. Thus for all its power the poem trails off to silence, "Denying they have been—." This is not the quiet click of closure. There is no resolution, just countless options, multiple to infinity, infinitely blank.

Dickinson pursued the implications. Critics have been careful to distinguish her applications of natural theology from Emerson's. Rightly so. Dickinson was nearer to the Trinitarian view that the facts of nature represent specific scripturally and doctrinally limited truths than she was to Emerson's notion of nature as a malleable manifold of signs that reveals a unitary truth to the intuitive insights of individuals. Of course, that view eventually led

Emerson to his own chastened recognition of the "artificiality of all cultures and texts." By her alternate route, Dickinson reached similar conclusions. But where Emerson, even at his most deflated, still hoped that truths could be grasped by "inspired sallies from diverse angles,"[64] Dickinson continued to suspect her instruments.

"The Brain—is wider than the Sky—" faces squarely the possibility that all reality—nature, meaning, even God—is no more than a construction of language and mind.

> The Brain—is wider than the Sky—
> For—put them side by side—
> The one the other will contain
> With ease—and You—beside—
>
> The Brain is deeper than the Sea—
> For—hold them—Blue to Blue—
> The one the other will absorb—
> As Sponges—Buckets—do—
>
> The Brain is just the weight of God—
> For—Heft them—Pound for Pound—
> And they will differ—if they do—
> As Syllable from Sound— (#632)

This has its own ambiguities. Still, the idea that the mind and words invent the only meaning available in the world centers a number of Dickinson's nature poems. In "Four Trees—upon a solitary Acre—" (#742), "A Light exists in Spring" (#812), and many others, the vocabulary of scriptural promise has disappeared, been attenuated, or become vestigial. With no guarantee of transcendence, nature is a ruin or a blank no vision can restore.

> There's a certain Slant of light,
> Winter Afternoons—
> That oppresses, like the Heft
> Of Cathedral Tunes—
>
> Heavenly Hurt, it gives us—
> We can find no scar,
> But internal difference,
> Where the Meanings, are—
>
> None may teach it—Any—
> 'Tis the Seal Despair—
> An imperial affliction
> Sent us of the Air—
>
> When it comes, the Landscape listens—
> Shadows—hold their breath—
> When it goes, 'tis like the Distance
> On the look of Death— (#258)

It is humanity's affliction—or "gift"—to need and seek significance. All we find are metaphors, projected from within. Even they depart. Thus Dickinson's skepticism could lead to even bleaker conclusions than her "Certainties of Noon." Now the God she had dared to challenge and even claimed to best may himself have disappeared. Dickinson followed the prescribed route to the center of being in nature. Freeing herself from preconceptions, she found the world a blank she could assert herself upon. In doing so, she knew she might have rendered meaning mere assertion.

She did not stop there, nor did she, very often, give in to silence or despair. Instead, she came back from solipsistic notions of invention as contrivance or imposition toward new modes of discovery, writing poems of "Finite infinity." Wolff suggests the ways in which Dickinson recovered from the implications for knowledge and for poetry of a world from which God's transcendence had been dismissed. For instance, in the many late poems of definition, she restores nature, now emptied of transcendence, to human and social significance. Such poems as "Presentiment—is that long Shadow—on the Lawn—" (#764), "Longing is like the Seed" (#1255), or "Hope is a subtle Glutton—" (#1547) make connections "between an insular self and the world of objects that exist outside of self, and they do so by finding what might loosely be termed an 'objective correlative' for one or another element of human consciousness." Another way in which the poet recovers from the loss of a putatively God-given and informing relationship with nature is by artfully recording her own delighted and privileged experience of nature's marvelously intense existence in the here and now. "Nature may be utterly indifferent to any mortal quandary; still, the poet can wring art from such a world, not by seeking transcendent truth in nature, but by capturing the play of brilliant surfaces that constitute its everything for us." Dickinson wrote many such poems. Perhaps the famous description of a hummingbird in "A Route of Evanescence" (#1463) is the finest of them. However, her poems of "untranscendent" or, as Wolff calls them, "post-Christian" nature are not limited to expressions of delight. Intensity is the key. "A narrow Fellow in the Grass" (#986) occasions no "transport / Of cordiality—," but "tighter breathing / And Zero at the Bone—." The fear is real, but it is a natural not a supernatural phenomenon. The heroic dimension available in Winthrop's narrative of the Puritan divine in combat with the serpent-Satan is lost, but the terror of absolute evil, with a metaphysical ground, is relieved. Paradoxically, "Zero" is somewhat warmed.

Each of these Dickinsons has been attractive to twentieth-century readers: the poet who challenged God with her negating "Certainties of Noon," the poet of radical doubt, and the literalist of imagination who celebrated "Finite infinity." We have been less aware that Dickinson did discover a God she could believe in—not the transcendent, mysterious stranger of the resurrection, but the earthly Jesus of the incarnation. "Christ becomes note-worthy not because he was divine, but because He was human; the mean-ing of Calvary is defined not by transcendent values, but by earthly ones." Implicit in such a view is a "subtle argument" that gives to Christianity not the absolute value of divine revelation, but the relative value of all other religions and myths. Its claim to attention is no longer unique; neither is it lost. "The touchstone of truth is not an unchanging and eternal God, but the reaction of many individual men and women: *human affirmation*, not re-vealed truth, confers importance upon a 'mythic' event. . . . The location of authority is thus reversed: before it had resided with God; now it resides in human nature."[65] This reversal is as important as reversals of the priority of world and Word or of nature and scripture. But I want to return briefly to the esthetic implications of Dickinson's skeptical epistemology. It is those aspects of her work that Frost, Stevens, Moore, and Bishop most fully inherit.

In a rare departure from his habitual pragmatic restraint, Emily Dickin-son's father, Edward Dickinson, once rang Amherst church bells to alert the sleeping town to a display of the northern lights. In "Of Bronze—and Blaze—," Dickinson re-searches the aurora, looking for signs of transcen-dent significance and human contact there. Its lights prove northern indeed.

> Of Bronze—and Blaze—
> The North—Tonight—
> So adequate—it forms—
> So preconcerted with itself—
> So distant—to alarms—
> An Unconcern so sovereign
> To Universe, or me—
> Infects my simple spirit
> With Taints of Majesty—
> Till I take vaster attitudes—
> And strut upon my stem—
> Disdaining Men, and Oxygen,
> For Arrogance of them—
>
> My Splendors, are Menagerie—
> But their Competeless Show
> Will entertain the Centuries
> When I, am long ago,
> An Island in dishonored Grass—
> Whom none but Beetles—know. (#290)

Nature, in the shape of the aurora borealis, is "adequate," but not in the sense that Trinitarian natural theology promised it would be. The northern lights do not suffice to answer human questions, provide signs of God's character and purpose, or give empirical support to faith. Their "Compete-less Show" is adequate only to itself. The light does not inform, "it forms," and the verb lacks an object. "The North" shapes no meaning to us, it simply shapes. It is self-reflexively "preconcerted," "distant," and sovereignly unconcerned. In some poems, Dickinson would take such indifference to be an attribute of God. Here, the universe is emptied of transcendence. That fact might have stunned her into silence, for the poet would seem to have no role in a meaningless world. Dickinson's frequent response to that problem was to set her own creative voice against nature, scripture, and God. But that maneuver, as she also recognized, could so empty the world of meaning as to leave meaning arbitrary and render the poet's act of creation a frivolous imposition. Both the response and the recognition reverberate here. If the poet cannot discover informing truth in nature, she can borrow from it a posture of majestic, disdainful indifference, refusing the pain of inhabiting an assertive but hollow world by forming an assertive, indifferent, and queenly identity of her own. Here, though, her self-importance is also hollow; her unwarranted "Arrogance" is punctured even as it swells. She describes her pride as an illness. Contracted from self-regarding nature, it "Infects" and "Taints." Her posturing is just that, a disdainful strut, comically constricted by its holdfast "stem." Her disregard for "Men and Oxygen" is a delusory self-reliance, at once solipsistic, antisocial, and suffocating.

The second stanza continues the critique. Bradstreet could outdo nature's superhuman glories by noting that where they would "perish, fade, and dye," "Man was made for endless immortality." Dickinson's world lacks the eternal dimension. It has only the near-timeless continuity of nature, and humanity's brief span. The poet's strutting splendors are "Menagerie," a tame and scrubby sideshow to nature's big top. They will disappear with her death and decay, while nature goes on entertaining "Centuries." But there is a countervoice here, too. Its barker's call is quiet, but enticing and clear. The "Competeless Show," taken above as belonging to the northern lights, may also be owned by the poet's "Splendors." The second stanza reduces but still asserts the worth of the poet's work. The claim is conventional enough: art confers what immortality I have; my work will last for centuries after my flesh has gone to grass. This "immortality" is but a semblance of the Christian promise of a personal eternity. And "Competeless" not only indicates that the poet's splendors have no competition but also that, with God gone, there is nothing for them to compete with, no reason *to* compete. The issues are not resolved. Many modern and postmodern poets continue to circulate among them, sharing—in their more secular contexts—Dickinson's concern with addressing nature in order to consider epistemology and esthetics, the meaning of meaning and the poet's role.

Nature's Nation

American poets who write about nature in order to engage epistemological and esthetic questions inevitably do so against the backdrop of broad cultural attitudes toward the natural world and the poet's social function. The most encompassing American notions about nature have to do with the conflict between nature and civilization. This is an issue in every culture, but geographical and chronological circumstances caused it to loom especially large in the United States. The Europeans who, as they saw it, discovered and settled the New World carried with them fundamental metaphors that implicitly defined their sense of the relationship of nature and culture. Leo Marx has shown that the most common and powerful of those metaphors figured America either as the earthly paradise or as a howling wilderness. Each version might be upheld by actual experience (a smooth or storm-tossed voyage, benign or malign terrain, yielding or hostile natives), but they had more to do with preconceptions about the human condition and the status of nature than they did with descriptive precision. Those preconceptions are themselves quite intricate, and they frequently interpenetrate in ways that conceal, ignore, or ostensibly reconcile their contradictions. A brief discussion requires drastic simplifications.

The view of American nature as Edenic was sometimes no more than propaganda used to promote discovery or colonization. More often it drew on deep-seated utopian aspirations and on a long tradition of imaginary, often westward-lying sites for the new golden age. The metaphor of the New World as New Eden is based on anticultural desires to escape from history—whether the protracted annals of European wars, oppression and rigid social hierarchy, or the unavoidable entailment of original sin. It expresses a desire "to cut loose from the constraints of a complex society" and to find—easily available to all in nature's simple, benevolent bower—an instinctive life of abundance, leisure, harmony, and freedom. This version of things stresses the individual and is anarchistic and primitivistic in its assumptions. It conceives of human nature, and of nature, as innately good, seeing corruption as an effect of civilization. Conversely, the metaphor of America as a howling wilderness is procultural. It sees the corruptions of nature and humanity as the result of the Fall. History and sin are real, and to some extent inescapable; nonetheless, it is the role of civilization to overcome as much as it can of nature's chaos and to replace it with order. In this version of things, the instinctive threatens to become irrationality and madness, leisure and freedom conduce to license, and abundance and harmony are to be achieved only by vigilance and laborious struggle. Such a view stresses community, requires the postponement of pleasure, and insists upon the need to establish and maintain rules and hierarchies. It considers the New World "a field for the exercise of power" and demands action for the manipulation and mastery of nature and of human nature.[66]

Those competing yet often conjoined metaphors have roots deep in Western cultural tradition—in the Bible, for instance. In Genesis, Adam and Eve are punished for their sin by expulsion from the paradisal garden. They are then compelled to live in wild nature. There, innocence and immortality are replaced by sin and death; ease and abundance are supplanted by labor and scarcity. Thus nature is associated with evil. In the book of Exodus, however, wild nature provides a place of escape from an oppressive and sinful civilization. It is the locus for encounters with God and an arena for purification and testing. Yet even in this relatively positive view, the experience of nature involves suffering and struggle. And the experience is a fundamentally transient one, the painful but necessary preparation for entry into the infinitely more desirable promised land. The pattern is typical. While a counterview is often dimly present, the idea of nature as an evil that civilization must resist and overcome (or pass through on the way to culture) has dominated Western thought. Medieval visionaries and saints went to nature to test and purify themselves, but from ancient times through the Middle Ages and beyond nature remained the home of the devil, the fearful haunt of Pan, the habitat of wild men and women no better than beasts. Roderick Nash demonstrates how slow, grudging, and equivocal has been the modification of this conception of nature as evil toward a conception of it as a presence to be appreciated, affirmed, and protected. That modification began in the Renaissance and continues into the present, where it is very far from complete. It involves large-scale transformations in intellectual history: the rise of humanism and science, the revaluation of materialism against medieval spiritualism and the doctrine of *contemptus mundi*, the reconception of the sublime, romantic primitivism and its interest in the exotic and the extreme, the transformation of cities from places of safety and comfort into industrialized urban jungles, and the elaboration of a conservation ethic and of the principles of ecology, to name a few.[67]

But this gets ahead of the story. In America, as in Europe, people typically chose civilization over nature. But in a sense, the very fact that there was a choice to be made remained invisible until the effects of the choosing had become extreme, until our protection of ourselves from nature reached the point where nature could be seen as needing protection from us—a fairly recent development. In any case, the opposition between nature and culture was rarely stated so baldly as I have framed it here. In the New World this conflict often involved a division of nature itself into the opposed categories of garden and wilderness. To an extent, the partition resolved the oppositions it described. The division is an ancient one, of course; it has biblical roots of its own and is the source of both pagan and Christian pastoral conventions. It had particular resonance in America. In its most common form, the division of nature into wilderness and garden implies a preference for cultivated nature over both civilization and wilderness. Thus, it satisfies the metaphor of the New World as Eden, rejecting the complications and corruptions of European society in favor of an American landscape that offers vast opportunities for starting over, for avoiding the errors of history, and for converting the wilderness into a newly paradisal garden. At the same time, the division of nature also satisfies the metaphor of the New World as a howling wilderness, since it retains the fundamental assumption of that view—the necessity for marshalling the forces of community and culture to exercise power over a natural wilderness dangerously tempting and hostile in its uncultivated state, yet with enormous potential for conversion. The choice of cultivated nature over both civilization and wilderness also received tremendous impetus from various versions of the faith that America was the site where the millennium would be achieved. It fit well, too, with eighteenth-century preferences for the middle way, and with the notion that humanity occupies a midpoint between the animals and the angels on the great chain of being.

Untouched wilderness always had its proponents, and there would remain a muted debate about whether the wilderness was somehow in fact already a garden or had to be made into one, but in general the ruralist preference for the cultivated middle landscape won out over competing versions. Daniel Boone would be invoked more often as the standard-bearer of agricultural settlement than as either the child of nature fleeing before society's advance or the founder of cities.[68] In Jefferson's agrarian vision, technology itself (say, the waterwheel) would harness nature and liberate human beings from onerous labor without destroying nature or subjugating humanity to the renewed feudalism of the European factory system. The image of the independent yeoman farmer, living a life of rural retreat within domesticated but undefeated nature (a situation that supposedly combined the inspiration of wilderness with the refinements of culture) persisted well after the factory system was solidly in place, that is, well into the nineteenth and twentieth centuries. The figure of the American Adam in the New World garden had become a national myth. It did not so much resolve as mask the conflict between nature and civilization.[69] Before we turn to that issue, though, there is another one to consider: the relationship between American nature and American nationalism.

From the beginning, American-European relations had been marked, on the American side, by an anxiety of influence. How could America, which purported to have thrown off the yoke of European history, hope to compete with the cultural glories which that history had achieved? One answer, of course, was the assertion that those supposed glories were in fact the sheen of corruption, that American primitivism in manners, means, and cultural production were the marks of primal innocence, of paradise regained. This response was never wholly satisfactory. Innocence was a two-edged sword: the unfallen Adam was also a country bumpkin. The Revolution intensified the problem: the United States could hardly justify its independence on the grounds of cultural attainment. Nature provided an alternative defense. American independence coincided with the revaluation of wilderness in Western thought. Despised for centuries as the hideously ugly and irregular consequence of the Fall, feared as a physical and spiritual threat, or simply regarded as useless until leveled, drained, or otherwise converted to human purposes, wilderness was reconceived as the unfallen remnant of a divine creation whose rugged glory had been concealed, marred, or destroyed by civilization. Wilderness was now seen as the landscape nearest to God; at times, it was seen *as* God. More typically, contact with the wilderness became the preferred route to spiritual knowledge and fulfillment, the place where material and spiritual truths would wholly coincide. This radical change was never so complete or widely agreed upon as this makes it sound; older attitudes still determined most economic and technological activity. Nonetheless, the altered view of nature was supported both by Enlightenment scientific notions of natural law and by romantic theory, and had enormous intellectual and popular currency. It provided America with a needed justification for its existence, with a claim to uniqueness among the nations. If wild nature was preferable to civilization, American civilization had wilderness aplenty. America was nature's nation,[70] and, by extension, God's nation as well, a notion supported by the myth of Puritan antecedence and, again, by the corollary faith that the millennium was destined to be realized here. By the mid-nineteenth century, in part as an escape from culture, in part as our particular version of it, nature had become the national religion. It was significant enough that the previously minor genre of the landscape could "assume the mantle of history painting."[71]

The actual situation was less clear-cut. Europe was already developed; its wilderness was a remnant. But if America had the advantage of possessing extensive wilderness, it also had a problem: wilderness was literally everywhere. The Revolution promised growth, development, expansion (in most versions, the millennium, too, would not simply occur but would have to be achieved). Expansive achievements could come only at the expense of wild nature, from its conversion into farm or town or city. American civilization, American greatness, could only be achieved by the destruction of the wilderness that gave American civilization its special claim to greatness. While settlement proceeded slowly and American resources appeared inexhaustible, the dilemma might be ignored. Eventually, though, it had to be faced. The simple inversion of the old choice, nature now preferred to culture, would not do. Once more, as with the more general tension between the claims of nature and civilization, the difficulty was ostensibly resolved by subtle shifts away from the celebration of wild nature and toward the depiction of cultivated nature as superior both to civilization (especially in the form of industrial cities) and to the untamed nature of wilderness. Again, this myth (and evasion) could hold so long as there was ample wilderness remaining to keep its contradictions concealed. Even today, the existence of national parks and national forests helps preserve the myth of virgin land intact. It seemed the perfect solution to conflicting claims. Perhaps its purest, and most knowing, expression is in Thoreau's statement that "[i]t would be some advantage to live a primitive and frontier life, though in the midst of outward civilization. . . ." Both the possibilities and limits of the myth can be seen there, as they can in the strategically placed tree stumps that dot the surfaces of so many American landscape paintings. They mark with frank or concealed ambiguity the tension the paintings seem to resolve. As Henry Nash Smith puts it, America's westward expansion provided opportunities both for "regretting the destruction of the primitive freedom of an untouched continent" and for celebrating "a glorious victory of civilization over savagery and barbarism."[72] The myth of the New World garden held the contradictions in check, but it did not so much resolve them as provide, however unintentionally, "a rhetorical screen under which the aggressive conquest of the country" could proceed unhindered.[73]

A major, usually ignored flaw in the myth of the New World garden is that it imposes an essentially static image on a dynamic process. In an age dominated by the notion (and fact) of progress, an age increasingly committed to scientific ideas that seemed to support "progressive" beliefs by showing that the world itself was not young and static but old and dynamic, the image of a rural landscape in stasis between civilization and wilderness could not be sustained, or, rather, it could be sustained only insofar as its contradictions were ignored. As many saw even then, the achievement of the middle-ground rural state required the destruction of the wild. That process would continue until there was no wilderness left. Furthermore, the rural did not exist in perpetuity but was apt to be on the way to becoming the alienating city that had made nature attractive in the first place. Some of our finest cultural historians have addressed those issues. Perry Miller is exemplary of them. In "Nature and the National Ego," he writes that although a survey of the 1840s reveals a "seemingly untroubled assurance about the great civilization America was hewing out of the wilderness," "the astonishing fact about this gigantic material thrust . . . is how few Americans would any longer venture . . . to explain, let alone to justify the expansion of civilization in any language . . . of utility." Rather, they viewed "the most utilitarian conquest known to history" not as "inspired by a calculus of rising land values and investments but . . . as an immense exertion of the spirit." The faster the forests were felled, the more emphatically poets, painters, and preachers strove to identify America with unspoiled nature, and in ways that, paradoxically, hastened its destruction. This gap between act and explanation can be understood in part by remarking the alienation of persons of sensibility within a rampantly materialistic society, but the gulf is wider and goes deeper than that. It points once more to the old American conflict between the claims of nature and culture and to the potent yet inevitably self-canceling solution to that conflict in the myth of the New World garden. Briefly, if America's uniqueness is a function of nature, then as nature is lost, so, too, is culture; yet if nature is left unaltered, culture cannot be established. The opposition ("between forest and town, spontaneity and calculation, heart and head, the unconscious and the self-conscious, the innocent and the debauched") could not be reconciled. It is the stuff of American consciousness, and of American art.[74]

The literary implications of these matters, especially for canonical nineteenth-century fiction, have been widely studied. R. W. B. Lewis takes the image of the American Adam as a concomitant of the image of America as a new Eden. He traces three responses to that figuration, the parties of hope, memory, and irony. The first two responses are often simplistic or naive, either hopeful that the innocent (male) hero will achieve his unlimited potential within unlimited nature, or saddened by his inevitable failure to do so in a society that destroys nature and human nature alike (alternatively, the innocent is lampooned for the callowness that makes him an easy dupe). The third response combines the first two in a sophisticated reaction that recognizes the tragedy inherent both in defining nature as culture and in the Adamic figure's supposed innocence—his hope to remain unfallen helps to bring about his inevitable fall. According to Lewis, this last establishes the pattern for American fiction.[75]

Leo Marx shows that American thought typically, and explosively, combines a pastoral preference for rural landscape with a Jeffersonian faith in limited, agrarian technology, a faith that is itself often confused with the more aggressive, progress-oriented, and essentially urban notions of the technological sublime (in which the industrial revolution will annihilate space and time and bring the heavenly city to earth). For most, the contradictions remained submerged in this heady mixture, but many American writers exploited its volatility, using irruptions of the machine into the garden as a fundamental metaphor to explode contradictions. They did so in interpretations that were variously transcendental, tragic, or vernacular. Marx further suggests that the incredibly rapid but slowly recognized transformation of America from a rural to an industrial nation helps explain the features of American fiction (they bear on American poetry as well) famously described by Richard Chase, including its tendency to leap over "everyday social experience into an abstract realm of morality and metaphysics" where reality is defined "as a contradiction between radically opposed forces."[76]

In a more narrowly focused treatment, Bernard Rosenthal suggests that the nineteenth-century American obsession with journeys to nature concealed the fact that the journey to nature is inevitably a journey to the city, since human presence makes the transformation of landscape inevitable. Similarly, it concealed the tension between science's picture of nature as a dynamic process of decay, indifference, and struggle and the Adamic picture of nature as a stable phenomenon. The transcendentalists resolved this dilemma by replacing the actual city building implied in the journey to nature with an internalized act of reconstruction, the restoration of the demolished self.[77] Perhaps the sense of rupture brought on by various versions of the tensions between nature and culture accounts for the quality Lawrence Buell notes in nineteenth-century American writing, in which Melville, Hawthorne, and Dickinson, and even Emerson and Longfellow, exhibit signs of the epistemological, linguistic, and esthetic unease characteristic of modernist and postmodernist thought.[78] In any case, along with the epistemological ones described above, these and related contexts help to define American nature poetry from the beginning through the nineteenth century. Versions of those contexts, along with new challenges to them, persist into the present. They continue to fuel our political debates, those between development and conservation, for instance, or between managed conservation and preservation. They provide an enduring backdrop for modern and postmodern nature poetry as well.

In nature's nation, what is the poet's, and poetry's, role? Again, the anxiety of influence bears on the issue. How could America's fledgling art compete with the soaring greatness of Europe's? The difficulty *could* be solved by asserting that Europe's cultural success is excess, the mark of corruption, but then art itself becomes suspect as "unnatural." At the same time, artistic achievements were among those deemed most necessary for justifying American claims to independence and for helping to create a sense of national identity. There were constant predictions of and demands for American works that would rival European ones, and that would somehow do so by being radically original and utterly different from them. Again, wild nature, which America possessed in abundance, and which was conceived of as a privileged route to the truth, seemed to offer a solution. But wild nature assumes the absence of art. The American landscape painters who recorded the transcendent sublimity of virgin wilderness typically accompanied expeditions for exploration, mapping, or surveying. Sponsored by government agencies or by railroad or mining companies, those expeditions had as their long-range goal the exploitation of wilderness and its conversion into civilization. The artists' celebration was inevitably mourning as well. The complications and contradictions implicit in these matters contribute to America's notorious ambivalence about the products of culture.

In developments from the Puritans to Emerson, the American poet moved from a peripheral and dependent position ringed about by doubt and distrust to an essential and definitive position confident of its claim to be without circumference. The poet who began as a minor acolyte to the priest became the priest. As to poetry, it had been at worst an idolatrous snare, and at best the modestly decorative, didactic conveyor of revealed truths, which, if they existed in nature at all, were inscribed there by God and decoded by scripture. Poetry became the most direct and essential mode of cognition, the discoverer or creator of truth in a natural world imbued with spirit, accessible to every individual, and nearer to God than even his book. In their various ways, the poets of the American renaissance promulgated and celebrated those elevations of their art. By the second half of the nineteenth century, American poets and poetry had achieved unprecedented positions of cultural value and respect. As Wolff puts it, poetry "was held to serve a significant intellectual function. The citizens of this still-new nation were willing to believe" that writers of serious verse might "teach them how to think." Poetry had a wide and enthusiastic audience: in 1858, one book of Longfellow's sold more than fifteen thousand copies on its first day in print. Furthermore, "for nearly twenty years Longfellow taught at Harvard and served as an arbiter of taste and thought among educated Americans." Emerson, although he rejected the church and the academy, lectured widely enough and was read by so many that he, too, "managed to fuse the roles of poet and intellectual leader." Even the iconoclastic Whitman, at first considered a disgrace, was being called the "Good Gray Poet" by the mid 1860s. In 1892, the year of his death, he, too, was acknowledged as a poet who had helped Americans to formulate their most important thoughts.[79]

Wolff makes these points to demonstrate that similar opportunities for intellectual, artistic, and cultural leadership were unavailable to women. Surely that is part of why Dickinson, from her peculiarly faithful position, renewed in radical terms the old challenge to notions upholding poetry's exalted cultural status, and at the very moment when that status was achieved. There are other reasons as well. For Dickinson, nature did not manifest benevolent divine or cosmic truths, nor was it merely a material obstacle to spirit that imagination might transcend or remove. If nature revealed God, it often revealed him as a cruel or tormenting master, or it revealed a blank indifference, nothing at all. Neither could "passing events in nature" be made "subservient to moral instruction" without dishonest distortions of the facts. Dickinson agreed that poetry and poets produce meaning, but she could not ignore the relativistic implications of subjectivity in romantic claims to discover or create the truth. Emerson and Whitman usually were confident that, in individualistic, self-reliant America, subjectivity is the sure sign of universality, that discovery and creation must of necessity coincide. Dickinson suspected that what was claimed as discovery might be creative invention, the imposition of meaning on what might have a quite different significance or no significance whatever. Again and again she questions the supposedly perfect fit between self and community, mind and nature, world and Word, words and world that upheld romantic assertions. Her poetry does not so much know as doubt. It finds whole and wholesome truth less often than rupture. Issues of publication aside, it was hardly the stuff to unify the nation, cement its moral and social conventions, or attach America's destiny to God's evolving plan in the light of nature's testimony. It could provide no comfort for the orthodox, nor could it serve as an idealistic mask for pragmatic depradations. It even abused the familiar, regular pleasures of rhythm and rhyme.

By the turn of the century, poetry's exalted cultural status was gone; poets were once more peripheral or irrelevant to American life. This was hardly the fault of Dickinson's honest critique. Such factors as the Civil War, urbanization, industrialization, immigration, economic rapaciousness, Darwinism, social Darwinism, the closing of the frontier, and the disappearance of wild or cultivated nature from the purview of most Americans all contributed to making both the guarantees of Dickinson's fellows and their ways of making them seem hopelessly naive, idealistic, and out of touch with American reality. Soon those seemed characteristics of poetry itself. As David Perkins says, by 1900 poetry was eclipsed by "the rising genre of the novel, which was seducing the audience of poetry and taking over many of its [poetry's] functions." For the moment, at least, realistic and naturalistic fiction seemed better able than poetry to deal with "the material aspects of existence," with "the facts of social environment and organization." Matter and spirit, what Emerson and Whitman had put together, came apart. Poetry was dominated by the genteel tradition and its attempt to compensate for the social and moral displacements of post–Civil War American life. Insecure with regard to European standards, and committed to literary conventions, the genteel poets felt that the involvement of realism and naturalism with the material facts of life came at the expense of more essential spiritual verities. They considered fiction vulgarly sensationalistic in its experimentalism and in its allegedly false emphasis on the violent and the low, the very world from which they hoped to redeem their readers. Thus the genteel poets recoiled from contemporary America. They sought comfort in a "vague idealism not much related to actual life" and in a faith in "culture" and its assumed "spiritual or quasi-religious value." Whatever their merits (their emphasis on formal craftsmanship, for instance), the dim idealism typical of their work joined other factors in tending to make poetry just one more "of the many spiritual, acknowledged irrelevancies on which Americans sometimes bestowed a few moments snatched from business."[80]

This need not have been the case. If Dickinson's challenge raised the question of what the poet's role would be in a world devoid of transcendence, she had also provided possible answers in her empiricism and humor, in her exploitation of dissonance and disjunction, in her deconstructions of the given, and in her reconstructive poems of finite infinity, definition, and description. It was still possible for poets to turn to nature to frame epistemological and esthetic questions, to do so with full awareness of contemporary reality—including social and scientific reality—and without sacrificing intellectual rigor, emotional clarity, or social purpose. It would be a generation before poets would do so again. When they did—Frost, Stevens, and Moore and, a little later, Bishop—the circumstances would differ, but the questions would be familiar ones: How do we know what we know? Is poetry most true or most feigning? Do we find or falsify, discover or invent? In the twentieth century those questions would coincide with some of the largest issues in Western culture.

CHAPTER TWO

ROBERT FROST

All virtue in "as if."

WHEN ROBERT FROST "returned" to New England in 1885, the region's agricultural economy had already dwindled toward the landscape of forsaken farms, empty cellar holes, and encroaching woods that figures so prominently in his poems. New England agriculture had reached its peak in the 1860s, when there was more cleared land than at any time since then—much of it carved with great difficulty from hilly and heavily forested terrain. By the 1870s, farms were being abandoned wholesale. The reasons for this were many. The New England topsoil was good enough, but scant; it was well mixed with rocks and concentrated in areas too small to support the large farm machinery then coming into use. The already powerful pull of vast tracts of cheap, level, easily cleared land in the west intensified when canals, steam navigation, and the railroads combined to provide inexpensive bulk transportation to markets in the east. Water-powered industry in New England's own river towns also drained people from the farms. The Civil War was another factor. By the 1880s the abandonment of farms—there were few buyers—was sufficiently advanced that the popular magazines of the period swelled with alarmist reports and hopeful proposals. The great national heritage of the family farm, located in what the public envisioned as an idyllic rural or "middle" landscape, was threatened by a flood of westward migration. Something had to be done to stem the tide. Nothing much was. Before long, deserted farmhouses decayed and collapsed; roads were abandoned; brush, and then trees, invaded the pastures and fields cleared by the heroic labor of New England pioneers. One New Hampshireman reported that when he was a child in 1865 he knew of nine old cellar holes within a mile's walk of his country school. In 1887, he counted twenty-three.[1]

Albert Gelpi has identified the pioneer myth as the "unifying conception" of Frost's poetry, "the source of his controlling images and metaphors."[2] Frost often does seem to side with the humanly "converted" landscape of the clearing in its battle against the woods, and his woods sometimes do represent the "howling wilderness" of indifferent nature and its dark encroachments on what little clearings and clarifications humans have wrested from it. But Frost's woods represent other aspects of nature's role in American mythology as well. They are sometimes a place of freedom from the oppressive constraints of too much civilization, for instance. On rare occasions in Frost's poetry, nature can seem (momentarily) Edenic in its own right. More important is that Frost recognizes those and other competing attitudes as being mythic or metaphorical projections, and in his work no one of them appears totally isolated from the others. Typically, several occur together, in the intricate Frostian arrangements William Pritchard designates by the term "designed inclusiveness."[3] An ambivalent sense of the relative values of clearings and woods is an essential aspect of Frost's work. It includes all the oppositions and "correspondences" his woods and clearings represent, among them mind (or poetry) and nature. The borders of clearings and woods are thus a site of what Frank Lentricchia calls Frost's "primary *agon*," "the struggle between the fiction-making imagination and the antifictive of the given environment."[4]

Insofar as Frost's clearings represent human conversions of shapeless nature into orderly form, and insofar as his woods represent nature's resistance to that conversion, their opposition can indicate the way in which Frost turns to nature to frame epistemological and esthetic questions. However, "opposition" is not the right word to describe the relationship of clearings to woods, or of mind to nature, or of form to "wildness" in his poems. "Complementarity" comes nearer.

Emerson believed that there were ontological, theological, and metaphysical validations for his imagined analogies ("the relation between the mind and matter stands in the will of God"; truth is present in nature, where we creatively perceive it). Dickinson doubted the existence of those validations, suspecting that analogies invent truths rather than perceive them; from that suspicion, and working with contraries, she made her finest poems. Frost thought that there are no validations, or that if there are, they are inaccessible to human consciousness. Any appearance of external validation for human meanings results from metaphoric impositions of pattern where none demonstrably exists, and from the human tendency to take those impositions as fact or gospel. Invention is a matter of imaginative creation rather than discovery. That view would have paralyzed Emerson. His freedom came from confidence that "perception is not whimsical, but fatal." "Any distrust of the permanence of laws" (that is, of the perfect fit between mind, nature, and God) "would paralyze the faculties of man." For Frost, the reverse is true. "Fatality" would immobilize the self. Frost's sense of meaning as humanly and provisionally constructed, rather than as absolute, permanent, and guaranteed by God, liberates him from Emerson's "fate" and from the tyranny of received ideas, including his own. But Frost's poems do not ignore the possibility of discovery. They frequently entertain the notion that creation and discovery *might* coincide. This is a source of their drama. Furthermore, Frost treats those oppositions more as complements than as contraries. Imagination's imposition of clarification or order, whether personal or cultural, is the defining characteristic of our humanity. It is as important to Frost as it was to Emerson; its exercise is as much as we have of saving grace. At the same time, however, to exercise it rigidly or with finality or certainty, as if "a solution to the riddle of the universe [were] just around the corner,"[5] is damnation. In Frost, the rage for order and the rage for chaos everywhere meet and challenge one another, and each has its human as well as natural sources.

Frost's comments on form can indicate the complexities of his attitude. Frost's enthusiasm for the human construction of form is famous. In his "Letter to *The Amherst Student*" he writes, "There is at least so much good in the world that it admits of form and the making of form. And not only admits of it, but calls for it. . . . When in doubt there is always form for us to go on with. . . . The artist[,] the poet[,] might be expected to be the most aware of such assurance. But it is really everybody's sanity to feel and live by it." The assurance resists a significant threat: "The background in hugeness and confusion shading away . . . into black and utter chaos." Against that threatening background stands "any small, man-made figure of order and concentration."[6] This is the well-known stuff of Frost's "momentary stay against confusion,"[7] and it represents a major aspect of his esthetic and "philosophical" position: faith in the human necessity to assert form against "natural" chaos. But when we notice the "diminished" language of Frost's statements and shift the emphasis from the "stay" itself to its "momentary" duration, we see the other side of his position. Were any specific "stay against confusion" to become permanent, then the very source of the form-giving urge that ensures our sanity—the "background in hugeness and confusion" calling out for form—would be lost. Frost considers both "man-made figures" and their background of chaos to be essential. Each exists, he says, the fictive and the antifictive, and "What pleasanter than that this should be so? . . . [W]e don't worry about this confusion. . . . [W]e like it, we were born to it, born used to it and have practical reasons for wanting it there." Making form is our sanity: that is Frost's "practical" reason for wanting the presence and "pressure" of chaos or confusion, its urging us on to form. "To me any little form I assert upon it is velvet, as the saying is, and to be considered for how much more it is than nothing." Too much success, though, would be just that, too much, and a kind of madness. Frost resists the desire for a perfect, permanent order: going on about the "little form" he admires for "how much more it is than nothing," he says, "If I were a Platonist I should have to consider it, I suppose, for how much less it is than everything."[8]

Although his remarks about the virtues of the form-giving imagination are better known, and perhaps better suited to his notorious desire to "reach out" to the widest possible audience rather than be "caviare to the crowd," Frost frequently stressed the dangers of too much form. "I'm very much in favor of unfinished business," he said in an interview. In a letter to a student, he wrote: "I'm less and less for systems and system-building in my old age. I'm afraid of too much structure. Some violence is always done to the wisdom you build a philosophy out of." These remarks about the danger of too much form were made in 1960 and 1927, respectively. Elsewhere, Frost suggests that his viewpoint developed over time: "I began life wanting perfection and determined to have it. I got so I ceased to expect it and could do without it. Now I find I actually crave the flaws of human handiwork. I gloat over imperfection." However that may have been, in the poetry those several attitudes are present in "designed inclusiveness" from early on. He put the matter rhetorically to Sidney Cox in 1937: "Why should I press home my conclusions everywhere." Reginald Cook recorded this comment in 1954: "We get so tired of meaning. . . . I'm sick of meaning. It's like a disease. . . . One of the relaxations must be back into chaos."[9]

Not that Frost could ever "distrust form as such"; that, he said, would be naive. He also said, "The freedom is ours to insist on meaning." But to insist too much, to trust meaning entirely, would be naive as well: "Only in a certain type of small scientific mind can there be found cocksureness, a conviction that a solution to the riddle of the universe is just around the corner." Frost's "passionate preference" is for formulas that do not quite formulate. He stated his preference to Louis Untermeyer as early as 1917: "You get more credit for thinking if you restate formulae or cite cases that fall in easily under formulae, but all the fun is outside saying things that suggest formulae that won't formulate—that almost but don't quite formulate." Frost's position is *between* the desire for form and the resistance to form's excesses, and not in the sense of any static balance. As he wrote to Lawrance Thompson about Thompson's *Fire and Ice*, "You gave me an anxious moment about my 'golden mean.' I should hate to get stuck in the golden mean. You make it all right in the end. You give me plenty of play between the tugs and the holdbacks."[10] The supposed New Critical pattern of perfect balance—a static structure held rigid by the struts of dichotomies in tension —was never the model of Frost's construction. His poems move by melting, build up while breaking down. They stay in motion; playing is their work.

Frost's definitions of the figure a poem makes always imply movement: "It begins in delight, it inclines to the impulse, . . . it runs a course of lucky events. . . ." Or, "Like a piece of ice on a hot stove the poem must ride on its own melting." In its way, the figure is erotic, "the same as for love," a rising and falling that bears, permits, calls out for repetition. "No one," Frost insists, "can really hold that the ecstasy should be static and stand still in one place." That would be the end of making, whether poems or love. Finality is what the poems avoid as they seek it. The "most exciting movement in nature is not progress, advance, but expansion and contraction. . . ." It is so for poetry as well: "Progress is not the aim, but circulation." This does not call for endlessly open-ended poems, however. Poems can be "finished" (contraction is as exciting as expansion), but they must be finished so as to remain somehow unfinished, so as to send up the *next* poem. Thinking and writing, Frost circulates between these poles: "The most conservative thing in the world is that like produces like. . . . The most radical thing is a certain dissatisfaction that that is so."[11]

The esthetic and epistemological implications of those attitudes emerge in Frost's "theory" of metaphor. The major prose expression of that theory is the essay "Education by Poetry," first delivered as a talk at Amherst College and then revised for publication in the February 1931 issue of the *Amherst Graduate's Quarterly*. Richard Poirier's penetrating observation that in Frost's best writing metaphor is a locus of energy, not a sign of meaning ultimately to be enforced, can serve as a summary of the essay's argument insofar as it affects or describes Frost's poetic practice.[12] But that gets ahead of the story.

American poets and poetry had attained unprecedented cultural status by the second half of the nineteenth century. An enthusiastic audience of readers believed that poetry had something important to tell and teach them (Frost's mother was such a reader). But in the late nineteenth and early twentieth centuries—the years of Frost's coming of age—poetry's exalted status drastically diminished. In those years, poetry was dominated by the genteel tradition, against which Frost's subject matter and diction were so dramatic a rebellion. Genteel poems seemed hopelessly out of touch with the major cultural developments of the time: urbanization, industrialization, immigration, and the cluster of ideas known as "naturalism" among them. Those developments were more often treated in fiction than in the now more marginal genre of verse. The increasingly evident and respected powers of science and technology also contributed to the decline of poetry's status. Frost's conversation and prose often display his sense that poetry is embattled by those forces and in need of advocacy and defense. In *Made in America*, Lisa Steinman shows how Stevens, Williams, and Moore attempted to rehabilitate poetry's fallen position precisely by redefining its practice in relation to science and technology.[13] "Education by Poetry" reflects a somewhat similar effort on Frost's part. It claims that both poetry and science are involved in the single activity of asserting provisional form upon a background of chaos. It also claims that they employ essentially the same method for doing so, the making—and unmaking—of metaphors.

Of course, Frost typically rejected any notion of the present age as somehow special: "[Y]ou will often hear it said that the age of the world we live in is particularly bad. I am impatient of such talk. . . . It is immodest of a man to think of himself as going down before the worst forces ever mobilized by God."[14] Therefore, "Education by Poetry" is as much a defense against Plato's attacks on poetry as against any more up-to-date ones. But whether he is countering Plato's charge that poetry obstructs knowledge and certitude, or the contemporary view of poetry as simply irrelevant to such ends, Frost's intention is to demonstrate that poetry is, in fact, a means to knowledge. Furthermore, the knowledge poetry discloses, while real and valuable, is a made thing, and always uncertain in any ultimate sense. The latter might seem to play directly into the enemy's hands, but Frost does not claim that only the knowledge *poetry* attains is fictive and uncertain: rather, *all* knowledge is tentative, provisional, and invented, a formula that won't quite formulate. In this Frost comes *near* accepting what has become a modern dogma: that the universe is meaningless and that any order "discovered" in it is the result of human imposition.[15]

For Frost (he speaks metaphorically, there being no other way), poetry is identical with metaphor: "There are many other things I have found myself saying about poetry, but the chiefest of these is that it is metaphor."[16] And metaphor is identical with thinking: "I have wanted in late years to go further and further in making metaphor the whole of thinking."[17] Poetry is not, then, the imprecise or fanciful opposite of hard-headed, practical science. Neither is it an obstacle to education, nor a mere entertainment or waste of time. Rather, since metaphor is the whole of thinking, science, like all human constructions, is a kind of poetry, and poetry is an essential means of education. Science and poetry both "attempt to say matter in terms of spirit, or spirit in terms of matter, to make the final unity. That is the greatest attempt that ever failed" (41). Failure to make the final unity is as essential as the attempt to make it, and it is as essential to science as it is to poetry. Any ultimate incarnational success would end the game for both. Frost rarely wrote about the physical details of modern life (say, cities, factories, or cars), but the ideas in his poems are quite another matter.

Because all thinking and knowing are metaphorical, and because poetry "is simply made of metaphor,"[18] poetry has epistemological and educational value. And because Frost identifies thinking with metaphor, his remarks about poetry are as much about epistemology as esthetics. "Education by poetry is education by metaphor" (35). Poetic education is vital because without it we are lost not only in poetry but in science and every other discipline as well. We do not know how we know and what the possibilities and limits of our knowing are. To support his claims, Frost borrows examples from history, from biology, and from physics both ancient and modern. The upshot is this: "[U]nless you are at home in the metaphor, unless you have had your proper poetical education in the metaphor, you are not safe anywhere. Because you are not at ease with figurative values: you don't know the metaphor in its strength and its weakness. You don't know how far you may expect to ride it and when it may break down with you. You are not safe in science; you are not safe in history" (39). You are not safe because you may ride the metaphor too far and end up lost. As Frost said about the dangers of political or ideological metaphors, "Fire flashes from the flint and steel of metaphor and if caught in lint it may be spread, but that is no reason why it should spread to burn the world. That is monomania or monometaphor."[19]

Frost gives an example from science. "Another metaphor that has interested us in our time and has done all our thinking for us is the metaphor of evolution. . . . The metaphor . . . of the growing plant or the growing thing. And somebody very brilliantly, quite a while ago, said that the whole universe, the whole of everything, was like unto a growing thing. That is all. . . . It is a very brilliant metaphor, I acknowledge, though I myself get too tired of the kind of essay that talks about the evolution of candy, we will say, or the evolution of elevators—the evolution of this, that, and the other. Everything is evolution" (38–39). This sort of extreme exercise of metaphor beyond its strength to bear is what education by poetry can rein us in from.

Of course, Frost does delight in the form-giving power of the human imagination making its metaphors. Form remains what we have to go on with, and "Great is he who imposes the metaphor."[20] In the essay, Frost takes enormous pleasure in the then-emerging metaphor of quantum physics and in its implications for the old debate between determinism and free will: "[H]ere it is on a platter. You know that you can't tell by name what persons in a certain class will be dead ten years after graduation, but you can tell actuarially how many will be dead. Now, just so this scientist says of the particles of matter flying at a screen, striking a screen; you can't tell what individual particles will come, but you can say in general that a certain number will strike in a given time. It shows, you see, that the individual particle can come freely" (38). The danger of such a metaphor, and of the pleasure and power it provides, is that it may harden into monometaphor, into Truth, as in the application of the metaphor of evolution to anything and everything. "We are all toadies to the fashionable metaphor of the hour."[21] Our protection from such madness, as from exhausted horses and wildfire, is a poetic education that teaches us to know the metaphor in its strength *and* weakness. Frost wants enthusiasm, a lively horse or a roaring fire, but "enthusiasm tamed by metaphor" (36), so that it neither runs down nor gets away from us.

> Let me ask you to watch a metaphor breaking down here before you.
>
> Somebody said to me a little while ago, "It is easy enough for me to think of the universe as a machine, as a mechanism."
>
> I said, "You mean the universe is like a machine?"
>
> He said, "No. I think it is one . . . Well, it is like . . . "
>
> "I think you mean the universe is like a machine."
>
> "All right. Let it go at that."
>
> I asked him, "Did you ever see a machine without a pedal for the foot, or a lever for the hand, or a button for the finger?"
>
> He said, "No—no."
>
> I said, "All right. Is the universe like that?"
>
> And he said, "No. I mean it's like a machine, only . . . "
>
> ". . . it is different from a machine," I said.
>
> He wanted to go just that far with that metaphor and no further. And so do we all. (40–41)

The weakness of a metaphor is as important as its strength: "All metaphor breaks down somewhere. That is the beauty of it" (41). This happy fact is Frost's secular version of *felix culpa*, the fortunate fall that permits such redemption as there is. Without it, the active assertion of form defining us as human would have ended long ago.

Poetry provides us the opportunity to live with metaphor long enough to "know when it is going" (going well or going off to die). Here again, as at Frost's borders of clearings and trees and in his comments about form, a complementary rather than oppositional relationship obtains. I suppose complementarity is *my* preferred metaphor for how Frost's esthetic and epistemological assumptions work in his poems. I have commented elsewhere on the parallel between Frost's epistemological notions and those suggested by Niels Bohr's theory of complementarity.[22] By 1918, Bohr had formulated the correspondence principle. It holds that the predictions of classical physics and quantum mechanics are not in conflict but correspond. Both are necessary to the description of the whole of experience: each is appropriate to a particular frame of reference; each, although it is in a sense opposite to the other, complements the other. Later, encouraged by Werner Heisenberg's description of the uncertainty or indeterminacy relation, and considering the phenomenon that "in the atomic domain, objects exhibit the . . . properties of both particles and waves, which in classical, macroscopic physics are mutually exclusive categories,"[23] Bohr began to use the term "complementarity" to describe his sense that irreconcilable views need not be contradictory, but may be, instead, complementary aspects of a single whole seen from different vantages.

Frost met and talked with Bohr at Amherst in 1923 and mentions him in "Education by Poetry." Both men were influenced by William James,[24] and they share James's tendency to think of opposites not so much as in conflict but as paradoxically compatible (if mutually exclusive) parts of wholes. The physicist R. V. Jones summarizes Bohr's position this way: "Following Bohr, most physicists have grown accustomed to having to accept the reconciliation of seemingly irreconcileable concepts [particles and waves, say, or objective and subjective theories of knowledge, or idealist and materialist viewpoints], to think constructively forward from the reconciliation, and to regard it as a recognition of the ultimately inevitable breakdown of any single model based on earlier experience."[25] For his part, Frost is taken by the beauty of metaphor's inevitable breakdown under the pressure of experience. He enjoys "seeing our theories knocked into cocked hats" ("What I like about Bergson and Fabre is that they have bothered our evolutionism so much with the cases of instinct they have brought up").[26] He likes just as well getting "up there high enough . . . [where] the differences that make controversy become only the two legs of a body the weight of which is on one leg in one period, on the other in the next. . . . I should think too much of myself to let any teacher fool me into taking sides on any of those oppositions."[27]

This argues affinity, not influence. Bohr shared Frost's tendency to think by metaphors that were tentatively held, as in his solar-system model of the atom or his liquid-drop nucleus. He conceived of human beings as "suspended in language" and could go so far as to say, "It is wrong to think that the task of physics is to find out how nature is. Physics concerns what we can say about nature." Those ideas imply a sense of the subjectivities of experience, knowledge, and language that is in tune with Frost's notions of metaphor. On the other hand (this, too, is a matter of complementarity), Bohr and Frost also share a strong desire for certitude. To that end, both hoped to extend the scope of description in such a way as to increase rather than reduce objectivity. Both would do this by multiplying reference frames and by remaining highly aware of the necessary partition, in any act of knowing or describing, between the communicating subject and the object communicated about. For both Frost and Bohr, the circumstance that, partition or no, there is apt to be an uncontrollable interaction between subject and object is at the heart of the problem of knowledge.[28]

Bohr's epistemological tool is the inclusive power of complementarity; Frost's is metaphor. Frost, by the way, tends to think of metaphor in the way that conventional literary definitions think of simile, that is, as emphasizing difference as well as similarity; he generally distrusts the romantic view of metaphor as asserting identity (in contemporary terms, Frost might be said to work at the border between metaphor and metonymy). In any case, and to repeat, for Frost metaphor is a way of knowing: when a given figure is experienced in its strength *and* weakness, it can lead us toward a more nearly complete, because more inclusive, or "complementary," grasp of our situation. Of course, where Bohr at least sometimes hopes to reduce the inherent ambiguity of language, Frost typically exploits that ambiguity. Nonetheless, the two work in parallel ways, enlarging description to include more reference frames and, therefore, more accuracy, while at the same time recognizing that any "whole" description can seem only momentarily determinate and will eventually break down. Bohr's willingness to seek out "flaws and deficiencies" in his own theories and to resist a too easy certitude is famous as the "Copenhagen" style of doing physics.[29] Frost had his own metropolis: asked once if he would not be better off in a city, where so much of the life of the mind was going on, Frost replied "Where I am, I go on."

Frost and Bohr shared William James's notion that attempts at introspective analysis are like "trying to turn up the gas quickly enough to see how the darkness looks." They shared as well his "suspicion" that what we know is not the world but models of the world, metaphors. James was assertive: all "definitions of the universe are but the deliberately adopted reactions of human characters upon it." "Classification, logic, and mathematics all result . . . from the mere play of the mind comparing its conceptions."[30] Most important in all of this (recalling, for contrast, Emerson's remark that "[a]ny distrust of the permanence of laws, would paralyze the faculties of man") is that neither Frost nor Bohr, any more than James, was incapacitated by his awareness that meaning may be a human imposition or construct, that the only cosmos is a willed shape set provisionally against chaos. Furthermore, neither Frost nor Bohr accepted or rejected outright the implications of his awareness of subjectivity. Each found it liberating *and* dizzying. They managed to live in and work with it by surrendering the demand for absolute certitude while still striving toward greater inclusiveness in knowledge, toward a larger grasp of James's "unity in manyness."

I have been emphasizing Frost's distrust of too much form, his awareness that metaphors ridden too far or taken as truth can betray and oppress us. Frost also considers the making of metaphors, the search for truth, or at least for trueness, to be essentially human ("I always think trueness better than truth. Trueness has a warmth about it. It's human.").[31] Frost's thinking, and his poems, occur between complementary views, at the border where metaphors are constantly building up and breaking down. Frost's commitment to the implications of that position was remarkably thorough. He mocked monism as "moanism," for instance, yet with a characteristic gesture of "bothering" reconsideration he also recalled that we can "take too much satisfaction in having once more remarked the two-endedness of things." "A melancholy dualism is the only soundness. The question is: is soundness of the essence." Similarly, Frost's awareness of the dangers of too much commitment is countered by his complementary admiration for "definiteness of position," his belief that, while "Every act is a great simplification," "You should go ahead on insufficient information." He counted as one of the freedoms "the wit to make unexpected connections"; he also said that the world is in parts, and that the separation of the parts is as important as the connection: the demand is for "good spacing."[32] Some readers find this "shiftiness" in Frost, his mixing of a heroic sense of the risks incurred in asserting form with a "diminishing" sense that it is all some interminable game, rather hard to take (asked if poets are born or made, Frost said, "Most people can't bear poets"). Frost's "duplicity" caused Yvor Winters to label him a "spiritual drifter." Frost's own summations put the matter better: "My ironies don't seem to iron out anything"; "I'm not confused; I'm only well-mixed"; "My motto for yesterday was Don't let being mixed make you feel confused. . . . Keep moving. Keep changing your motto."[33]

Having said all this, it is tempting to skip over the vexed question of Frost's modernity and make him out a postmodernist, aware that human systems of order are the only orders we have and that those orders, carried so far that they are taken to be inevitable or natural, become modes of oppression that limit our freedom; aware, too, that we are all inevitably implicated in the making and consecrating of systems of order.[34] But as radically provisional as Frost's poetry is, his differences from the postmodernists are many. His urge to form, however richly qualified it is, is never finally distrusted or despised. So, too, with his sense of authorship and authority. And Frost incorporates the past by other means than appropriation. He is too content with the rules of the game as laid down to fit postmodernist norms, too filled with "vulgar" vitality[35]—with confidence that playing well is sufficient satisfaction and that no government or god could change the rules, too certain of the priority, presence, and continuity of the individual person and of his or her power to work successfully within given limits. Anticipating, say, Thomas Kuhn's *The Structure of Scientific Revolutions*, Frost drew a parallel between the methods of poetry and those of science: both, he thought, are ever in motion, building metaphors up and breaking them down in response to the "anti-fictive of the given environment." That motion, expansion *and* contraction, is our life.

However much or little we are willing to grant Frost his claims, they provide an invaluable definition of how his own poems typically work.

Frost's poems are often constructed so that in them a metaphor offering clarification is built up, but built up in such a way that the counters which predict or imply its breaking down, or which suggest the limits of its clarification, are present as well. The presence of both these "forces" indicates a ceaseless process of adjustment on the part of the writer, and demands a similar process from the reader. Frost thought reaching conclusions was perilous. "May I live to the end", he said, "in premises and rest in processes."[36] The paradox is instructive.

Frost's poems are made of opposites. This is true of everything about them, from the esthetics that support them to their techniques, settings, and themes. The point of this long aside about some of Frost's ideas has been to suggest that the "designed inclusiveness" of his poems, including the many poems that turn to nature to pose epistemological and esthetic questions, typically treats opposites as complements: clearings and woods, night and day, storm and hearth, nature and culture, individual and society, freedom and responsibility, form and formlessness, meaninglessness and meaning. Frost once wrote that "[s]uccess in taking figures of speech is as intoxicating as success in making figures of speech."[37] This puts the reader squarely *in* the process. The challenge is to take the poems—Frost's metaphors—as they were made, with a complementary sense of their building up and breaking down, and with an awareness of the various indeterminacies of their instruments and observers: their metrics and forms, their characters and speakers. As in Frost's remarks on form, motion is the prerequisite: "I should be sorry if a single one of my poems stopped . . . anywhere."[38] Frost's poems are not so much objects as events. They work, not "out" to resolution, but in a kind of permanently mobile suspension where the complementary counters of *mens animi*, the feeling thought of the active mind, are at play. But then of course the poems are objects, too: "Everything is an event now. Another metaphor. A thing, they say, is an event. Do you believe it is? Not quite. I believe it is almost an event. But I like the comparison of a thing with an event" (38).

On New Year's Day 1917, Frost wrote Louis Untermeyer that he "should like to be so subtle" at the game of suggesting formulas that "almost but don't quite formulate" "as to seem to the casual person altogether obvious. The casual person would assume that I meant nothing or else I came near enough meaning something he was familiar with to mean it for all practical purposes. Well well well."[39] Some readers find this attitude evasive, even a little predatory. Nonetheless, it defines the way Frost takes himself: his style. As Richard Poirier puts it, "Frost is a poet of genius because he could so often make his subtleties inextricable from an apparent availability."[40] Many recent critics have noticed the nearly biblical mixture of revelation and concealment in Frost's work. For a long while, though, Frost's subtlety veiled the extent to which his poems share certain modernist philosophical and esthetic concerns, perhaps because of his "insistently ordinary" subject matter: as Poirier says, Frost "chose resolutely, even defiantly, to work . . . within the circumstantially or topically familiar. . . ." Because of that, his poetry "appears to be written *against* that kind . . . which is an interpretation of itself and of its potentialities."[41] In fact, Frost often, even typically, concerns himself with what, how, and how certainly we know, and with the power and limitations of poetry's ability to impose or discover order. This is especially true of his "nature poems." It is precisely because the definition "nature poet" seems to preclude such concerns that Frost bridled at it so: "I'm not a nature poet. There's always something else in my poetry."[42]

Reuben Brower unveiled a large portion of that "something else" when he wrote, "In the sense that for Frost 'revealing' is 'making,' all revelation has been his."[43] That sentence—Frank Lentricchia calls it the best ever written about Frost[44]—points directly to Frost's essential concern with the relationship between knowing as discovery and knowing as creative imposition. And since for Frost making metaphors is the whole of poetry as well as of knowing or thinking, it also points directly to his esthetic concern with the possibilities and limitations of poems. Lentricchia has defined the philosophical context of those concerns, relating Frost to the pragmatist adjustments of Kantian idealism in such forerunners of phenomenology as William James and Hans Vaihinger. Frost's insistence that metaphorical structures condition all modes of discourse *might* seem to align him with neo-Kantian notions of symbolic forms, or to suggest a dismissal of referentiality in language. But his viewpoint is always double. Redemptive consciousness, the imagination that makes metaphor, overmastering matter and giving to chaos a saving form, "is matched by an ironic, referential consciousness that recognizes the world of objects for what it is, for better or for worse." To invert the emphasis, "It is peculiarly the strength of pragmatism to recognize a difficult and real world that plays some determinative role in our lives, while also allowing for the possibility of the active consciousness to carve out, to a certain extent, the world of its desire."[45] Such thinking is a source of Frost's certainties *and* uncertainties, of his double sense of "making believe." Frost's confidence in the self's ability to believe things into existence, to make them come true, stands in complementary relationship to his suspicion that making is mere makeshift, the self's ungrounded yet practical response to the psychic need for a system of meaning the world will not supply. To repeat, this circumstance neither immobilizes Frost nor leads him to despair. He likes it that way; it keeps him moving, urging him to form and to resistance to too much form, to formulas that won't quite formulate.

Frost is neither and both an idealist and an empiricist. He distrusts systems, yet feels the need to make them; having made them, he feels the need to test them against "facts," and to do so while remaining aware that "facts" are often themselves projections of consciousness, made things. In this sense, Frost is a synecdochist. Paul de Man defines synecdoche as a "borderline figure" that "creates an ambivalent zone between metaphor and metonymy," where metaphor implies a "vertical" identity guaranteed by a metaphysical absolute or system, and metonymy implies a "horizontal" association with no such guarantee.[46] In that rough zone, Frost makes believe, not as Emerson's heroic prophet-poet, but by "braving alien entanglements."[47]

Frost's earliest nature poems take a somewhat less complementary view of matters than the one I have been laying out. "Storm Fear" is largely governed by the traditional pioneer view of nature: it is a "howling wilderness" meant to be resisted by human structures—home, hearth, dooryard, road, "comforting barn"—and by the human self, which, however "subdued" it becomes, remains able to take the storm's measure, "to mark / How the cold creeps as the fire dies at length—." But even in this poem, the extravagance with which the storm's howling is rendered wolfishly, doggedly literal—it "whispers with a sort of stifled bark, / The beast"—suggests that the storm's malevolence is as much a projection of human consciousness upon indifferent nature as are the acts of counting and marking that resist it. The storm's *spoken* invitation or order to "'Come out!'" also betrays a human consciousness at work, so that both the threat of wildness and the temptation to join it are made subjective, and thereby subject to control. Most of the poem is given over to strategies of control, but this is ambiguous, too: both heroic and straining for effect. The greatest fear—"Whether 'tis in us to arise with day / And save ourselves unaided"—is a good deal less apocalyptic than it sounds, more a fear of needing help than of there being none. The line that introduces those two, "And my heart owns a doubt," mixes a frightened admission with the sort of confident self-possession and self-containment that puts fears to rout.[48]

Insofar as "Storm Fear" presents nature as a "howling wilderness," "Rose Pogonias" tenders it as the New World garden, a recovered Eden. Bryant-like, Frost describes a sacramental clearing in the trees.

> A saturated meadow,
>   Sun-shaped and jewel-small,
> A circle scarcely wider
>   Than the trees around were tall;
> Where winds were quite excluded,
>   And the air was stifling sweet
> With the breath of many flowers—
>   A temple of the heat.

Then we bowed us in the burning,
　As the sun's right worship is,
To pick where none could miss them
　A thousand orchises;
For though the grass was scattered
　Yet every second spear
Seemed tipped with wings of color
　That tinged the atmosphere.

We raised a simple prayer
　Before we left the spot,
That in the general mowing
　That place might be forgot;
Or if not all so favored,
　Obtain such grace of hours
That none should mow the grass there
　While so confused with flowers.

As in most of Frost's poems of Edenic nature, the speaker is accompanied; the poem's voice is intimately plural, suggesting two lovers in a bower of bliss. But this Eden is already fallen: the poem is in the past tense, and the place has been left, soon or late, to the "general mowing" and its lapsarian and Marvellian intimations of mortality. The highly poetic devices of the piece—symbolic numbers, a "tinged" atmosphere, "pretty" or decorative lineation—all suggest an imaginary as much as an actual space (natural and human conjoin and impinge in "Sun-shaped and jewel-small"). The clearing's precious privacy has its constricted and constricting qualities, too, forecasting Frost's later tendency to regard closed spaces as both secure and stifling, and open ones as both encouraging freedom and threatening chaos. Syntactically, the human presence in the poem, the would-be, ought-to-be mower, is as much "confused with flowers" as the grass is. Those remarks are too heavy-handed for so delicate a poem, but it is worth noting that the poem's delicacy is upheld by the recognition that even our lost Edens are at least partially invented.

　The finest early expression of Frost's emerging attitudes about nature's meaningfulness and meaninglessness, and about poetry's great and restricted powers, is "Mowing," an experimental sonnet. The whispering of a mower's scythe cutting hay creates a border between nature's silence and the human need for meaningful speech; it joins them and keeps them apart, as the poet-speaker ponders implications. At first the poem is remarkably hesitant, right down to the intensifying vagueness of referent emerging from the repeated pronoun "it": "What was it it whispered? I knew not well myself; / Perhaps it was something about the heat of the sun, / Something, perhaps, about the lack of sound—." The identity of the whisperer, technically the scythe, becomes increasingly ambiguous. As to what it whispers, there is poetry ("the heat of the sun" is Shakespeare), and there is silence, a natural world with nothing to say to human beings, no response. No redeeming romantic conversation between human and natural spheres takes place, except in the speaker's imagination, as the repetition of "perhaps" exposes. Still, the whisper is there and demands interpretation. With deliberate self-consciousness, the poet provides one, telling what poetry, perhaps explicitly nature poetry, ought to be, or, rather, ought not to be (Poirier has indicated Frost's tendency to move toward the visionary by means of negation,[49] undermining as he asserts): "no dream of the gift of idle hours, / Or easy gold at the hand of fay or elf: / Anything more than the truth would have seemed too weak." Too much meaning, "more than the truth," won't do; there's no hesitation in that. But neither, it seems, will too little: the words "too weak" suggest some role for strength ("the earnest love that laid the swale in rows" and "scared" a snake). Here, the mower takes the orchises that "Rose Pogonias" preserved. Meanwhile, dream and gift, gold and elf have made their presence felt, even in denial. Finally, an assertion does emerge: "The fact is the sweetest dream that labor knows." But it is unclear whether this "message" is revealed by nature or imposed by the human observer. As do so many of Frost's concluding epigrams, this one slips from closure toward enigma: the words "fact" and "dream," and "labor" and "knows," should sort uneasily together, yet here they seem held easy enough in the supple harness of "definitive" sentence structure. The last line lets go: "My long scythe whispered and left the hay to make." The hay has its making; the mower has his. The poet has his, as well. Nothing is resolved. Nature stays silent, yet seems to speak. Fact and dream both blur and stay apart. "Mowing" is a nearly perfect expression of some of Frost's essential themes. He knew it, and feared he might never do better. He returned to such matters in every one of his books.

Buckminster Fuller attended Harvard a generation after Frost did. In a memoir, he suggests changing the college's motto from "Veritas" to "Veeritas," in order to reflect his doubts about certified truth and his preference for the self-correcting cybernetic process of navigation he so admired. Fuller's example is walking, our veering to the left, then right, as our way to go straight forward. Frost might have agreed. He liked walking (he walked out of two colleges; one of them was Harvard), and he liked both worn paths and out of the way extravagance. Scientific confidence aside, Fuller's notion is as Jamesian as anything in Frost. In *The Will to Believe*, James wrote: "[T]here is really no scientific or other method by which men can steer safely between the opposite dangers of believing too little and believing too much. To face such dangers is apparently our duty, and to hit the right channel between them is a measure of our wisdom as men." Poirier describes Frost's greatness as in large part dependent upon "his actually seeking out opportunities for being in untenable positions" in which some steering will be required: "To 'hit the right channel' between believing too little and too much is to be always more or less in carefully navigated motion."[50] Rarely at sea, Frost stayed metrical; he did his navigation on foot.

For present purposes, the most important poem in *North of Boston*, Frost's second book ("Storm Fear," "Rose Pogonias," and "Mowing" are all from *A Boy's Will*, his first), is a walking poem, "The Wood-Pile." David Perkins has listed the many ways Frost invokes the attitudes of romantic poets in order to "unsay" them.[51] Saying and unsaying, "The Wood-Pile" uses several. To simplify a bit, romantic poets often criticize and correct the exaggerated regularities of human structures (including "regular" poems) by contrasting them with the organic shapes of nature. They escape the oppressiveness of regularity by going into nature, finding variety and solace there. Frost's speakers often go out to walk in the woods when the security of domestic space turns confining. As often, they eventually find "natural" space to be threatening as well as liberating, and go back home, refreshed, perhaps, but rarely solaced. In "The Wood-Pile," a poem about being lost in which the return is only implied, nature is not so much organic as regular in its own terms, and those terms are not necessarily "sympathetic," instructive, or beneficial.

Drawn in Frost's familiar black and white, and typically mingling to gray, "The Wood-Pile" is a winter poem, about a walk in an alien, sometimes unstable landscape: a "frozen swamp" where "now and then / One foot went through" the crusted snow. The initial tone is casual ("Out walking"), but soon the speaker has traveled far enough to get lost. What he loses are landmarks, the differences that locate us in space. It is the regularity of the woods that makes them strange.

> The view was all in lines
> Straight up and down of tall slim trees
> Too much alike to mark or name a place by
> So as to say for certain I was here
> Or somewhere else. . . .

The absent punctuation enforces sameness in a kind of syntactic blur. In one sense, this is the classic pioneer situation: the self is alone amid alien nature, shorn of the human processes of marking and naming that inscribe nature with human significance; he will either reimpose those processes or die. (That drama has more to do with the New England landscape of abandoned cellar holes and encroaching woods than with the more permanently rural landscape of the English romantics, where the city is the threat, as it is likely to be for later generations of American poets, too.) Frost's speaker retains his self-control, or, rather, appears to, by the deliberately transparent stratagem of projecting his fear, disorientation, even paranoia, on the bird that flies before him (probably a junco, it is unidentified—naming is what the speaker cannot do). Anthony Hecht notes the intricacy of Frost's "projective" maneuver here when he defines paranoia as "itself an illness consisting of projecting baseless feelings upon others."[52]

Eventually, by accident (on the one hand, it is precisely that: no divine plan or intervention is working here; on the other hand, following through on his own imaginative projection is what directs the speaker's gaze), the speaker comes upon an abandoned wood-pile. This sign of someone else's exercise of the shaping process he had missed among the trees prompts the speaker's own exertion: he names, marks, and measures. The wood is specified as maple, and as if by a kind of spell sameness begins to retreat. The beats fall like ax strokes; the words stack tight as logs in a solid cord: "It was a cord of maple, cut and split / And piled—and measured, four by four by eight." For a moment, order is restored. But the measurement is imagined. Seen up close, the wood-pile's shapeliness retreats in time and in dimension. The intensification is dramatic. The wood-pile is singular and isolated. It grows old before our eyes. The woods begin to take it back. It shrinks, sags, decays, its purpose lost, its only heat cold comfort for any human want.

> And not another like it could I see.
> No runner tracks in this year's snow looped near it.
> And it was older sure than this year's cutting,
> Or even last year's or the year's before.
> The wood was gray and the bark warping off it
> And the pile somewhat sunken. Clematis
> Had wound strings round and round it like a bundle.
> What held it, though, on one side was a tree
> Still growing, and on one a stake and prop,
> These latter about to fall.

There is some resurgence of shaping power here: the artifice of "strings" and "bundle." But "like" exposes the ruse it deploys. For now, the pile is held between natural and human forces, living tree and "stake and prop." It is the latter that are about to fall. For now, though, the balance holds. The speaker has found no shortcut home, but he seems self-possessed enough to survive. Still, there is no benevolent plan, no ministering nature. Nature has no signs but the ones we impose upon it; those it sloughs off as it can. Wood-pile and woods, human and natural, shaping and shapelessness, meaning and meaninglessness, neither defeats the other (in this Frost is very unlike a pioneer): the metaphors are "loci of energies, not . . . meanings ultimately to be enforced."

True enough. But Frost still feels the tug toward moral interpretation exerted by a long New England habit in poems describing nature. Lawrence Buell has plotted this drive in nineteenth-century American poetry, where its vector is often toward "doctrinal codification." Buell charts another force as well, a tendency to resist closure by a variety of means. This is Frost's line.[53]

> I thought that only
> Someone who lived in turning to fresh tasks
> Could so forget his handiwork on which
> He spent himself, the labor of his ax,
> And leave it there far from a useful fireplace
> To warm the frozen swamp as best it could
> With the slow smokeless burning of decay.

Here, loss (the long slide to shapelessness and death) and the human capacity to keep moving (the ability to survive, to turn to other tasks, to assert form, then let it go before it entraps the self and overwhelms the formlessness that sends it up) are complementary forces.

Frost's third book, *Mountain Interval*, has three poems especially pertinent to the range of issues just discussed, "Hyla Brook," "The Oven Bird," and "Birches." Whereas in "The Wood-Pile" esthetic implications are relatively muted, in each of these poems epistemological oppositions occur in complementary patterns that also have fairly direct implications for esthetics.

Frost's next-to-last public appearance was a talk and reading given at Dartmouth College. The talk was later published as "On Extravagance." In it, Frost said of his poems, "So many of them have literary criticism in them—*in* them. And yet I wouldn't admit it. I try to hide it."[54] "Hyla Brook" fits the description; it works as a commentary on a particular literary tradition, the representation of nature as instructing humanity with significant expression. Among its texts are Shakespeare's "books in the running brooks," with its image of nature as a benevolent nurturer, and Tennyson's "The Brook," in which a stream goes on babbling volubly and forever against a background of human pain and transience. Those texts represent two quite different versions of expressive nature. In one, nature is itself a trustworthy text, God's book, a world inscribed with meaning; in the other, nature's voice is wholly indifferent, its only message is meaninglessness. More important here, though, is that each brook *has* a message, one which is somehow verbal, whether conceived of as writing or as speech. Frost's poem announces its own intentions by defining those streams as "brooks taken otherwhere in song." "Hyla Brook" will be taken somewhere else; it will be at once both more and less literal and more and less literary than they are.

"Hyla Brook" begins with a monosyllabic negation. Whatever voice nature once had is gone now: "By June our brook's run out of song and speed." The poem's final sentence is also complete in a line—the fifteenth, it brims the sonnet's banks in affirmation: "We love the things we love for what they are." This suggests a movement in the poem from loss (a sense of nature emptied of the human significance or concern that Shakespeare's line conveys) to accommodation (a chastened but satisfied acceptance of things as they are that gets beyond Tennyson's disillusioned melancholy). However, even in that framework, the poem's oppositions are blurred. The opening negation is qualified by the brook's once having had both song and speed. The seasonal reference suggests the possibility of recurrence. "Run" has its own energy, particularly in the context of Frost's assertion that "[s]trongly spent is synonymous with kept."[55] And "our" predicts the affection the final line asserts. Similarly, the closing affirmation is qualified by the negative implications of the phrase "for what they are."

As in "Mowing," meaningful sound is the issue for much of "Hyla Brook." A traditional source of inspiration, the brook is here a spring freshet, dried up by early summer, its song and motion stilled. Its other voice is gone as well, the call of the tree frog or *hyla crucifer*, which gives the brook its name. Already muted by parentheses, the lines describing the frogs' remembered song catch its odd mixture of volume and evanescence and convey the haunting qualities of a once enlivened scene now eerily silent: they "shouted in the mist a month ago, / Like ghost of sleigh bells in a ghost of snow." So described, the poem seems to this point a lament for a natural world once communicative and inspiring in human terms (a place where the natural and human sounds of frogs and bells were able to consort); it is a world now lost in empty stillness. But the stillness is not complete; the scene is haunted by remnant sound, and a counterforce is at work in the poem from its beginning. A human consciousness that seeks the brook after its silencing *will* find it out.

> By June our brook's run out of song and speed.
> Sought for much after that, it will be found
> Either to have gone groping underground
> . . . .
> Or flourished and come up in jewelweed. . . .

Those discoveries are visual, not aural, reminding us that nature is "textual" in more than one way. The willful seeking implied suggests that what seems to be discovered is in fact imagined. Or perhaps it is a matter of remembrance, whether of things discovered or imagined. Frost keeps all those possibilities before us. In any case, whatever meaning or presence the brook may now be said to have seems to be the projection of a questing human mind. Consciousness will find something, that is certain enough. The form that something will take will depend upon the observer, and perhaps on the moment of observation as well, as in the distance between Shakespeare's brook and Tennyson's. Options are given: the brook will be found either "to have gone groping underground" or to have "come up in jewelweed." Those seem like opposites, up or down, life or death, but each overflows with competing implications, and those implications link as well as separate the pair. For instance, to find the brook "gone groping underground" might suggest a naturalistic explanation for its disappearance, its return to the water table it came from. It might equally well suggest something so literary as a heroic journey to an underground realm where frog-choked rivers provide the traditional locus for ritual death and rebirth. This sort of extravagance is very much to Frost's point. The flourishing jewelweed pays tribute both to fact—a dry streambed might well send up such flowers—and to imagination, to a certain sort of consciousness those flowers might seem to have "come up" in accordance with laws of compensation. Meanwhile, the punning excess, the verbal willfulness of flowers flourishing, undercuts such claims, as do both the fact-denying assertiveness ("against the way its waters went") and the actual weakness ("foliage that is blown upon and bent") of the jewelweed's resistance.

With such issues entertained and unresolved, the poem returns to descriptive declaration, then offers what seems to be a concluding esthetic principle.

> Its bed is left a faded paper sheet
> Of dead leaves stuck together by the heat—
> A brook to none but who remember long.
> This as it will be seen is other far
> Than with brooks taken otherwhere in song.
> We love the things we love for what they are.

A blank and pulpy mass, the brook has nothing to say; it seems unable even to announce itself. Its very identity is dependent on the constructions of human memory. This denial of any meaning inherent *in* nature seems to lead to the concluding line, in which the poem celebrates its own rejection of the pathetic fallacy (whether it gives us nature as nurturing text or indifferent babbling) and claims to love nature for its blank self and for nothing "ulterior." But the comparison of the brookbed with writing paper, so that nature's value is in part as a surface for encouraging and receiving human impositions complicates that view. So, too, does the fact that we cannot look at nature without recalling the human and natural history that inscribes it (just as the scene is haunted by remembered sound, the streambed's "paper sheet" is not so much blank as "faded"; the "leaves" of its book are "stuck together" but not dissolved). The phrase "what they are" (the brook has become representatively plural) includes all that is natural and human in nature, factual blankness and the growth that preceded and will succeed it, growth that is figurative as well as actual. In this context, the phrase "as will be seen" suggests both verification and imagination. Factual and visionary, ordinary and extravagant, the poem is itself a song written *on* those dead and bookish leaves. We can no more find nature a perfect blank than we can avoid inscribing it ourselves. Language renders nature bookish even as it denies its bookishness. Literal and literary share their root.

Paired with "Hyla Brook" is "The Oven Bird." It, too, is a summer sonnet, concerned with the seasonal reduction of natural song and with the esthetic implications of that reduction. The literary tradition involved is that of the bird as inspiring muse—skylark or nightingale. Unlike those full-throated singers, the oven bird has a talky song (field guides render it as words: *cher* tea-*cher* tea-*cher*). Sung not in spring but summer, its burden is diminishment:

> He says that leaves are old and that for flowers
> Mid-summer is to spring as one to ten.
> He says the early petal-fall is past, . . .
> . . . .
> He says the highway dust is over all.

Because of its "song," the oven bird is sometimes called the teacher bird. As rendered here, its tune is repetitive and flat; it seems to speak to the modern condition in which poetry must adjust to a nature emptied of inspiration and meaning, a world in which Emerson's Overall is dust. The bird adjusts by reducing its voice from lyric flights to ordinary speech, by knowing "in singing not to sing." Thus the oven bird is often taken as a sign of Frost's deliberate diminishment of romantic claims for poetry, his symbol of a colloquial, realistic esthetic that manages to continue to produce art in a pedestrian time by knowing what to make of a diminished thing.

There is a good deal in this, of course, but it reads Frost's metaphor too simply, for this is another case of Frost creating a metaphor while at the same time suggesting the counters that will break it down. Frost admired Thoreau as a "most noticing man," and Frost was a most noticing man himself (although, like Thoreau, he sometimes noticed wrong: his misinformed discussion of geese roosting in trees cost him his job with the publication *Farm-Poultry*). Frost's "noticing" awareness of those aspects of the oven bird's appearance and behavior that make it an apt emblem for a diminished kind of verse is sure enough: its talky song, its drab coloration, its pedestrian tendency to walk rather than to hop or to soar in flight all make the point. Yet this sort of analogizing requires caution; there are other facts about the oven bird that suggest a more intricate picture. The poem's first line should put us on our guard. The "fact" it asserts—"There is a singer everyone has heard"—is very unlikely, but it may be a warning about what sort of knowledge is required for reading the poem. In any case, the oven bird has characteristics that qualify its "diminished" aspect. For instance, in addition to its summer talk-song, it also has a beautiful mating call, a nightingale-like outpouring of rapturous melody that is accompanied by a most unpedestrian skylark-like flight upward. The oven bird is probably Thoreau's mysterious night warbler; its drab plumage conceals a bright orange crown.

Recalling that Frost resisted any notion of the present age as particularly bad, and given his tendency to use seasonal duration as much to induce hope of reprieves from time as to express submission to it,[56] we may take "The Oven Bird" as resisting a too-literary depiction of nature in any season, but also as insisting on the power of poetic creation no matter what circumstance surrounds it. This view is buttressed by the poem's insistence on the "constructed" aspect of all our treatments of nature, diminished or otherwise. There is, for instance, its assertion that our seasonal categories are themselves imagined and subject to revision: spring has its own fall, a "petal-fall"; later "comes that other fall we name the fall." Naming is and is not definitive. A similar strategy occurs in this line: he "makes the solid tree trunks sound again." Primary here is the oven bird's "re-sounding" persistence in singing out of season. But "sound" suggests solidity or soundness as well as singing, indicating a creative force that grants reality its substance. This extravagant claim is nearly silenced at the very moment when it is expressed: the trees are described as being solid even before they are made sound again, as if poetic power were at once real and redundant. This sort of play with the possibilities and limitations of creative power is far from any chastened acceptance of diminishment; neither does it make excessive claims. No "natural" creature considers such matters. The bird has no words, however close it comes to speech. It has "all but words." Its sayings are our inventions. Only the speaker has language, and all the poem's "frames" are his, made things, signs of creative power and of willful imposition, whether assertions, questions, or symbolic birds. Whether we see nature as inspiring or diminished, we do not see nature itself, but our projections on it. For Frost such play has a saving grace so long as it is entertained and not enforced.[57]

"Birches" also plays the literal against the literary; again they overlap. When he sees birch trees arched over in the woods, the speaker would like to think they have been bent down by some boy's swinging on them. But he willingly submits this rather poetic preference to the harshly authoritative voice of "Truth," which is certain that "swinging doesn't bend them down to stay / As ice storms do." Yet Truth's "matter of fact" speech proves remarkably poetic. The ice-bound trees drop "Such heaps of broken glass to sweep away / You'd think the inner dome of heaven had fallen," an allusion (a critical one) to Shelley's *Adonais*. The trees that ice weighed down to stay are described by the extravagant, even visionary image of a row of kneeling girls throwing "their hair / Before them over their heads to dry in the sun."

Having paid this apparent homage to truth and fact, the speaker now feels free to return to his own construction of the scene: "But I was going to say when Truth broke in / With all her matter of fact about the ice storm, / I should prefer to have some boy bend them." The supposedly fanciful description that follows is remarkably physical; whether factual or not, its brilliant handling of detail and of the rhythms of letting go and holding back gives it the feel of experience, so that the voice of fanciful preference carries some of the weight of fact, just as the voice of fact is qualified by its use of literary allusion and poetic extravagance.

> One by one he subdued his father's trees
> By riding them down over and over again
> Until he took the stiffness out of them,
> And not one but hung limp, not one was left
> For him to conquer. He learned all there was
> To learn about not launching out too soon
> And so not carrying the tree away
> Clear to the ground. He always kept his poise
> To the top branches, climbing carefully
> With the same pains you use to fill a cup
> Up to the brim, and even above the brim.
> Then he flung outward, feet first, with a swish,
> Kicking his way down through the air to the ground.

This passage involves the exercise of human power over nature; its key words are "subdued" and "conquer." But the power described is of a special kind. We might call it a poet's power, but "it is really everybody's sanity," the capacity to assert form in such a way as to conquer, not as ice storms do (or facts), but as a momentary stay against confusion. Human form is imposed on nature's background of chaos (it is said that the arch is based on the body's shape), but not permanently so, for to wholly conquer nature would end the game, whether of swinging trees or writing poems. I may seem to have exagerrated the degree to which conquest here is partial. After all, the insistence on thoroughness is extensive ("not one but hung limp"). But an important function of the opening section is to insist that a boy's swinging on trees, no matter how thorough it may seem, does not bend them down to stay, any more than a well-made poem can permanently shape the world. This is one source of the speaker's preference, the form of his resistance to the temptations of a finality or perfection that would disable any future acts. Again, motion is the key, and not just the poet's motion, or the boy's, but everyone's. The commonplace simile of filling a cup to the brim and beyond extends the range of graceful action in such a way as to include us all.

It is a mark of Frost's genius as a poet that he can make this passage convincing as the description of a farmboy swinging birch trees and as a metaphor for the poet's art. It is a mark of the coming change in his style that the poem does not end there. "Birches" concludes with a kind of commentator's coda that is both localizing ("So was I once myself a swinger of birches") and generalizing ("Earth's the right place for love"). It explains, insists upon, even enforces its own complementary practices. In doing so, it shifts away from presenting the act of moving gracefully between contraries, and toward the declaration of that motion as an esthetic and philosophical rule. It *applies* its metaphor, and thus to some extent freezes it in place, locking the poem's motions of body and mind into a kind of tableau, making its ecstasy static. The shift from enactment to commentary is clear in the italicized "Toward" that punctuates the poem's conclusion. Now the poem instructs by precept. The saving act of ceaseless motion between opposites conceived as complements has become an idea, a principle of life.

> I'd like to go by climbing a birch tree,
> And climb black branches up a snow-white trunk
> *Toward* heaven, till the tree could bear no more,
> But dipped its top and set me down again.
> That would be good both going and coming back.
> One could do worse than be a swinger of birches.

There is a beautiful calm in this shift toward abstraction, but also some seepage of smugness. The change points toward both the attractions and the flaws of Frost's later style, toward the wise and witty versifier and the self-regarding expert with too-palpable designs upon us. In this sense, "Birches" marks a change in the way Frost turns to nature in order to consider epistemological and esthetic issues. Many of his later poems are marked by a self-consciousness about inclusion that can lead to such static, programmatic, and deliberately philosophical and didactic versions of complementarity as "West-Running Brook." In a related development, the later poems often display a new willingness to take sides, to move away from complementary views toward assertiveness and closure. The causes of those changes are many, among them a move toward more "social" or "light" verse.[58] Frost had always admired "definiteness of position," and the pressures of age, of personal suffering, of political developments, and of public and critical responses to his work may all have urged a change in poetic posture. Perhaps his original inspiration was lost or altered ("Hyla Brook," "The Oven Bird," and "Birches" make a trio of poems trying out ways to compensate for flagging inspiration). But although those changes are real, and although their effects increasingly dominate in the volumes from *New Hampshire* onward, Frost did continue, until the very end of his career, to produce provisional nature poems in which a complementary treatment of apparent opposites is used to consider the ability of consciousness to know the world and the power of poetry to assert or discover some measure of form. It is those that concern us here.

Any list of such poems would include these: "A Fountain, a Bottle, a Donkey's Ears, and Some Books," "Nothing Gold Can Stay," "The Aim Was Song," "Stopping by Woods on a Snowy Evening," "The Onset," "Looking for a Sunset Bird in Winter," "A Boundless Moment," "The Need of Being Versed in Country Things," "Spring Pools," "The Last Mowing," "Desert Places," "The Master Speed," "Design," "Afterflakes," "All Revelation," "Come In," and "Never Again Would Birds' Song Be the Same." Three more are especially important: "For Once, Then, Something," "The Most of It," and "Directive."

"For Once, Then, Something" is marked by an astonishing mixture of tones. Poirier points out the way the title begins assertively ("For Once, Then"), only to modulate quickly toward the hesitant word "Something."[59] At one time Frost had thought of calling the poem "Well." In addition to specifying the poem's location, that word carries with it some of the tone of the "Well well well" Frost pronounced upon readers who would think he meant something so familiar to them that for all practical purposes he did mean that. The word "well" is as likely to pose a question as to introduce conclusions. Assertiveness about the world's significance and hesitation before its mystery are very much the issue here. Even the poem's meter, with its many "weak" line endings, contributes to the play of assertion and doubt (the poem is written in hendecasyllabics, perhaps in tribute to its classical, Narcissistic subject).

"For Once, Then, Something" begins with a self-portrait. It depicts the speaker as solipsistically self-absorbed, kneeling before his own image reflected "godlike" in a wreathing frame of fern and cloud that is at once "classical," naturalistic, and baroque. The picture is comic, to be sure, but there are other elements as well. Many of Frost's speakers worry about the judgments of others who might be watching them engage in the sort of supposedly idle looking that is part of a poet's work. The most famous example is in "Stopping by Woods on a Snowy Evening," where the speaker fears he will be seen watching another's woods fill up with snow. The same dread of judgment is present here: "Others taunt me with having knelt at well-curbs / Always wrong to the light." Among other things, they taunt him for wasting time, for being superficial, for "never seeing / Deeper down." But "taunt" also suggests that the ones doing the judging are them-selves being superficial, childlike, or petty: a taunt is a particularly jeering sort of judgment. Furthermore, the self-exposure of the poem's opening is marked by an extraordinary poise and self-possession. The taunts are in a way put off by the very fact of their being so easily mentioned, and there is something in all of this of the tone of "In Neglect," where the lovers, who are supposed to feel like social outcasts for failing to live by others' expecta-tions, sit "With mischievous, vagrant, seraphic look, / And *try* if [they] cannot feel forsaken." Mischief, vagrancy, and the seraphic are all on show in this poem, too, as are a willingness and a refusal to be judged by "com-munity standards." In any case, the speaker offers an explanation of sorts for his behavior. What appears to others as idle self-absorption may well be something else.

If the speaker kneels at well-curbs now it is because doing so had once brought him a glimpse of that something "Deeper down" he is accused of never seeing (the word "once" is in italics, emphasizing both the certainty of the experience and the absolute singularity of its occurrence).

> *Once*, when trying with chin against a well-curb,
> I discerned, as I thought, beyond the picture,
> Through the picture, a something white, uncertain,
> Something more of the depths—and then I lost it.
> Water came to rebuke the too clear water.
> One drop fell from a fern, and lo, a ripple
> Shook whatever it was lay there at bottom,
> Blurred it, blotted it out. What was that whiteness?
> Truth? A pebble of quartz? For once, then, something.

The word "discerned" suggests a powerful, even visionary, seeing through or into. "Beyond" implies access to a transcendental or metaphysical realm underlying this one. This is the poet's traditional apology for "idleness"; it claims for the artist a social role as the discoverer or disseminator of truth. The effort to replicate discernment is thus a heroic exercise of intellect and imagination in the service of human knowledge. But the very phrase that claims the speaker's involvement in that effort, "as I thought," suggests not only that the vision came *while* the speaker was thinking but also that he only *thought* it came. The word "trying" implies the sort of willful seeing that often leads to at once attractive and suspect envisionings in Frost's poems. The posture he describes in self-defense is self-deflatingly comic as well as noble. In the end, the envisioned object he recalls to validate his quest proves vague and indefinite: "a something white, uncertain, / Something. . . ." It disappeared as soon as it was seen: "and then I lost it." Nature seems willfully to have resisted any human discernment: "Water came to rebuke the too clear water," as though the glimpse were of something actually there but not meant for us to see. This might swell the Promethean note, but the sense of a sublime moment tragically lost or snatched away is another extravagance that is quickly undercut. In this poem, the archaic poeticism "lo," with its visionary tone and its air of announcing a portentous conclusion to come, seems as much a punster's joke as not. The speaker's sense that nature rebukes itself and him ("rebuke" is a companion word to "taunt") adds to the solipsism the poem exposes (and itself rebukes or taunts). The drop of water that fell from the fern is as likely to have done so by accident or because the fern was jostled by the peering speaker as it is to have been willed to do so by some mysterious force resisting human attempts at discernment.

The result is unprecedentedly thorough. The water never clears again. The ripple that spread from that fallen drop not only shook the "something white" and "Blurred it." It "blotted it out." All that remain are questions: "What was that whiteness? / Truth? A pebble of quartz?" This hesitates between large metaphysical claims (the potential for discovering truth that would validate the artist's quest as a heroic seeking) and the merely material (if the world is just surface, then the artist's quest is quixotic, an idle exercise in swollen self-delusion). "For Once, Then, Something" began assertively and modulated toward hesitation. Now the hesitation implied in those unanswered questions modulates back toward assertion, as the interrogatives are replaced by confident declaration. It does so only to hesitate again; the poem comes full circle, framing yet one more perspective: "For once, then, something."

In a sense, this poem is a version of the story of the Fall, an example of Frost's natural supernaturalism, his using the *structures* of faith without the faith that filled them. *Once*, human beings had access to truth and could discern it through the world's transparent surface. But then some drop, some fall, occurred. The world became opaque, so that now it gives us back no more than the image of ourselves, our own projections. Still, the memory of that one-time penetrating glimpse keeps us kneeling religiously, heroically at well-curbs, writing poems or philosophies, seeking the something "deeper" we know we may never see. But this is a little too neat. The poem is not the story of the Fall. The prelapsarian condition the Fall demands is itself in doubt. The poem's tragic dimensions are eroded by the comic notion that our noble effort to see into, through, or beyond the surface of the world may itself be based upon caprice, a willful sense that there ought to be something deeper, something more. This is the poem's compelling blasphemy. Even the memory on which our quest is based remains uncertain. Was it truth or a pebble of quartz? The singular insight underlying all our seeking may have glimpsed nothing more than some gleaming stone, not even a stone, a pebble.

Frost's "whiteness" approaches the whiteness of Melville's whale, a something meaning everything and nothing all at once. But Frost's response differs from Melville's disillusionment in attitude as well as in scale. Frost likes the world all right the way it is. He treats the confusion of tragic, comic, and even absurd elements in the human and creative condition seriously, playfully, and with equanimity. "[W]e don't worry about this confusion. . . . [W]e like it, we were born to it, born used to it and have practical reasons for wanting it there." Not the least of those reasons is that the confusion demands more poems, more kneeling at well-curbs to look into tantalizing surfaces. Poems create meanings, yes, and this is their value, but if their meanings are to have any substance at all they must avoid having too much substance. Otherwise their meanings harden into "fact," the world has a permanent shape, and there is nothing left for poets or anyone else to do. Seen this way, the poet's role is silly *and* important, an exercise in folly and an engagement of our deepest human needs. For Frost, a poem most satisfies when it persists in making form but does not too much insist that its form is "Truth."

"The Most of It" is a kind of companion piece to "For Once, Then, Something." It treats similar themes, and with a similar intricacy of attitude and idea, but its approach is tonally more consistent, less comic, and a good deal more distanced: its governing pronoun is "he," not "me." The question of how we know what we know, of whether nature is a source of truth or a meaningless other on which we impose any meaning we purportedly find there, is again the issue. In "For Once, Then, Something," the world's reflections of our projections on it are visual; here, they have to do with sound as well as vision, an emphasis that provides "The Most of It" with an explicitly poetic dimension. Assertion and doubt are once more kept suspended, in this case between the poem's narrative drive (with its perfected mechanics of alternating rhyme) and its hesitant diction: "thought," "some," "Unless."

> He thought he kept the universe alone;
> For all the voice in answer he could wake
> Was but the mocking echo of his own
> From some tree-hidden cliff across the lake.
> Some morning from the boulder-broken beach
> He would cry out on life, that what it wants
> Is not its own love back in copy speech,
> But counter-love, original response.
> And nothing ever came of what he cried
> Unless it was the embodiment that crashed
> In the cliff's talus on the other side,
> And then in the far-distant water splashed,
> But after a time allowed for it to swim,
> Instead of proving human when it neared

And someone else additional to him,
As a great buck it powerfully appeared,
Pushing the crumpled water up ahead,
And landed pouring like a waterfall,
And stumbled through the rocks with horny tread,
And forced the underbrush—and that was all.

Frost is up to his habitual technique of "perspectivizing" here. The term is Harold Bloom's; it indicates a process by which the occurrence a poem ostensibly describes is filtered through layers of language and depiction that deliberately conflate the visual and the visionary, that confuse actual with imaginary perceptions, as in "After Apple-Picking." In "The Most of It," phrases we expect to be especially precise (those that specify location in time and space, for example) are in fact remarkably vague: "*Some* morning"; "*some* tree-hidden cliff." The poem even risks exposing the machinery of its own conventions, in this particular case the conventions of realism. The phrase "after a time allowed for it to swim" lets show manipulations ordinarily concealed, so that the poem tests its documentary qualities by insisting on its artificial aspects, too. In a related manner, the word "would" in the phrase "He would cry out" suggests that even the extremely realistic events that appear to follow upon that cry are "as if" considerations, things that might take place if the crying out occurred. Even the seemingly central question of whether the buck is in fact a response to the character's appeal to nature for "original response," or is simply an accidental appearance as indifferent to human concerns as the landscape itself, turns on a word that merges possibility and doubt: "Unless." As usual, Frost's interest is in entertaining, not in enforcing, ideas.

The speaker in "For Once, Then, Something" practices his version of solipsism in a relatively comfortable, or at least comprehended, social situation. The character in "The Most of It" is in the more extreme circumstance of the traditional American Adam, an isolated figure dwarfed by an immense landscape that is at once sublime and alien. Here, though, his situation is less a matter of fact than a construction of consciousness: "He *thought* he kept the universe alone." He has reasons for his suspicion; the only response he can evoke from nature is meaningless mimesis, a "mocking echo" of his own demand for meaning. Nonetheless, both his solipsism and his attempt to evade it are intensely willed: "He *would* cry out on life." He would cry out both to demand the "counter-love" that would indicate the existence in nature of a human dimension and to object to the utter and painful absence of that dimension. His willfulness projects the power of the human need to discover meanings embedded in the world. It indicates as well the human tendency to impose those meanings where none exist. In any case, "nothing ever came of what he cried." This suggests the Frost whom Harold Bloom describes as never being "surprised that life is a sensible emptiness."[60]

But the poem does not end there. The word "Unless" reopens the possibility that nature does respond to human needs. This notion is immediately undone by the syntactical likelihood that if the buck embodies anything at all it embodies "nothing," but that fact is easily lost in the burst of activity surrounding the buck's magnificent arrival. The creature is pure energy and force, as the words "crashed," "splashed," "pushing," "crumpled," "landed," "pouring," and "forced" all show; that its manifestation is as much auditory as visual enhances the possibility that it comes in response to the speaker's cry. At the same time, the buck's representation of a kind of sonic chaos contrasts significantly with the character's "verbal" expectations and with the poem's own careful management of sound.

For all of its qualifications, "The Most of It" insists on entertaining the possibility that the buck's appearance is a response to the character's demand for meaning. Insofar as it is, it ought to provide some comfort; imaginary or not, the buck answers our need for "counter-love, original response." Surely this is better than the "mocking echo" of "copy speech." But of course the buck is too original for words, too "counter" for comfort. Its entire appearance belies what we require: the buck is an expression of energy and force, not of language or of love. As Robert Pinsky says, the buck embodies "the absence of conceptual meaning"; it is "literally insignificant," "a series of details."[61] As to love, the buck is utterly without affection. It has a sexual dimension—it moves with a "horny tread" and forces the underbrush, but it expresses sexuality as indifferent power, not as love. Those matters are all intensified by the character's Adamic situation. Alone in the New World garden, he seeks companionship, affection, a kind of marriage. But no marriage of the natural and the human is possible here. Nature is at one with itself as we are not—either with ourselves or with it.

Any terror the manifestation of the buck evokes is presented as itself a projection of human concerns, concerns to which nature is quite indifferent. Only the willful human presence in the landscape—poet's, reader's, and character's—takes the buck's appearance as any sort of reponse at all. This suggests that we might escape from the terror of nature conceived as pure energy or force by recognizing that conception as yet another of our own projections. Of course, one effect of that is to locate the terror within ourselves (as in "Desert Places," this sort of self-possession scares us as it comforts). It also returns us to a situation in which the world offers no response at all. (Something similar occurs in "Design," where the strategy intended to free us from the implications of our own arguments traps us as well; the possibility that design may not govern in a thing so small as a spider, a moth, or a flower resists the thought that design is as likely to prove the existence of a malevolent as of a benevolent God, but it inexorably evokes the equally disturbing possibility that there is no design whatever. "The Most of It" has a similar plot.)

Only an imposing imagination could construe the buck as a "response" to its own summons, whether comforting or fearful. The words "imposing imagination" suggest the right mixture of gloriously creative power and radical self-delusion, but whom do those qualities describe? One of the more remarkable "perspectivizings" of "The Most of It" is the virtual absence of any interpreting voice between the poem's events and the reader. After the first few lines we hear no more of the character's views, and the poem scrupulously avoids authorial comment or intrusion. There is no commanding presence to instruct us. However, the poem does have a kind of remnant coda in the broken phrase "and that was all." Here is yet another way in which "The Most of It" is a poem with literary criticism *in* it. The phrase "and that was all" functions as a frayed remembrance of the nineteenth-century nature poem's habitual move from description to commentary, application, and closure. It is a remembrance that undoes what it recalls at the moment it recalls it. Its attenuated form makes its own point: almost literally tagged on after the final dash, the concluding words seem unable to escape their own context and evaluate it from a distance, as if commentary were overwhelmed by the immense and fleshly presence it presumes to comment on. On the other hand, the phrase's brevity signals summary completion, and its apparent claim is itself immense: as a generalization it makes the buck's appearance represent nature at large; the buck becomes an emblem of the world, the universe. The poem's conclusion, then, is both an appeal to and an attack on the tradition in nature poems of moving from depiction to "doctrinal codification." It is a diminished statement on the one hand: "and that was all"; there was nothing more (just surface, energy, force—no meaning, no response)—or if a meaning, then the announcement that there is no meaning. At the same time, it recalls such poems as Emerson's "Each and All," which discover God or Truth in the smallest details of creation. Taken this way, though, Frost's already attenuated closing shrinks further still—the meaning *this* sign points too is "all" with a vengeance: the entire universe means what the buck means, that is, it means nothing at all. Or perhaps the conclusion simply refuses any comment whatsoever. The poem reports and then withdraws, leaving us to our own conclusions, to our own imposing imaginations at work with metaphors that exist not to explain or to resolve, but to explore and to be tested.

"Directive" is the most distinguished of Frost's late poems. In it, the instructive voice that dominates his later work turns in upon itself. Contemporary criticism directs us to read suspiciously, to consider the poet not as an avatar of truth but as yet another cultural producer, a maker of systems, which, when they are taken as inevitable or natural, are oppressive. Frost valued the poet's work too much to go so far in quite those terms. He retained an almost relentless authorial control throughout his career, even in his most self-subversive poems. Yet Frost often exerts control in ways that deliberately challenge and undermine it. In "Directive," the poet-speaker is set up as a guide with such extreme self-consciousness, the reader is addressed so baldly, and the quest motif is so thoroughly over-determined that the poem casts doubt on the very roles it announces. The speaker of "Directive" delivers his instructions in ways that call them physically, metaphysically, and esthetically into question. Thus the "instructed" reader is in fact given responsibility for the provisional construction of the poem and of his or her own journey and "salvation."

"Directive" does offer salvation of a sort, but not by recommending any single system of meaning. Part of the literary criticism *in* the poem, as its water goblet Grail and playhouse chapel-perilous suggest, subverts Eliot's recommendation of a specific religious solution to the problem of chaos. For Frost, paradise is not to be regained. The root circumstance of the human condition requires that we function within the context of chaos, not that we overcome chaos and replace it with some perfect and permanent order. Thus "Directive" recommends no specific system of meaning. Instead, it offers multiple ones, privileging none over the others. The value of each system is real, but less for its particular ideas of order than for the more general human urge to order it represents. In this sense, the systems of meaning invoked in the poem are synecdoches for all human attempts at meaning. It is the process, the building up of meaning and its breaking down, that matters, not any particular version of the process, let alone any final product of it. By presenting a multiplicity of systems while pretending to offer a single "way" to salvation, the poem both celebrates the human making of systems and avoids any reductive or premature closure. The effect of this is not mere confusion. The poem performs what it advises. Any stay against confusion must be momentary, a provisional construct not to be enforced; yet some stay, some order, is desirable and possible. It must be continually enacted rather than locked permanently in place. "Directive" is such an enactment. Its conflicting systems are held together by the speaker's remarkably authoritative voice, by the use of conventional narrative and didactic strategies, and by the reader's response to them. At the same time, those strategies are themselves recognized as provisional systems of order, and they come in for the same sort of celebration *and* undermining as all the other systems in the poem. This suggests yet another sort of literary criticism in "Directive," a commentary on habits of writing and reading that make their goal a unified and wholly coherent interpretation.[62]

"Directive" might be called a "summary" poem. As Yeats does in "The Circus Animals' Desertion," Frost in "Directive" enumerates old themes, putting his menagerie all on show: his sites and stratagems, his metaphors, his perspectivizing frames for the questing play of human consciousness as it artfully asserts itself and plots the limits of its artifice. The scene is familiar— a landscape once converted to human purposes and meanings has been abandoned; nature reclaims it as its own: "The only field / Now left's no bigger than a harness gall"; the house is gone; the cellar hole is "slowly closing like a dent in dough." In that context the human imagination is both overawed and invited to reassert itself. A glacier terrifies us with its indifference, but even its scarifying chill can be reduced by a creative maneuver. Personification tames the glacier by converting it into the controllable stuff of a comical tall tale: he "braced his feet against the Arctic Pole"; "You must not mind a certain coolness from him." As elsewhere in Frost, such strategies have dangers. The recognition that even the "coolness" of nature's indifference to us is our own projection on it—the result of our making it literary—is as likely to intensify our sense of nature's chilly disregard for our concerns as to reduce it. Similarly, our distress at the trees, which seem to vaunt their "excitement over" us, their conquering exaltation in having displaced the orchard and its more "human" trees, can be reduced by our noting their limited duration: "Where were they all not twenty years ago?" There is comfort in this. There is also a discomfiting reminder of how brief our own durations are and of how quickly nature moves to eradicate our signs. The question wouldn't work so well on glaciers. Competing constructions of the meaning of duration are another aspect of the poem's play with literary "systems."

"Directive"'s advice to use the traces of human marks on the landscape as a source of companionable comfort and as a goad to creative assertions of our own is offered seriously: "Make yourself up a cheering song of how / Someone's road home from work this once was." But this also suggests that our inventions, made up as they are, are little more than whistling in the dark. Because those lines invoke strategies employed in Frost's own poems—"The Tuft of Flowers," for instance, or "The Wood-Pile"—they also suggest that the entire poetic project is a matter not of truth, resolution, or solution, but instead a kind of useful, provisional make-believe. This is the familiar stuff of Frost's pragmatism, his sense of poetry's possibilities and limits. He believes that "a difficult and real world . . . plays some determinative role in our lives"; he also allows "for the possibility of the active consciousness to carve out, to a certain extent, the world of its desire."

This carving out—and its extent—is what "Directive" wants to exercise and measure, and what it wants to teach us how to do as well: to sculpt the world of our desire while appreciating both our carving's limitations and extent. It does so by an exemplary demonstration in which the poem's apparent precepts remain assertive while challenging their own assertions. "Directive" uses all of Frost's tricks for calling itself into question in the act of its own utterance. Its descriptions blur presence and absence, subverting the diegetic conventions they deploy: "There is a house that is no more a house / Upon a farm that is no more a farm / And in a town that is no more a town." The visual and visionary merge; what seems to be seen is made present by negation. Elements of "realistic" depiction are deliberately confused with the willfully fanciful and extravagant, so that the conventions of local color fiction mix with those of the fairy tale and the quest romance ("serial ordeal"). Again and again the realistic surface is complicated by details and comparisons that remind us of the artifice of the poem's procedures. The writerliness of the world, the impossibility of our seeing it other than through the perspectivizing filters of past and present cultural constructions, is conveyed throughout, as details are borrowed from fairy tales ("Under a spell"), childhood games ("the children's house of make-believe"), Bible stories ("St. Mark"), quest literature (a "goblet like the Grail"), and, of course, from Frost's own poems. The town that is not a town is itself a literary phenomenon: "there's a story in a book about it." The story has a human dimension (the comforting, sorrowful line-like ruts worn in by years of passing wagons); it has an utterly inhuman one as well: "Besides the wear of iron wagon wheels / The ledges show lines ruled southeast-northwest, / The chisel work of an enormous Glacier." If the world is a text to be read in some way beyond our own inscriptions on it, its message may not be what human will desires. Here Frost reflects his early interests—his awareness of how geological inscriptions provided the time frame for undoing scriptural absolutes and giving evolution time to work. Geological, natural "writing" stays intact the way that wagon ruts, gravestones, or poems will not—*they* are eroding already. Of course, it takes humans to read the glacier's marks, or to think they do. The same may be true for poems. In any case, the glacier's "ruled" "lines" contrast with the marks of human culture in dimension and duration. The chisel work of glacial time reduces human carving not quite to insignificance—we still can read the impulse—but to blurred significance. We make memorials, "permanent" signs of our own durations—the human chisel work of "graveyard marble sculpture" marked by names and by dates of birth and death. But by glacial, geological, "natural" standards, those records last the merest moment before their detail is "burned, dissolved, and broken off." Even were we to concentrate on seemingly more manageable categories, say, the human ones of archaeology and anthropology, no full control of loss, or restoration of the past, would be possible. Not one but two village cultures were here; they "faded / Into each other. Both of them are lost."

"Directive" is a fairly typical Frost poem insofar as it asserts form without insisting on any solution to the riddle of the universe. But "Directive" appears to go further, to offer a "way" beyond such difficult considerations, a path to salvation. The rutted road it describes "May seem as if it should have been a quarry." This suggests that even the immensity of geology might be mined or managed. It also suggests that the "way" is more a quarry to be sought than an end to be dug up or achieved. Still, the poem's conclusion seems to offer the reader a kind of paradisal resolution, however much the play of poetry substitutes for more traditional modes of grace: "Here are your waters and your watering place / Drink and be whole again beyond confusion." Only "the wrong ones" will swallow the "message" straight. The place where this healing draught is to be drunk is inevitably a place that is no more a place. The cup that is offered is broken. The whole business may not quite hold water. In "The Most of It," authorial comment is nearly absent; in "Directive," its presence everywhere obtrudes. The effect is very nearly the same.

The "way" of "Directive" is offered by a guide "Who only has at heart your getting lost." There is an element of natural supernaturalism in this, a secular version of the Christian notion that we must be lost to ourselves and the world to find ourselves in God. And Frost is serious in suggesting that we need to lose our absolutes and find the saving play of metaphors. But getting lost is a never-ending process. No metaphor is final. There is no resting place. If you stop for water, you stop in order to go on. You drink to be whole again beyond confusion only in order to return to the confusion that keeps you lost and searching, that keeps you involved in the process of making and unmaking meanings that defines us as human. The poem's end turns back to its beginning, which indicates that being whole beyond confusion is a provisional and artificial, not a permanent or actual, condition or place. The stream as ultimate source is a destination or destiny only in the magical, *literary* world the poem's prologue announces; only there, in the fictive world of art, out of the actual antifictive that sometimes is too much for us, does magic work and abide:

> Back out of all this now too much for us,
> Back in a time made simple by the loss
> Of detail, burned, dissolved, and broken off
> Like graveyard marble sculpture in the weather. . . .

Loss is the engendering circumstance. Frost resists it without pretending to overwhelm it in any but artificial ways, in the necessary simplifications of poems. Those, momentarily, suffice. Part of the purpose of the opening lines is to make clear that it is not only "natural" chaos that encourages as it threatens human making. Human constructs, including writers' and readers' interpretations, carry the germs of their own dissolution. That happy fault keeps the conditions for future creativity in place. I have implied that "Directive" is a "writerly" text, for all its authorial control. This is so in an unexpected sense. In *The Waste Land*, as in many modernist poems, shifting speakers and a fragmented surface ultimately present a coherent vision and a single significance. In "Directive," a single, old-fashioned didactic voice and a coherent narrative surface reveal a swirling collage of competing systems of meaning. If there is any hierarchy among them, it is only asserted, and only for the moment, by the poet or the reader; there is no authority to reveal or guarantee it.

Throughout his long career, Frost turned to nature to consider epistemological and esthetic questions. His responses belie the contraries in which those questions usually are framed: knowledge either discovers truth that is actually in the world or it imposes "truth" on chaos; poetry has the power to discover or create or is an empty artifice. In Frost's work, opposites are kept in complementary motion. This is as true of his dramatic narratives and their depictions of tragedy without blame as of the sort of nature lyrics discussed here. Lawrance Thompson once connected Frost to his Calvinist and transcendentalist ancestors by saying that in his poetry any fact is "viewed as a type or emblem or symbol of some element in the divine plan."[63] Poirier makes the right correction, noting that where such an inclination does exist in Frost, so, too, does a strong resistance to it. "Frost's sense of fact does not elucidate an idea so much as a state of mind about the proper *way* to think and to perceive, the proper way to 'educate' yourself by the reading and the writing of poetry, and by the dramatic trying out of metaphor. You may save your soul in the process, because it is the process that will save it, not any theological faith prior to it."[64] Emerson revealed his radical faith *or* solipsism once, asking impatiently what difference it makes "whether Orion is up there in heaven, or some god paints the image in the firmament of the soul." Lacking a heavenly absolute to help him choose between or fuse those oppositions, Frost stayed in play between them, whether they were expressed in terms of woods and clearings, nature and culture, or women and men. He knew "as if" considerations put together stars.

CHAPTER THREE

WALLACE STEVENS

And we feel, in a way apart, for a moment, as if
There was a bright scienza *outside of ourselves,*
A gaiety that is being, not merely knowing. . . .

WALLACE STEVENS called nature his "source of supply" as a poet.[1] It remained so long after his early transcendentalism became vestigial. Stevens's youthful journals abound with descriptions of and reflections on nature, most of them taken from his long country walks on the outskirts of Reading, Pennsylvania, and New York City. Many of those journal entries have a transcendentalist cast, and they reflect conventional late nineteenth-century pieties: nature is a relief from the drudgery of the world of work, a refuge from the crowds and triviality of town and city life, and an authentic alternative to the derivative artificiality of literature and the other arts. It is the place where the spirit finds range and refreshment in contact with the beautiful and the sublime. A single example can gauge the depth of the young Stevens's immersion in the watery transcendentalism of his day, here the commonplace that nature is a book with priority over other books: "I wondered why people took books into the woods to read in summertime when there was so much else to be read there that one could not find in books."[2]

But Stevens's early transcendentalism was not just a convention. The transcendental belief that nature grants contact with the divine provided him with an alternative to the Presbyterianism of his boyhood. It helped him toward the "alliance . . . between naturalism and a visionary faculty"[3] that defines his career as a poet, toward his characteristic conjunction of a poetry of earth with a poetry of transcendental desire. Transcendentalist ideas prepared the way for Stevens's break with established religion; they helped him to respond to the materialistic and naturalistic conceptions of his age and to indulge his emerging skepticism without requiring him to surrender his faith in something "beyond." He wrote: "I believe, as unhesitatingly as I believe anything, in the efficacy and necessity of fact meeting fact—with a background of the ideal"; "I'm completely satisfied that behind every physical fact there is a divine force. Don't, therefore, look *at* facts, but *through* them"; and "[A]s I went tramping through the fields and woods I beheld every leaf and blade of grass revealing or rather betokening the Invisible."[4] Those assertions ring with received transcendentalist emotions, ideas, and vocabulary—Stevens's 1898 Christmas gift from his mother was a copy of Emerson's *Addresses and Lectures*; he read and marked it thoroughly.[5]

Of course, even Stevens's creedal invocations of Emerson's axiom that God reveals himself in nature expose his thoughts and feelings about the matter as less than axiomatic: "unhesitatingly" and "completely" may protest too much; "force" (replacing "presence" or "being") has naturalistic connotations; and the corrective phrase "or rather" contracts the confident claim of grand revelations grandly beheld to a vague statement about diminutive hints rather dimly perceived. In marking a passage from the "Language" section of Emerson's *Nature*, it was not this sentence: "For the universe becomes transparent, and the light of higher laws than its own shines through it," but this one, which Stevens placed a line beside: "There sits the Sphinx at the roadside, and from age to age, as each prophet comes by, he tries his fortune at reading her riddle."[6]

Whatever the extent of his confidence in them, though, Stevens's transcendentalist notions were crucial to his early development, particularly his response to the religious crisis he expressed in this poignant journal entry for the first day of the new century: "I was trying to say a prayer but could not."[7] Much of Christian dogma had become incredible to Stevens by then, and his satisfaction that there is a divine force discernible behind every physical fact permitted him to abandon most of his doctrinal beliefs without conceding the emotional heightening made available to him by faith in a transcendent Something or Someone. For a time in these years, Stevens believed in both nature and the church as routes to the divine.

> Last night I spent an hour in the dark transept of St. Patrick's Cathedral where I go now and then in my more lonely moods. An old argument with me is that the true religious force in the world is not the church but the world itself: the mysterious callings of Nature and our responses. What incessant murmurs fill that ever-laboring, tireless church! But to-day in my walk I thought that after all there is no conflict of forces but rather a contrast. In the cathedral I felt one presence; on the highway I felt another. Two different deities

presented themselves; and, though I have only cloudy visions of either, yet I now feel the distinction between them. The priest in me worshipped one God at one shrine; the poet another God at another shrine. The priest worshipped Mercy and Love; the poet, Beauty and Might. In the shadows of the church I could hear the prayers of men and women; in the shadows of the trees nothing human mingled with Divinity. As I sat dreaming with the Congregation I felt how the glittering altar worked on my senses stimulating and consoling them; and as I went tramping through the fields and woods I beheld every leaf and blade of grass revealing or rather betokening the Invisible.[8]

However, by 1907, after several years of loneliness and struggles with work in New York, Stevens's views of both the church and nature had considerably altered; his "cloudy visions" became opaque. In March of that year, he wrote to Elsie Moll (whom he would marry in 1909) that although churches remain nonetheless "beautiful and full of comfort and moral help," it is "undoubtedly true" that they "'influence'" none "but the 'stupid.'" The church is an "exquisite device," and "[o]ne can get a thousand benefits from churches that one cannot get outside of them," but churches have nothing to do with truth: "I don't care whether the churches are all alike or whether they're right or wrong. It is not important." He instructs Elsie, or pleads with her, "Don't care about the Truth." Stevens's valuation of the church is now sharply reduced: it remains a socially useful "device," but the church no longer provides absolute knowledge or access to divinity. Nature is also devalued, but, as so often in Stevens, that reduction involves an expansion as well. He writes, "I am not in the least religious. The sun clears my spirit, if I may say that, and an occasional sight of the sea, and thinking of blue valleys, and the odor of the earth, and many things. Such things make a god of a man. . . ."[9] Nature is diminished here. As with religion, it no longer provides access to a god beyond the material world. But in losing one value, nature gains another in its place: now nature's transports make human beings feel godlike themselves.

This position involves some familiar difficulties. If the transports experienced in nature are not the result of contact with a transcendent divinity who guarantees their validity and gives them their meaning, then those transports are no more—and no less—than projections of the self and of its needs and moods. It is precisely this "diminishing" fact that elevates the self to godhood, making it the creator-discoverer of the transports it perceives, the author-reader of nature's "book." Thus nature's transports are radically exalting. But they are radically provisional as well, projections of wish and of will rather than discoveries of truth or ways of knowing that are underwritten by God. Stevens arrived at no easy or early resolution of this "prob-

lem." Variations on it and related issues would involve his poetry and think-
ing to the end.

Other aspects of Stevens's emerging view of nature also become apparent
at this time. In 1906, he had recorded in his journal his yearning for the kind
of definite and permanent knowledge religion and transcendentalism used
to provide: "To laugh at a Roman awe-stricken in a sacred grove is to laugh
at something to-day. I wish that groves still *were* sacred—or, at least, that
something was: that there was still something free from doubt. . . ."[10] Later,
Stevens called it "a habit of mind with [him] to be thinking of some sub-
stitute for religion."[11] Nontranscendental nature was one of the replace-
ments he thought of. But nature's more sublime manifestations and larger
consistencies—the sea and the seasons, say—involve the same mechanical
monotony that sent Stevens to nature for relief in the first place. Thus,
occasional sights of the sea are the transporting ones. He wrote to Elsie in
1909: "You wonder why I didn't go into the country to see apple-blossoms
and the like. The truth is, or seems to be, that it is chiefly the surprise of
blossoms that I like. After I have seen them for a week . . . I am ready for
the leaves that come after them—for the tree unfolded, full of sound and
shade."[12] This esthetic of surprise, with its emphasis on "local" moments of
change, solves the problem of repetition and monotony implicit in nature,
but it does so at the cost of precisely the permanence Stevens sometimes
desired. That difficulty, too, would remain a continuing subject of his work.

Of course, Stevens's attitude toward nature in these years was not all, in
fact only a little, the stuff of religious and philosophical speculation. Nature
remained a pleasure for its own sake and for its refreshment of his spirits.
And Stevens rarely lost his sense of humor in considering larger matters.
Even in the heartfelt passage about the sacred groves, he mocks his rage for
order: "I think I'd enjoy being an executioner or a Russian policeman." As
he became more and more concerned with what would be a lifelong interest
in the theory of poetry as the theory of life, Stevens continued to find one of
his most important refreshments in his own ability to attend to nature
closely and to render it with precision in ways that were Thoreauvian with-
out being transcendental: "The fronds of a fern were dangling over my
knees and I felt lazy and content. Once as I looked up I saw a big, pure drop
of rain slip from leaf to leaf of a clematis vine. . . . It was certainly a mon-
strous pleasure to be able to be specific about such a thing."[13]

To return to Stevens's religious development, George Lensing points out
that the logical third step in the progression from Presbyterian orthodoxy
through transcendentalism—the step required to complete Stevens's rejec-
tion of institutional religion—might seem to be an unqualified atheism.
That was not the step he took. Instead, Stevens began to work out the
theory of fictions that would give his poetry its subject and, eventually, its

style. In a 1909 letter, Stevens describes the church as "largely a relic," which has lost its "vitality" by being so far out of touch with its source in Palestine. This view, and its concomitant sense of Jesus as a historical rather than divine figure, did not so much destroy as redefine the idea of God for Stevens:

> Reading the life of Jesus, too, makes one distinguish the separate idea of God. Before today I do not think I have ever realized that God was distinct from Jesus. It enlarges the matter almost beyond comprehension. People doubt the existence of Jesus—at least they doubt incidents of his life, such as, say, the Ascension into Heaven after his death. But I do not understand that they deny God. I think everyone admits that in some form or other.—The thought makes the world sweeter—even if God be no more than the mystery of Life.[14]

It was an easy development from those notions to the idea that God—and any other system of meaning—is constructed by human beings in order to make "the world sweeter." Phrased in this way, Stevens's ability to reject religion as truth while retaining faith in the value of the religious impulse sounds a good deal like escapism. The degree to which it was is another issue that occupied him for most of his life. The crucial point is that by the time Stevens began to write his mature poetry, he had lost his faith in both God and nature as transcendent sources of the sublime, without giving up his faith in the experience of the sublime, whether in moments of contact with nature or, as he would come to see it, in the act of creating and believing in such supreme fictions as God.

In the years from 1909 to 1916, Stevens married; moved within and at the circumference of the avant-garde Arensberg circle in New York (coming into contact with a number of modernist "isms"); found—after several false starts—his career as a lawyer specializing in surety bonds; moved to Hartford, Connecticut, where he spent the rest of his life; and transformed himself from the author of the private juvenilia of "The Little June Book" into the published poet of "Peter Quince at the Clavier" and "Sunday Morning." During those same years, Stevens's speculations about religion became more clearly what in one sense they always had been, speculations about poetry. The development was conventional; it was a commonplace of the period that poetry would replace religion, either as a system of order, didactic poetry, or the realm of feeling, *poésie pure* (Stevens was interested in both). But conventional or not, Stevens's shift from theology to esthetics represented a turning point in his thinking and writing.

Harold Bloom has expressed his annoyance at critical attempts to find a

Christian sensibility in Stevens. Certainly it is true that by the time Stevens began to write his mature poetry his starting point was the one Bloom describes: "God and the gods are dead, quite dead, but the Sublime survives anyway."[15] And by then Stevens's lifelong respect for the church as a social institution had nothing to do with divinity or transcendence. Nonetheless, Stevens arrived at his "starting point" from conventional religious beginnings and by way of transcendentalism as well as a combination of unsystematic naturalism and hedonism. Those facts help to explain the stubborn persistence of the sublime in Stevens, what Bloom calls the not-easy-to-understand "alliance in [him] between naturalism and a visionary faculty." Stevens was raised on the sublime. By background, education, and cultural habit, as well as by temperament, he needed the sublime somehow to survive the death of the gods, just as his corrosive intelligence and innate skepticism had to accept the evidence of his experience and education that the gods were gone. In a late poem Stevens characterized his own relationship to the gods and other versions of the sublime when he described a walker in New Haven as "Free from their majesty and yet in need / Of majesty."

Stevens is sometimes presented either as an acid, whimsical, or reveling debunker of outworn myths who then seeks satisfactions in the here and now (all guises of the poet of the earth), or as a mystically affirming or majestically failed quester after sublime unifications (both figures of the poet as a noble wrestler with the angels of the imagination and reality). Stevens is all of those things, and usually all or most of them at once. Criticism recognizes this and typically presents his antinomies as parts of a whole; however, in doing so it often tends toward a dialectical configuration in which opposed theses move rather too grandly and inexorably toward synthesis. Helen Vendler has commented on the limitations of the pattern: the "dialectical model . . . , in which a recognition of antitheses, however full, usually leads to a diapason of synthesis, seems to me oddly at variance with the taste of much of the poetry on the tongue, a taste at once more astringent and more provisional than that offered by either antithesis or synthesis."[16] Concentration on Stevens as a nature poet for whom nature fulfills and foils the human need for "majesty" may offer a less foreordained approach.

Stevens typically "attends the moments of natural change."[17] In doing so, he continues a long American tradition. Early on, Stevens found in nature a transcendentally grounded substitute for the religious satisfactions eroded by Darwinism and its materialist and naturalistic attendants. Soon, though, the transcendentalist notion of nature as a book written by God and providing immediate access to the Logos behind matter was equally eroded, and by the same or similar forces. Nonetheless, Stevens continued to attend to nature, if not to seek there for the absolute itself, then to seek for the feelings it had once engendered. Like Dickinson and Frost, he turned to nature to put epistemological questions while shifting those questions from the meaning of God toward the meaning of meaning. Of course, Stevens moved more quickly and conclusively than Dickinson or Frost toward the declaration that God is dead (a grand but nonetheless merely human construct now no longer able to compel belief). And, in searching nature for satisfactions, Stevens shifted his emphasis from the epistemological to the esthetic more often and more thoroughly than they did. At the same time, though, while his skeptic's emphasis on subjectivity certainly equaled theirs, Stevens surpassed Dickinson and even Frost in his affirmative hope that the epistemological doubts engendered by recognizing all meaning as human invention—including God and a transcendental vision of nature—might itself lead to sufficient if not transcendent transfigurations.

In 1946 Stevens wrote to his young Cuban correspondent José Rodríguez Feo, "One of my firm beliefs is that Life and Nature are one."[18] The equation indicates the difficulty of separating Stevens's attitudes toward nature from his other concerns, and the need to attend to his ideas and ways of thinking in broader contexts before focusing on his epistemological (or postepistemological) nature poetry. It can also suggest why his finely nuanced thought is so difficult to clarify. Stevens is not in the usual sense a particularly coherent or consistent thinker; "I don't have ideas that are permanently fixed," he told Ronald Lane Latimer.[19] Stevens's ideas do have a shape. He said that "[t]hought tends to collect in pools," and his own thoughts pool around certain problems and possible solutions—the imagination-reality or subject-object relation, issues of belief and of "fictions," the nature and function of poetry and the poet. But the coherence of Stevens's thinking stems less from philosophical consistency than from "the unity of his nature," the force to which Stevens attributes the coherence of a writer's poems.[20]

Denis Donoghue describes the mutability of Stevens's ideas: "[T]he philosophic positions registered in Stevens' poems are severally in contradiction. If we were to list every variant reading in the argument of epistemology, for instance, we could quote a poem by Stevens in favor of each." And no single philosophical position, materialist, idealist, symbolist, pragmatist, or phenomenological, can account for the rich variety of his work. Donoghue offers one explanation for those facts when he describes Stevens as "devoted to the human imagination in its marvellous range, its plenitude, its manifold powers." Elsewhere he implies that a kind of principle—a preference for process—underlies Stevens's apparent lack of ideational accord: "Stevens loved to declare a theme, and then go walking around it as if it were a cathedral or a blackbird; he loved the process of thinking, not the thought that presses for a conclusion." Donoghue also suggests an analogy for Stevens's sort of thinking: the physicists' principle of complementarity, which, as an epistemological position, calls for the recognition and acceptance of "the simultaneous presence of incompatibles on the field of action."[21] All of those descriptions are to the point, for at times it seems as if Stevens took as his model for thinking the enmeshed ambiguities of natural process itself: birth, growth, decay, death—the edgeless overlap of perfectings and dissolutions.

In his youth Stevens had advised his fiancée not to care about "the Truth." Years later when Latimer pressed him too hard for reductive expla- nations, Stevens replied, "What you don't allow for is the fact that one moves in many directions at once." And again: "I never thought that it was a fixed philosophical proposition that life was a mass of irrelevancies any more than I now think that it is a fixed philosophical proposition that every man introduces his own order as part of a general order. Those are tentative ideas for the purposes of poetry."[22] The remarks are characteristic. In a familiar American formula they reject consistency as the highest standard for thought, and they "contradict" Stevens's own desire "to have things definite."[23] They also suggest that for Stevens incompatibles are not only simultaneously present but also themselves mutable and involved in pro- cess.

As that implies, Stevens tends to think in terms both of objects, discrete entities, *and* of events, in which there are no discrete entities but only interactions. Late in his career he would quote C. E. M. Joad on Bergson in support of the latter view: " 'Every body, every quality of a body resolves itself into an enormous number of vibrations, movements, changes. What is it that vibrates, moves, is changed? There is no answer. Philosophy has long dismissed the notion of substance and modern physics has endorsed the dismissal. . . . How, then, does the world come to appear to us as a collection of solid, static objects extended in space? Because of the intellect, which presents us with a false view of it.' " In a 1940 letter to Hi Simons, Stevens describes his transfer of allegiance from one view to the other as a matter of personal growth: "When I was a boy I used to think that things progressed by contrasts, that there was a law of contrasts. But this was building the world out of blocks. Afterwards I came to think more of the energizing that comes from mere interplay, interaction."[24] The conclusion of "An Ordinary Evening in New Haven" puts it this way:

> It is not in the premise that reality
> Is a solid. It may be a shade that traverses
> A dust, a force that traverses a shade.[25]

The shift of emphasis was real and important; it is the crucial factor in Stevens's development as a thinker and artist. However, it was never so dramatic or complete as he makes out. Stevens had always thought in terms of process, and throughout his career the intellect continued to present its "false view." As he said, "one moves in many directions at once," and Stevens could shift from "object thinking" to "event thinking" and back again without much sense of contradiction.

Lisa Steinman describes Stevens's intellectual and poetic project as exploring the relationship between imagination and reality while refusing to settle the terms of that relationship.[26] Recalling that by the time of his mature poetry both religion and nature were dead for Stevens as sources of absolute truth—and that he was therefore thrown back upon himself (the imagination) and the world (reality) in his search for sublime satisfactions—and recalling as well that Stevens thought in terms of both objects and events, Steinman's description can suggest some essential aspects of his poetry and thought. For instance, when Stevens thinks of the imagination and reality as discrete entities, they remain divided, engaged in a conflict in which one or the other may have the upper hand at any given moment. When he holds reality to be "real" or "true," for instance, then the emphasis is on a materialistic or naturalistic view of things, and the ideas and poetry are decreative, that is, they show the imagination's "discoveries" of feelings, ideas, or patterns in nature as impositions that falsify the way things are—say, the facts of indifference, meaninglessness, and entropic decay. When he holds the imagination to be "real" or "true," on the other hand, then the emphasis is on an idealist, often solipsistic, view of things, and the ideas and poetry are recreative, that is, they show how the imagination can compose an integral, meaningful, and satisfying order and successfully impose it on an otherwise blank reality. Those are the characteristic patterns of Stevens's early work. However, when Stevens thinks of the imagination and reality not as discrete entities but as interacting aspects of events, as he typically does in his later work, then issues of conflict and of power and priority based on mutually exclusive categories of truth and falsity retreat. Now the emphasis is phenomenological, and the ideas and poetry describe and celebrate the marriage of the imagination and reality in a union that dissolves contradiction and satisfies our deepest needs. But that is not the end of matters either. Because the emphasis now is phenomenological rather than symbolist, that is, because it describes what seems to be rather than what is, because there is no absolute to guarantee the "rightness" of any particular marriage of mind and world, it characteristically occurs to Stevens that the union is just another imaginative and imaginary projection that gives delusory comfort. "Object thinking" and issues of conflict and truth return, and the poetry describes divorce. As a further complication, the collapse of union occasions not only sorrow but also a renewed hope for "salvation," for now new attempts at union are both required and enabled. Of course, those attempts, should they succeed, will collapse as well. In much of Stevens's thinking and poetry, most or all of those perspectives are active in sequence or all at once. This makes for enormously rich and subtle textures of idea, language, and feeling, and for a good deal of difficulty. As Stevens put it: "Everything must go on at once," and "everything needs expounding all the time."[27]

This might all be put in another way. Stevens is at times a complementary thinker for whom conflicting truths may be compatible aspects of experience. However, his complementarity has its own complement: the desire for simple or sublime clarities, for finality and permanence, for ultimate solution. Stevens was not only able to accept contradictory aspects of experience as compatible truths; he was also tempted to merge them in one or another idealist, symbolist, or phenomenological monad. The critical word is "tempted." Stevens gave in to the temptation only as a matter of process and not as a means to conclusion, for while he often reflects the vocabulary of romanticism and its stress on the imagination as dissolving contraries into containing and transcending unities, he also consistently deflects that vocabulary away from attainment to potential, from final unions to provisional interactions. In a late autobiographical note, Stevens retroactively insisted that the "many poems relating to the interactions between reality and the imagination . . . are to be regarded as marginal" to his "central theme": "the possibility of a supreme fiction, recognized as a fiction, in which men could propose to themselves a fulfilment."[28] As the words "possibility," "fiction," and "propose" make clear, he refused "to settle."

Repeatedly in Stevens, the recognition and acceptance that ever-shifting "incompatibles" might both or all be true is joined to the desire to merge incompatibles in a final unity beyond contradiction and change, which is joined in turn to the recognition that any such projected merger must stop short of realization. Any final unity would be fixed, therefore removed from process, therefore dead. And not only dead, but deadly, since it would destroy the urge that encouraged it. The human desire for final unities is inevitable (in this sense, Stevens is an essentialist). Because the human desire for ultimates is "natural," ultimates must be projected, but because any final realization would mean the death of desire—something unnatural—their realization must remain propositional, our "fulfilment" must come from the idea of ultimates and the effort to conceive them, from the "feel" of desire and its projections, not from any actual object or faith.

By thinking in such ways, Stevens serves his naturalistic awareness that any specific, "realized" sublime is dead, a merely human projection, *and* his nonetheless persistent sense that the desire for the sublime and the projection of it are essentially and nobly human. In effect, this transfers the transcendent from a single, finally knowable and therefore oppressive and dull absolute "out there" to a flicker of thought and feeling "in here," capable of repeated creations and satisfactions although (and because) it is incapable of any *final* satisfaction. Remarks from Stevens's last years underscore the point: "I have no wish to arrive at a conclusion. Sometimes I believe most in the imagination for a long time and then, without reasoning about it, turn to reality and believe in that and that alone. But both of those things project themselves endlessly and I want them to do just that." In a letter written just a few months before he died, Stevens declared (with a whiff of graveyard humor): "The last thing in the world that I should want to do would be to formulate a system." Stevens spent much of his career in formulating systems; he formulated them in ways that demolish systems while honoring the urge to make them. He puts his several paradoxes best himself when he says, "We never arrive intellectually. But emotionally we arrive constantly (as in poetry, happiness, high mountains, vistas)."[29]

Stevens's habits of thought account for much of the complexity of his work, and they explain a number of its characteristics; for instance: the conjunctions of hedonism and asceticism; the characteristic merging of formalist and organicist theories of composition and of experimental and traditional techniques; the frequent use of the terms of certainty, such words as "must" and "should," as ways of expressing doubt;[30] the sense that the radically provisional and fictive nature of all human knowledge is a source of both sorrow *and* "salvation"; the emphasis on the imagination as decreative *and* recreative; the wholly prospective cast of all his later conceptions of potential substitutes for religion. Stevens's playing (both playfully and in earnest) among analytical, complementary, and synthetic paradigms also sheds light on his "contradictory" ideas about language. Stevens sometimes believes that words make the world, or at least cooperate in its realization, that "[t]he tongue is an eye" or that "words of the world are the life of the world." He also complains about the impossibility of rendering the world in words, about the gap between signifier and signified, about the way words and ideas about the world obscure the world as it is: "Life is not free from its forms."[31]

Similarly, Stevens can conceive of metaphor in romantic terms: "It is important," he says, "to believe that the visible is the equivalent of the invisible." But he can also conceive of it in ways nearer to current notions of metonymy than to metaphor, insisting that metaphor has no transcendent dimension: "We are not dealing with identity."[32] Stevens retains the romantic *desire* for transcendent metaphors in which the visible and the invisible become one, but by denying the existence of an absolute that could guarantee identity he also circumscribes metaphor so that it can never *achieve* that union. If it did, then the "universe of reproduction" would become a tedious "assembly line" instead of a joyously "incessant creation."³³ That is why Stevens makes metaphors *and* comments on them self-referentially. It is the same with his myths or figurations. In that as in other ways, Stevens not only records the loss of transcendent faith and the effort to create provisional replacements for it, he also interrogates the processes of decreation and recreation he enacts. Susan Weston's summary of the matter is both accurate and affecting; it captures the tragicomic fact that for Stevens our dearest objects of desire are always fictions: "Though I would prefer to conclude by saying that what Stevens gives us when he is at his best and we at ours is a 'new knowledge of reality,' in fact he gives us something more rare: the courage to accept the possibility that our every definition of reality is a regulative and saving fiction—an 'as if,' a 'like.'"³⁴ It is in this sense that Stevens, for all his epistemological concerns, might be called a postepistemological poet.

Stevens is famously a poet of ideas, a philosophical poet in the sense that metaphysical and epistemological paradigms condition his poems. The categories of Stevens's ideas most important for our purposes here are those involving the interwoven issues of God, belief, and fictions and those concerned with the powers and purposes of poetry and the poet. Of course, in discussing the form of Stevens's thinking I have often implied its content. Given his adage that style and subject are one ("A change of style is a change of subject"), it could hardly be otherwise. Still, it is worth risking some repetition in order to concentrate on a few of Stevens's intellectual "subjects." His starting point as a poet is that there is no God. God and every other system of belief, including transcendental nature, is a fiction; thus there is nothing to believe in but fictions, and fictions are by definition (until they are redefined) lies unworthy of belief. Since poetry's traditional value is that, among other things, it tells the truth, both poetry and poets are threatened by irrelevance if there is no truth for them to tell (of course, there is the truthful task of exposing untruths, as well as the possibility of a poetry of pleasure rather than one of truth). In any case, Stevens's entire career can be seen as an attempt to face the loss of absolutes, and to do so while still exercising the will to believe. This attempt involves a redefinition of fictions as neither false nor true but as provisional "truths" that help us to live, and that do so without being merely escapist (Stevens distinguishes illusion in the pejorative sense—"elusion"—from "benign illusion," a something credible that helps us to live our lives: "God," he says, "is an instance of benign illusion").³⁵ Finally, Stevens's attempt to accept both the loss of absolutes and the "naturalness" of the will to believe also involves a defense of the roles of poetry and the poet: they are among the creators and conveyors of the conditional sanctions that give life whatever meaning and value it has.

Stevens retained vestiges of the idea of God as defining something "actual" well into his twenties, but eventually that idea eroded and "God" became nothing more than a word for "the mystery of Life." This led to what became Stevens's view of the matter from then on. It is not that God is simply dead, or untrue: "The idea of God is a thing of the imagination. We no longer think that God was, but was imagined."[36] God is a human creation, a fiction. Stevens said it again and again, not only of God, but of every system of belief, from transcendentalism to political systems and even literary history. Every system is a projected fiction, a human invention, not the discovery of an actual and transcendent "inhuman more" beyond the "inhuman less" of the merely material. Here it is in an aphorism: "The death of one god is the death of all."[37] The demonstration of that point makes up some portion of all of Stevens's poetry, the decreative portion. But his assertions that God and the idea of nature as a route to transcendence are dead are typically made in ways that emphasize not only death but also the requirement that some substitute be created for what God and nature once provided—an explanation of life and death, an object of belief, a sanction. Stevens put it this way in a letter: "if we are to eliminate systems as we go along (and it is obvious that everyone is fairly busy doing that) we have got to replace them."[38]

This is not a simple matter of replacing a less true system with a truer one; Stevens's paradigm is not the traditional scientific model of progress. The old systems die precisely because they are fictions ("I think that the history of belief will show that it has always been in a fiction").[39] But for Stevens, at least, it follows that any new systems created to replace the old ones will also be fictions. Life still requires the sanction of belief, but, because all objects of belief are fictive, we will have to believe in fictions. Stevens's own summary of the matter is definitive: "The final belief is to believe in a fiction, which you know to be a fiction, there being nothing else. The exquisite truth is to know that it is a fiction and that you believe in it willingly."[40]

This means that denial will be part of every affirmation and involves rather stringent difficulties, as Stevens knew. In an anecdote he suggests a way beyond them.

> One evening, a week or so ago, a student at Trinity College came to the office and walked home with me. . . . I said that I thought that we had reached a point at which we could no longer really believe in anything unless we recognized that it was a fiction. The student said that that was an impossibility, that there was no such thing as believing in something that one knew was not true. It is obvious, however, that we are doing that all the time. There are things with respect to which we willingly suspend disbelief; if there is instinctive in us a will to believe, or if there is a will to believe,

whether or not it is instinctive, it seems to me that we can suspend disbelief with reference to a fiction as easily as we can suspend it with respect to anything else.[41]

Perhaps Stevens has in mind here the legal fictions he worked with every day at the office.[42] Certainly a number of the philosophers who influenced him support the idea that "as if" fictions are the only "truths" we have (James, Santayana, Bergson, Nietzsche, Heidegger, Husserl, Whitehead, Vaihinger, and Wittgenstein are the ones most frequently mentioned). In any case, Stevens redefines fictions in his own terms. They are not to be judged as true or false in relation to some absolute; there is no absolute. But we need the sanction for life that fictive absolutes supply, and so we believe in them willingly, recognizing their fictive nature for what it is. This does not mean that every fiction is equally worthy of our willed assent. There is a standard of evaluation. But it is not an absolute standard guaranteed by some author, presence, or principle beyond the here and now. Instead, evaluation is guided by a pragmatist rule—a fiction is credible to the degree to which it satisfies our needs and helps us to live our lives. Stevens puts it in terms of poetry: "The incredible is not a part of poetic truth. On the contrary, what concerns us in poetry, as in everything else, is the belief of credible people in credible things. It follows that the truth of poetry is the truth of credible things, not so much that it is actually so, as that it must be so." To compel the belief of credible people in credible things, the poet—as a type of the capable imagination that makes sufficient fictions—will require both a potent imagination and all the skills of the craft, for the audience the poet has to satisfy is sublimely demanding: "The deepening need for words to express our thoughts and feelings which, we are sure, are all the truth that we shall ever experience, having no illusions, makes us listen to the words when we hear them, loving them and feeling them, makes us search the sound of them, for a finality, a perfection, an unalterable vibration, which it is only in the power of the acutest poet to give them."[43]

Stevens shared the modernist need to defend poetry and the poet against charges of irrelevance. He does so by defining them as providing the fictive sanctions we crave and require. The poet's social value once stemmed either from the ability to convey already known or revealed truths in an ornamented or memorable fashion, or from an especially insightful or creative access to truths inscribed in nature: God or a system of correspondences. Neither source of authority is available now. Stevens's poet has contemporary social value precisely because, in the circumstance that there is no ultimately knowable truth, the poet's ability to make fictions that satisfy the human need for sanctions (without turning them into dogma) is what we require. Similarly, poetry is enormously important: "a purging of the world's poverty and change and death." But its achievements are momentary and must be newly enacted again and again. When they settle into dogma, they must be decreated. Poverty, change, and death are permanent; thus poetry is no more and no less than "a present perfecting, a satisfaction in the irremediable poverty of life."[44]

Given those circumstances, poetry and the poet have two tasks. One is decreative, to recognize that the film covering the world and our experience of it is the residue of once effective but now no longer credible fictions, and to use the imagination to cleanse that film: "The world has been painted; most modern activity is getting rid of the paint to get at the world itself."[45] The other task is recreative, to construct out of the particulars of this time and place a system of meaning that will satisfy the self and others. Those tasks are further complicated by the always lurking fact that the replacement fiction is itself liable to become obscuring paint demanding decreative scraping, an awareness that Stevens's poems typically include. This is the source of the endless hesitations of Stevens's voice, his "and yet, and yet, and yet." He must expose dead fictions as dead while recognizing their value as manifestations of the energy of creation, and he must create replacement fictions while exposing the fictive nature of those replacements and the process that creates them, not least because that exposure permits the next fictive act, the act without which poetry and life would end.

Stevens's defenses of poetry and the poet are often accompanied by a shift in emphasis from objects to process. In "The Noble Rider and the Sound of Words," he argues that the idea of nobility remains possible in spite of the fact that "poetry is a cemetery of nobilities" precisely because, as he said elsewhere, "It is the belief and not the god that counts."[46] The point is clearest in this analogy: "as a wave is a force and not the water of which it is composed, which is never the same, so nobility is a force and not the manifestations of which it is composed, which are never the same."[47] This rescues not only nobility but also poetry, belief, and other idealizations from the junkpile of their specific manifestations. By shifting emphasis from inevitably dead or dying objects to the act of proposing objects, including the poet and the poem, Stevens keeps the activity alive without making any particular manifestation or product of the activity absolute or inevitable. This is Stevens's center. The old epistemological and esthetic questions about the power of poetry to discover in nature evidence of God or meaning or truth are dying, dispatched, or dead in his work, but their ghosts are everywhere in its essential subject: the power (and limitations) of poetry as it invents, imposes, and decreates the fictive absolutes we require in order to live felicitous lives.

"The world is completely waste," Stevens wrote in a letter, "but it is a waste always full of portentous lustres."[48] He might have been summarizing the attitudes toward nature in his poems. The emphasis in *Harmonium*, his first book, is often naturalistic, and in a number of decreative poems Stevens reveals nature as a world of waste whose truths are monstrous and whose comforts are frauds. The revelations are delivered in tones ranging from disillusioned outrage to insouciance. "The Worms at Heaven's Gate" is sardonic. It composts the promise of eternal life, making a wormy joke of the rites of resurrection. The worms speak:

> Out of the tomb, we bring Badroulbadour,
> Within our bellies, we her chariot.
> Here is an eye. And here are, one by one,
> The lashes of that eye and its white lid.

And so on. The clash of the cosmic and cartoonish, of processional dignity and a toneless yet gleeful dissectionist's report, is skillful; the droolingly dour name is fine. And if the odor of twenties' irreverence hangs too thick in the poem's air, the reduction of spirit to flesh in the phrase "The genius of that cheek" does earthy work.

"The Man Whose Pharynx Was Bad" is *Harmonium*'s definitive poem on nature's lesson that there is no soul and death is all. It deflates the tradition that nature inspires the poet. The poet is asleep; the aeolian harp has become a shutter; the wind wakes neither. The companion tradition that the poet animates nature is equally undone: unstirred, he is "diffident," "too dumbly in [his] being pent." The romantic echo amplifies his speechlessness. Both the poet and the seasons have "grown indifferent." "Grown" is bitterly ironic; it groans, and difference is dissolved: decay and growth, winter and summer merge in a lifeless mass. Process and stasis, those romantic cynosures, have recurred until they have become "The malady of the quotidian." Poet and nature alike are routed by routine. The "grand ideas" that once redeemed the rutted round are dead; they toll in idle repetition. This is dejection indeed, but it is not quite complete. The poet finds his voice in voicing voicelessness. And he hopes for an intensity of negation in nature that would move him to fuller speech, speech that would in turn give nature significant shape:

> Perhaps, if winter once could penetrate
> Through all its purples to the final slate,
> Persisting bleakly in an icy haze,
>
> One might in turn become less diffident,
> Out of such mildew plucking neater mould
> And spouting new orations of the cold.
> One might. One might. But time will not relent.

What the speaker hopes for here—although hope is hardly the word—is an abasement of the world to a bleakness so total, a slate so blank, that it would make room for the possibility of original writing or speech. This is Stevens's notion of reduction to the "first idea," a cleansing of preconceptions thorough enough to undo repetition and permit a new beginning. In this poem, though, that hope is qualified to the brink of negation. The "I" of the first stanza has become an impersonal "One." And, as each new term conditions the next, "Perhaps," "if," "might," and "less" create a semantics and syntax of radical doubt. The word "plucking" does restore the shuttered harp; "spouting" recalls the fountain, another conventional romantic image for overflowing inspiration; and "neater mould" suggests efficient shaping. But plucking mildew makes meager picking and a strange bouquet; in the company of "orations," "spouting" augurs the rhetoric of fraud; and "mould" is merely mildew by another name. For now, at least, a dull recurrence is all there is, and "time will not relent."

Helen Vendler has remarked on the degree to which Stevens merges religious, philosophical, and esthetic crises with personal ones involving love: "Never was there a more devout believer—in love, in the transcendent, in truth, in poetry—than Stevens. And never was there a more corrosive disbeliever—disillusioned in love, deprived of religious belief, and rejecting in disgust at their credulousness the 'trash' of previous poems."[49] Surely disillusionment accounts for the enraged energy of some of the decreative poems in *Harmonium*. "Le Monocle de Mon Oncle" savages the belief that love, religion, art, or nature can offer absolutes or solace. The speaker imagines a permanent object for his desires in the image of "A damsel heightened by eternal bloom." The damsel represents love and the beloved, and as the words "heightened" and "eternal" show she represents religious and other absolute and permanent truths as well, including poetic ones. But the crucial word is "bloom." The romantic or transcendentalist habit of transferring to nature those idealist and Christian traditions that promise requital of our desires for permanence and perfection is here turned on itself. Stevens takes the trope seriously and finds it trivial. Like Keats's "forlorn," the word "bloom" tolls him back from the realms of romantic fantasia and evokes an angry clamor of Shakespearean and Keatsian pastiche in which every promised permanence is exposed as a gruesome cheat, and by the very natural processes traditionally intended to prove it otherwise. The beloved, the object of desire, is a bloom. Therefore it is this way with love and every other ripeness:

> It comes, it blooms, it bears its fruit and dies.
> This trivial trope reveals a way of truth.
> Our bloom is gone. We are the fruit thereof.
> Two golden gourds distended on our vines,
> Into the autumn weather, splashed with frost,
> Distorted by hale fatness, turned grotesque.

We hang like warty squashes, streaked and rayed,
The laughing sky will see the two of us
Washed into rinds by rotting winter rains.

Birth, copulation, and death: process is all there is. If it brings moments of beauty or pleasure, it obliterates them as they come. Of course, as the monocle of the title suggests, this is looking at things with a single, weary eye. If the speaker is Stevens's relation, he is not quite Stevens. And this is neither the poem's nor the poet's final word on the matter. It is, though, a note struck often in *Harmonium*, and it is never finally stilled.

Several poems in *Harmonium* practice decreation while they also examine the idea that nature might provide transcendence or substitutes for it. In "The Paltry Nude Starts on a Spring Voyage," the sun itself is the nude. Meager in spring, she stands without pediment and moves without pomp, setting forth "on the first-found weed," not as a deity but "like one more wave." She is a natural phenomenon, "Archaic" and self-sufficient in her nakedness. But "She too is discontent." "Too" gives the human position in the matter and exposes Stevens's strategy. The sun is personified to replace outdated modes of transcendence—Botticelli's Venus or mythic figures of the seasons—and to represent our own hopes and discontents as we seek a proper object of desire. At first it seems as though self-sufficient nature might replace our fallen gods. But both we and the image that expresses us, the sun, are discontent. We want things clothed in godly or transcendent circumstance, "purple stuff upon her arms" and a wider arena than the world of surfaces provides: "Tired of the salty harbors," we are "Eager for the brine and bellowing / Of the high interiors of the sea." As the season swells, the sun's domain expands; she moves toward open water, becoming the more imperial, godlier, "goldener nude" of summer. Fulfillment seems at hand. But the image fails. Our hopes fail with it. The sun's circuit is not transcendent but contained in "the circle of her traverse." Her motion is neither her own nor ours ("The wind speeds her"), and she is powerless to alter her course, not a queen but the "Scullion of fate." When she comes, as she will, to her summer height, the moment that "feels" transcendent, she will be as unable to stop there as at any other point. The solstice is a lie. She can only rise and set, brighten and fade, come and "go," "ceaselessly, / Upon her irretrievable way." Nature has its beauties and attractions, but it remains an empty, mechanical cycle, unable to ease our discontent or satisfy desire.

At other times, in the way "The Man Whose Pharynx Was Bad" implies it might, nature's nude indifference engenders elation, not discontent, as in these vatic lines from "Nuances of a Theme by Williams," addressed to the morning star:

Shine alone, shine nakedly, shine like bronze,
that reflects neither my face nor any inner part
of my being, shine like fire, that mirrors nothing.

Here, speech inspires reduction, and reduction inspires speech. In "The
Paltry Nude," Stevens stripped off the sun's old costumes only to dress "her"
in another. For this star, a final bareness is proposed. Williams's "theme"
makes the morning star a metaphor for human courage in a lonely and
indifferent world. Stevens rejects every figuration as false. He pleads with
nature to be neither the mirror of our selves nor the object of our imagina-
tive transformations: "Lend no part to any humanity that suffuses / you in
its own light." To be a myth ("chimera") is to be tamed and tired out, "Like a
widow's bird / Or an old horse." The poem's apostrophe celebrates absence:
there is no one and nothing to address, and Stevens deflates even his own
afflatus, descending from burnished bronze to canaries and nags. Yet the
form of the poem is a prayer. Our need to make something of nature, to
converse with it, is strong. It requires constant undoing, and even undoing
makes its plea. This is a nuance Stevens makes much of.

The great poem of decreation in *Harmonium* is "The Snow Man." Twenty
years after its publication, Stevens would say, "It is not the individual alone
that indulges himself in the pathetic fallacy. It is the race."[50] From that
definition of the fallacy as no fallacy at all but the expression of a natural
human need, he would construct his belief that the urge to meaning must
constantly be exercised as well as restrained. For now, though, as in
"Nuances," restraint is almost everything. Stevens wants to freeze the pa-
thetic fallacy to death, to so severely purge the self of indulgent and painful
preconceptions that only pure perceptions will remain. Then, seeing nature,
we would behold "Nothing that is not there and the nothing that is," and
see the world clear, bare and barren of feeling, value, or figuration: a blank
surface with nothing on or behind it, giving no ground for interpretation.
The title counts the cost: a snow man is no man at all. As Keats and Stevens
knew, when we cease to hear nature's noise as requiem we are dead to
ourselves, a sod. To hear the winter wind and "not to think / Of any misery
in the sound" is to escape our fears of life and death, our fretful need for
meaning. It is also to die to our humanity. To know nothing and to feel
nothing is to be nothing.

That Stevens can imagine the state and find it attractive, even elating,
calibrates his needs, including his need for a final truth, however scarifying.
Of course, "The Snow Man" only declares the conditions for achieving that
state; it cannot in fact achieve it. All those pointing boughs recall how our
desires for nature to point beyond itself are encoded in the way we see and
in our speech, as in "behold" or "distant glitter." And the poem is as "full of

portentous lustres" as of waste: "pine trees crusted with snow," "junipers shagged with ice," "The spruces rough in the distant glitter." The language enlivens as it goes, and it makes present what it wishes to deny; "behold" is a little warmer than "regard." But here, at least, the temptation to make of the "distant glitter" any sort of gold is chillingly withstood.

Harmonium has still other responses to nature's nothingness. In 1904 or 1905, Stevens had told Elsie Moll that "with a bucket of sand and a wishing lamp I could create a world in half a second that would make this one look like a hunk of mud."[51] This is the mood of "Tea at the Palaz of Hoon." In "The Snow Man," imagination empties the world of itself. In "Tea at the Palaz of Hoon," it flows until it overflows and contains the world that would contain it. Here, the posturing self cavorts; things are a solipsist's toy; the world is us and what we say it is. In this poem of prepositions ("on," "beside," "through," "Out," "in"), inner and outer, self and world, dissolve and coincide:

> Out of my mind the golden ointment rained,
> And my ears made the blowing hymns they heard.
> I was myself the compass of the sea:
>
> I was the world in which I walked. . . .

But the poem is as much a parody as a triumphal parade. Its coronation of the self is a tea ceremony. Reign gets mixed in with the rain. "Out of my mind" has, like Hoon, a loony sound. Still, solipsism offers a mode of discovery. Making its own world, the self can say, "And there I found myself more truly and more strange."

Other poems in *Harmonium* abandon metaphysical pleas or posturings for pure or nearly pure description. These are painterly poems, in which the pleasures of observation and of the resemblances the eye or ear discovers or creates provide sufficient satisfactions in themselves, such poems as "The Load of Sugar Cane" or "Sea Surface Full of Clouds." More often, though, the pressure for metaphysical knowledge asserts itself, either by way of its explicit presence or by the various exertions meant to engineer its absence. Occasionally, as in "Sunday Morning," nature provides a replacement faith for the metaphysics naturalism has erased. The pagan and Christian gods, all the gods, are dead—the poem spends much of its time in killing them off, setting us "unsponsored, free." But the requirements they satisfied persist: we feel "The need of some imperishable bliss," "fulfilment to our dreams / And our desires." The poem offers two substitutes for traditional religion. One is a mode of worship in which the object of worship, the sun, is recognized as a metaphor with no transcendent dimension: "a boisterous devotion to the sun, / Not as a god, but as a god might be." The other also involves natural beauty and change, but now not so much as an object of worship as of appreciation, appreciation for the world as it is, beautiful or pleasant, portentous in its lustres, but ambiguous, always expanding and always going to waste:

> Deer walk upon our mountains, and the quail
> Whistle about us their spontaneous cries;
> Sweet berries ripen in the wilderness;
> And, in the isolation of the sky,
> At evening, casual flocks of pigeons make
> Ambiguous undulations as they sink,
> Downward to darkness, on extended wings.

Those swelling cadences evoke the satisfactions of transcendental feeling while disclaiming any transcendent realm to guarantee them; they consecrate an apt accord between human needs and the sorrows, comforts, and elations nature offers. Such sacraments are rare in *Harmonium*. More typical here is the self-deprecating "Anecdote of the Jar," in which nature's ends and ours stay radically disjunct. The jar tames and organizes nature ("It made the slovenly wilderness / Surround that hill"), but it does so at the cost of a lifeless exercise of power:

> It took dominion everywhere.
> The jar was gray and bare.
> It did not give of bird or bush,
> Like nothing else in Tennessee.

Nature, on the other hand, can reproduce; it is alive as no work of art, no human object or product, ever can be. It gives life. But it resists order. Even when colonized and made to straighten up, it sprawls around. Here, no choice is made between the poles of nature and culture; no side is taken. Transcendentalism had promised a Logos or realm beyond to certify the fit between the self, its words, and the world. In *Harmonium*, there is no Logos, no transcendent realm. The fit between the self, its poems, and the world is usually a misfit. In this poem, even the form helps say so: quatrains and consonance give the effect of symmetry, but there is no fixed pattern.[52] Nature is blank and alive. Art is significant and artificial.

Stevens rarely leaves it at that. He keeps watching for the curtains of the world to lift, as in the Dickinson-like "The Curtains in the House of the Metaphysician." Trained to expect transcendent revelations, he sometimes hopes for those; more often he is "bold to see" "Deflations of distance" and to hear, not a heavenly voice, but only the silence dropping. When the final curtain, the veil of "the firmament," lifts away, it "bares" an emptiness "beyond us," "The last largeness." Apocalypse uncovers no new world, just nothingness, an empty sky, a paltriest nude, a blank. In the words of "Cy Est

Pourtraicte, Madame Ste Ursule, et Les Unze Mille Vierges," "This is not writ / In any book." Holy Writ, both the Bible and God's other book, the natural world of transcendent revelations, is a lie. In 1907 Stevens wrote about his spring housecleaning: "I went through my things . . . and threw away a pile of useless stuff. How hard it is to do it! One of the things was my Bible. . . . I hate the looks of a Bible. . . . I'm glad the silly thing is gone."[53]

By the time of *Harmonium*, all of Stevens's bibles were gone or going; religion, transcendental nature, and previous poetry, too, were dead as sources of truth. Only nontranscendental nature and its dissolving round of birth and growth, decay and death, is left. It is a plenum, but one so exhausted of meaning as to sometimes seem a vacuum. *Harmonium* erases other books. Its responses to the blankness it uncovers are diverse. There is disillusioned anguish and anger—a sense of betrayal and loss at being left "unsponsored" in a world the poet had been taught would give him succor. There are delighted discoveries that the burden of the past is dead, ranging from a somewhat self-regarding pleasure in debunking the follies—the pathetic fallacies—of fools and dupes, to the happy recognition that the blank left by the erasure of all authoritative writ can set the poet "free" and grant him both the confidence and the room to write his own "scriptures"—a gift that exacts in exchange for the giving the surrender of every hope of authority and permanence. Finally, there are efforts to restore old satisfactions, either by stripping the world of the layers of falsifying paint that religion, transcendentalism, and prior art applied, or by performing solipsistic feats of unbounded creation, or by seeking substitutes for religion that will be metaphorical but not metaphysical, substitutes that will meet our needs without exceeding our limits. In a sense, *Harmonium* is theatrical, an actor's trunk, "full of strange creatures, new & old."[54] In it the actor rummages around, looking for a costume, a gesture, a voice to suit the role he already has: to discover how to accommodate the loss of absolutes and exercise his freedom in a world completely waste and full of portentous lustres.

Harmonium was followed by a long silence as Stevens adjusted to drab reviews and meager royalties, consolidated his legal career and his household, and became a father. It is often suggested that with "The Comedian as the Letter C" Stevens had reached a dead end, that the poet was left stranded when Crispin's desire for "relentless contact" with reality failed, causing him to give up on the imagination and to settle for quotidian pleasures. Perhaps so. In any event, when Stevens finally returned to poetry— he began to publish again in 1930—it was in the context of the economic and social troubles of the Great Depression. The political and other systems then in place had caused or failed to prevent human suffering on a massive scale, and they were now failing to ameliorate that suffering. To the more "proletarian" reviewers of the time, with their demand that art have direct social content and application, Stevens's spiffy poetry of ideas seemed useless and self-indulgent, even dangerous or parasitical. Nonetheless, *Ideas of Order*—which appeared in a limited edition in 1935 and in a slightly expanded trade edition a year later—does respond to its social context. A new concern with the poet's responsibility in a time of cultural collapse restored Stevens's interest in his old subjects and set him writing again, or so it seems in retrospect. Of course, Stevens's sense of the poet's social role would hardly have satisfied his critics: he insisted that the poet has no sociological or political obligation. Still, Stevens believed that the poet is inevitably contemporaneous.[55] However abstractly, the poems of *Ideas of Order* are consistently concerned both with the facts and consequences of the failure of cultural systems and with the artist's responsibility to human happiness. That they envision no collective solution in any usual sense and that they address crises other than economic ones is another matter.

In poem after poem, Stevens records the collapse of structures that had once lent meaning and value to human life. Nature is both one of those "structures" and a means of resistance to their collapse; but because in this volume the unity of "Life and Nature" of which Stevens spoke to Rodríguez Feo obtains so very much, it is necessary to widen our focus a bit before returning to concentrate on Stevens as a nature poet. In any case, to use the language of "Sailing after Lunch," in *Ideas of Order* most sources of transcendence are shown to be "wholly the vapidest fake[s]." "Sad Strains of a Gay Waltz" phrases it this way: the "epic of disbelief / Blares oftener" these days, destroying every "Mode of desire," every sufficient idea, action, or image. Nature, religion, political systems, the arts, the social virtues, and even material rewards and animal vitality fail to provide the sanctions life requires. For instance, the comforts of tropical lushness turn to hateful ash in "Farewell to Florida." In "The Reader," the only truth to be read in the book of nature is the entropic fact that "everything / Falls back to coldness." In "Waving Adieu, Adieu, Adieu," we wave goodbye to God and inhabit "a world without heaven to follow." In "Dance of the Macabre Mice," every political or social system becomes a verminous ruin. And in "Lions in Sweden," all our "sovereign images"—lofty phrases, the personified public virtues of faith, justice, fortitude, and patience, even "savings banks" and "the sculptor's prize"—decline to "souvenirs." In the empirical view of "Botanist on Alp (No. 1)," nothing can sustain us, not pastoral interactions of the human and natural: "Panoramas are not what they used to be"; not nature itself: "Marx has ruined Nature"; and not the whole long history of human building—classical, religious, or secular: "The pillars are prostrate, the arches are haggard, / The hotel is boarded and bare." As for art, "Claude has been dead a long time."

Everywhere in *Ideas of Order* there is decline, destruction, and death. There is resistance, too. "Botanist on Alp (No. 1)" rejects "despair." "Lions in Sweden" says that although our "sovereign images" have become mere "souvenirs," "The vegetation still abounds with forms." And "Autumn Refrain" insists that "beneath / The stillness of everything gone," "something resides, / Some skreaking and skrittering residuum." But as those inhuman sounds suggest, nature's cyclical returns promise nothing for individual human beings. For us, there is no rejuvenation; "time will not relent." In "Anglais Mort à Florence," the coming of spring brings only "A little less," so that the spirit grows "uncertain of delight." Still, "Autumn Refrain" offers some hope for resistance to its season of personal, historical, and natural decline. The word "Refrain" suggests apt response as well as exhausted repetitions or retiring refusals. *Ideas of Order* responds particularly to the question posed in "The American Sublime": "What wine does one drink? / What bread does one eat?" That is, what secular communion can abide the loss of all our sacraments and somehow "sanctify" our lives.

Several responses, stoic and hedonist at once, are familiar from *Harmonium*. In "The Brave Man" a willingness to accept the natural world as it is and to live "without meditation" is offered as exemplary. In "Delightful Evening," the too-rational or too-contemplative self, "Herr Doktor," who grieves that the twilight is "overfull / Of wormy metaphors," is reminded that it is "A very felicitous eve, / . . . and that's enough." Also familiar is the response of "Dance of the Macabre Mice," where decreative enthusiasm cheers the collapse of oppressive systems of order, mocking the human vanity expressed in any "arm of bronze outstretched against all evil!" "How to Live. What to Do" is reminiscent of "The Man Whose Pharynx Was Bad" and "The Snow Man"; it celebrates the absence of chorister and priest that leaves the self alone with reality's high, bare rock. But a nearly opposite response is more usual in *Ideas of Order*, where Stevens often turns to just such figures as chorister, priest, and poet in his search for sustenance in a time of loss.

Stevens believed that every system of order, precisely because it is fixed as a system, will collapse when it fails to keep pace with change. Sometimes, as in "Delightful Evening," "The Brave Man," or "How to Live. What to Do," he imagined that we might survive without any systems at all and find the world as it is "enough." More often, he thought that we are unable to live meaningful or bearable lives without something to give them the "benign illusion" of significance or shape. From this vantage, although old systems must be abandoned as they die, new ones can and should be created constantly. That is why "Lions in Sweden" advises discarding moth-eaten trophies and renewing the hunt for forms. This "cure" for a sick spirit in an "unpropitious place" is the one that *Ideas of Order* most frequently invokes. And here the cure is usually thought of as being performed by one or another special figure who will redeem the rest of us from the depression of decline by inventing a new "benign illusion" or "sovereign" form. This figure, this poet or other creator of systems, effects cures by making his imagination "the light in the minds of others"; he "helps people to live their lives" "by making them see the world through his eyes."[56] This process can be either coercive or saving. When the poet's order becomes rigid, it, too, becomes a souvenir or a mouse-ridden statue, a useless trinket or an oppressive weight. But when it provides the "fresh romantic," then "the most casual things take on transcendence." For Stevens, the "fresh romantic" is the essence of poetry: the reverse of what is commonly and pejoratively spoken of as the romantic, it is created by the elimination of the false romantic and is "something constantly new."[57]

Several poems in *Ideas of Order* call upon figures of "capable imagination" to restore us to contentment by eliminating the false and providing the "fresh romantic." "Sad Strains of a Gay Waltz" summons a "harmonious skeptic" to revive the dance as one of the "Modes of desire," to "unite these figures of men" so that "their shapes / Will glisten again with motion." "The Sun This March" prays to a rabbi to "fend" the supplicant's soul. In "Academic Discourse at Havana," the figure of hope is a poet:

> As part of nature he is part of us.
> His rarities are ours: may they be fit
> And reconcile us to our selves in those
> True reconcilings, dark, pacific words,
> And the adroiter harmonies of their fall.

In "Mozart, 1935," a musician is instructed to discard the past, to perform as a universal, ritualistic "thou," and to "Strike the piercing chord" that will divert us from despair in this difficult time of breadlines and bad weather when "The snow is falling / And the streets are full of cries."

The role of the poet-priest in creating "benign illusions" that can help us to live in a natural world that lacks a transcendent dimension and that deranges every system we set against its chaos is a central subject in *Ideas of Order*. "The Idea of Order at Key West" is its essential poem. It explores the relationship between the human imagination and natural reality in terms of Stevens's desire for a "benign illusion" that would transfigure our lives without ignoring nature's indifference or succumbing to one or another malign "elusion." Stevens had long seen naturalism or solipsism as two possible responses to the departure of the gods from heaven and nature. "The Idea of Order at Key West" continues to consider those views, and it celebrates the imagination's power to transform the meaningless indifference of nature into significant measures. Here, though, that power is not only celebrated but also corrected and, in some of its forms, supplanted.

The implied narrative of "The Idea of Order at Key West" is a conventionally romantic one. The speaker and his rather ghostly companion overhear a woman singing as she walks along the beach. At first the speaker is tempted to discover in her music a romantic unification of singer, sea, and song, a unification familiar from the transcendentalist faith that there is a God or Logos present behind this world to certify that when we sing in harmony with nature we discover and convey a saving knowledge of transforming truth. It is a temptation the speaker resists as he expresses it, and his ambivalence is condensed in the opening line, "She sang beyond the genius of the sea," where the word "beyond" has its traditional transcendentalist connotations *and* denies any possibility of transcendence by insisting on a radical disjunction between the singer's song and the natural world. The speaker's hopes and doubts are also conveyed in his haltingly assertive speech. He shifts from confident declarations (some of them in conflict with others) to qualifications and back again in a kind of blur of precisions: "The water never formed to mind or voice, . . . and yet"; "The song and water were not medleyed sound / Even if . . . "; "It may be that" nature "stirred" "in all her phrases," "But it was she and not the sea we heard." And so on.

Whatever surviving transcendental hopes the speaker harbors, they are quickly drowned. The opening sections of "The Idea of Order at Key West" define the natural world as an empty force that offers neither comfort nor knowledge. "[E]ver-hooded" and "tragic-gestured," "heaving," "dark," and filled with "meaningless plungings," nature's voice is a wordless cry, a wild and vacuous howl. There is no presence behind or beyond nature; its only truth is chaos. There is, though, an alternative to this naturalistic vision, and the speaker now hears the singer's song as an act of solipsistic creativity so potent that the sea "became the self / That was her song." This moves and even inspires him, and it gives rise to passages of nearly ecstatic celebration. The force of her imagination is impressive; it appears to transmute the "meaningless plungings" of the "veritable ocean" into a meaningful shape, and to do so not only for her, but for her audience as well:

> It was her voice that made
> The sky acutest at its vanishing.
> She measured to the hour its solitude.
> She was the single artificer of the world
> In which she sang. And when she sang, the sea,
> Whatever self it had, became the self
> That was her song, for she was the maker.

As so often in *Ideas of Order*, "piercing" sounds transform nature, as if the world were (or, as Stevens might say, is) measured by the singer's measures. Eventually, the speaker is so elated by the burden of the singer's song that his own speech is transfigured. The halting assertions with which he began the poem become a fluent question rising from interrogation toward avowal:

> Ramon Fernandez, tell me, if you know,
> Why, when the singing ended and we turned
> Toward the town, tell why the glassy lights,
> The lights in the fishing boats at anchor there,
> As the night descended, tilting in the air,
> Mastered the night and portioned out the sea,
> Fixing emblazoned zones and fiery poles,
> Arranging, deepening, enchanting night.

Those passages are a flourish of praise in which a litany of terms—"made," "measured," "artificer," "became," "maker," "Mastered," "portioned out," "Fixing," "Arranging," "enchanting"—commemorates the imagination's ascension over reality. But for all the celebration, the speaker has already begun a "corrective" commentary on the "singer's" solipsism and his response to it. That she is a solipsist is a given: "there never was a world for her / Except the one she sang and, singing, made." Of course, we have only the speaker's and not the singer's word for this. In fact, we never hear the singer's words or music in the poem at all, nor do we hear her comment on them. As several critics have noticed, Stevens made a dramatic shift from female to male figures of imaginative power in these years.[58] The mistrust feminism has taught us to feel in the presence of masculine mufflings and displacements of the female muse might be brought to bear on the poem. However much the singer's ability to transform nature into a humanly satisfying shape moves and even inspires the speaker, he also resists the notion that her song replaces the "veritable ocean" with itself. For her, he tells us, the sea, "Whatever self it had, became the self / That was her song." For a time, this seems to be so for him as well, but a number of matters undermine the idea, until he comes to see her song as added to rather than replacing the world as it is. The speaker's emphasis on the meaningless indifference of the actual sea, and his extended effort to define precisely the relationship of her song to the "veritable ocean," indicates that for him there *is* a world other than the "one she sang and singing, made," that the sea retained "whatever self it had" no matter how powerful her song.

As the poem moves toward its conclusion, the focus shifts away from the singer's song to its consequences for the speaker. As it does, it becomes clear that the speaker's earlier praise of the singer includes incipient corrections and supplantings of her voice. In the first passage quoted above, for instance, the word "solitude" is a reminder of the cost of a solipsistic response to nature's indifference; similarly, "vanishing" suggests dissolution and loss as well as magical power, and "artificer" hints at fabrication as well as creative skill. From the perspective of the poem's final stanza, those qualifications seem like the speaker's retroactive emendations. In the second passage quoted above this feeling intensifies. Now the song is over and the speaker and his companion move away from it in time and space, turning "toward the town." In one sense, and this is a measure of Stevens's subtlety here, the speaker's praise for the singer's achievement seems magnified; the shaping force of her song appears to persist even after the song is over, so that the lights on the fishing boats "Mastered the night and portioned out the sea." This does suggest an extension of mastery, but in fact the source of mastery is now located somewhere else, probably in the speaker himself. The singer disappears from the poem, and, more dramatically than before, the speaker takes over both her voice and her power to master chaos and resist the night. This is not, I think, a simple or somehow scandalous usurpation. The singer's inspiration of the speaker is never denied, nor is his power any more free of qualifications than hers is: the words "Mastered," "portioned out," "Fixing," and "Arranging" are strongly challenged by the words "fiery," "deepening," and "enchanting," especially the last, with its implication of fraudulent imposition. Nonetheless, just as the speaker's transcendental hopes were drowned, so is "her" claim that solipsistic creativity might provide a satisfactory response to the vacancy of nature. Her song has not replaced the world, and it has not persisted beyond the moment of its uttering. It does, though, inspire another act of ordering, one that celebrates her song *and* replaces it with a new act of ordering that is more inclusive of naturalistic facts.

What I am suggesting is that the qualifications included in the speaker's words of praise for the singer are the result of his continuing awareness of the presence of indifferent, meaningless reality and of his rejection of the singer's supposed replacement of it, a rejection that nevertheless admires her imaginative strength. Since we lack her actual song, it is difficult to be sure of this view, but it seems borne out by the final section of the poem, where the speaker's correction becomes explicit and illuminates what goes before. By the end of the poem, inspired by but dissatisfied with the singer's idea of order, the scholarly speaker is no longer content merely to describe and interpret her enlivening song. Now, in an exclamatory celebration of the creative urge as a kind of general instinct or will, avowal is transformed into a vowel of praise, and the speaker becomes a singer himself. He supplants his muse while praising and appraising her, and shapes his own myth to resist the chaos of the world: the myth of the artist who satisfies our need for the sublime by providing transforming but not transcending or solipsistic knowledge of ourselves and of the world, a myth for which she provides a positive and negative model, a paragon to be both imitated and replaced:

> Oh! Blessed rage for order, pale Ramon,
> The maker's rage to order words of the sea,
> Words of the fragrant portals, dimly-starred,
> And of ourselves and of our origins,
> In ghostlier demarcations, keener sounds.

There are ambiguities and inclusions here that her more fixed and finished song could not embrace. The lovely hesitation of "dimly-starred," the ambiguous connotations of "rage," and the paradoxical equation of "ghostlier" and "keener" revise such "final" words as "Mastered." The speaker's song includes precisely the naturalistic knowledge of nature's inhuman indifference the female singer had appeared to replace. It also contains the "illusion" of the sublime she had so impressively evoked, and it does so without the "elusion" of solipsism she seemed to employ.

In effect, the speaker redefines the nature and degree of the singer's achievement so as to criticize its solipsistic disregarding of naturalistic facts while still admiring its transcendental urge, and while finding in her flawed expression inspiration for attempting an expression of his own, an expression less flawed precisely because it accepts its limitations. Satisfied with neither naturalism, transcendentalism, nor solipsism, the speaker attempts a further refinement, a song that will recognize both the fraudulence of any system of transcendence and our genuine and noble need to make such systems. In the end, it is not her song itself as a finished product of the rage for order that the speaker celebrates. Rather it is the rage for order itself: the "force and not the manifestations of which it is composed." As Stevens put it in another context, "It is the belief and not the god that counts." That is why her song can continue to inspire him as he corrects and supplants her voice and moves toward fuller definitions of an "ideal artist" who will imagine potently but without a solipsistic dismissal of naturalistic facts. Those definitions will be less "final" and more provisional and prospective than any managed here.

Harold Bloom has said that "The Idea of Order at Key West" may be impossible to interpret fully.[59] Certainly this reading is more orderly than the poem. Nonetheless, it points the direction in which Stevens is heading, away from finished products and single systems of order toward emerging and plural acts of ordering, away from the rhetoric of closure toward something more provisional and open to revision, away from an actual and present artist toward the self-consciously mythical myths of the "impossible possible philosopher's man" or the "supreme fiction," which are to be proposed but not attained. Stevens's next several volumes take it as their task to define the "acutest poet" who can, to say it once again, provide his audience with the transfiguring "illusion" it requires without yielding to the "elusion" of solipsism or transcendence.

As if to correct "The Idea of Order at Key West," the volume title *Ideas of Order* has already shifted the singular to the plural. Several poems in the book indicate the route Stevens will take in attempting to move beyond his current impasse. In them, the figure of the "redemptive" artist remains optative, someone to be imagined and hoped for rather than discovered or described. In "Sad Strains of a Gay Waltz," the future tense dominates. Expectation rather than attainment controls the various instructive voices of "Some Friends from Pascagoula," "Mozart, 1935," and "Academic Discourse at Havana" as they seek the artist of "dazzling" words or "piercing" sounds whose "reconcilings" "May . . . be fit." The figures and actions those poems project are also described in language that deliberately joins possibility to limitation. In "Sad Strains," the musician will be "Some harmonious skeptic" playing "a skeptical music." In "Academic Discourse," the poet's words will be "dark, pacific" ones, and there "pacific" is as much of the veritable ocean as of any peaceful speech.

The clearest statement of these matters in *Ideas of Order* is in "Evening without Angels." The assertion that "Air is air" undoes our dreams of seraphs (in our sadness, we concoct them from the glory of the sun; nature is the source of all our projections of supernatural beings and realms). Yet the same assertion allows us to use "the voice that is great within us" (redefined now as a natural urge, not a reverberation with the supernatural). We use the voice to make our home in the world, to compose our bare reality as we can. The final section of "Like Decorations in a Nigger Cemetery" puts it this way: "the wise man" builds "his city in snow," resisting the change he accepts as sovereign. "[P]erhaps for no more significant reason than that poets come and go,"[60] Stevens is moving toward a new definition of poetry and the poet, a definition in which they neither discover sovereign meaning and order already present in nature nor sovereignly create and impose meaning and order on a natural world that lacks them. Instead, poetry and the poet must do something else. They must somehow create, impose, and subvert their prospective patterns all at once, so that they fade as they emerge, while still providing sufficient solace for their audience of many or of one.

By the time of *The Man with the Blue Guitar* in 1937, Stevens's major themes were firmly in place. God, transcendental nature, and every other idea of order is a fiction. Such fictions are literally "false." But the term loses exactness in the absence of absolutes, and, to the extent that they satisfy fundamental human needs, fictions are true, or "credible." Thus we are "unsponsored," with no absolute realm beyond this world to guarantee the truth of our inventions; that is a source of desolation. We are also "free" to create; that is a source of joy. In "The Well Dressed Man with a Beard," Stevens writes, "After the final no there comes a yes. / And on that yes the future world depends." For Stevens, "yes" is affirmed in the making of fictions. It is in the character of fictions that, once made, they become "definite" over time, lose their power to satisfy, and prove obscuring or oppressive, that is, each given "yes" becomes "the final no." It is also in the character of fictions that they can constantly be replaced; this, as things go round, is Stevens's "yes" beyond finality. For the poet, those circumstances ("It can never be satisfied, the mind, never") demand that old fictions—and every new fiction is soon old—must continually be decreated and replaced with credible new fictions that might provide the public with the satisfactions it requires. Because all systems are ephemeral human inventions, the poet and the poem must gratify those needs in ways that incorporate both the fictive and the temporary character of whatever satisfactions they offer.

Stevens spends the next phase of his career trying to imagine such a poet and such poetry. He imagines them not so much as an actual person or poem—although surely in some sense he hopes to be that poet and write that poem—but as quasi-mythical projections. In a way, those projections are themselves to be thought of as invented substitutes for religion and other dead or dying systems of meaning. To that extent, Stevens is employing more or less standard notions of the artist as culture hero or secular savior and of art as a replacement for religion. But he swerves from those notions by insisting on the invented and impermanent status of his projections. In doing so, he still keeps in mind the human desire for objects of belief, but he typically shifts his emphasis from the definite (as in *"the* final no") to the indefinite (as in "there comes *a* yes"). He moves from an emphasis on creating specific or permanent objects of belief toward an emphasis on imagining their creation. This leads to considerations of the sources of our desire for such objects and to descriptions of optative and provisional acts of believing. In a development that began in *Ideas of Order*, the reader is not asked to believe in the myths of ideal poet and poem as actual replacements for faith in God or in nature. Instead, the reader should accept and enjoy those substitutes—and especially the process of their projection—for whatever momentary pragmatic satisfactions they provide, and should do so while recognizing that the substitutes are themselves provisional fictions, caught in the endlessly sorrowful and joyous act of being made, unmade, and made anew.

In "The Man with the Blue Guitar" and the other long poems of his next-to-last period, as well as in many shorter poems, Stevens rehearses all of his major themes in a new key. Nature continues to be his "source of supply." It frequently provides the context for his new forms and other stylistic devices—more about those in a moment. It also provides the context for the ambiguities those devices express about the possibilities and limits of meaning and knowledge and about the function and value of poetry and the poet. The aspects of nature explored in those poems are familiar ones: its beauty, blankness, and constant change; its revelation as a naturalistic force when purged of the "wormy metaphors" that gave it meaning; its role as the unresisting material that the solipsistic imagination teases into satisfying shapes; and its counterrole as the resistant actual world that challenges and refreshes the imagination when it loses contact with the real and goes stale. Furthermore, nature's lack of human meaning remains Stevens's central discovery. It engenders all of his attempts to replace the ideas of God and transcendence with self-consciously fictive and provisional myths, myths that, particularly in the form of the always projected but never realized figures of "major man" and "the supreme fiction," begin to decreate themselves as they emerge.

Most of the continuities and developments of the later period appear in "The Man with the Blue Guitar." A sequence of thirty-three sections, it continues from *Ideas of Order* a concern with the poet's social or cultural responsibility. For Stevens, the current form of that obligation arises from the demise of the gods and from the fact that the earth is not a nurturing mother but a comfortless stone. In the world of "The Man with the Blue Guitar," social and political systems are as unable as religious and philosophical ones to provide solace or elicit belief. We live in "Oxidia, banal suburb, / One-half of all its installments paid." The politician, whether churchman or statesman, is a fake, "him whom none believes," "A pagan in a varnished car . . . hoo-ing the slick trombones." Collectivist schemes involve a killing equation of people and things: "Women become / / The cities, children become the fields / And men in waves become the sea." This leaves art or poetry as a possible source of contentment. However, the poems of the past are as useless as everything else. The public instructs its poet: "Do not speak to us of the greatness of poetry, / Of the torches wisping in the underground, / / Of the structure of vaults upon a point of light." Homer, Virgil, Dante, and Milton are all discarded here. The poems of heaven and hell are no longer credible; they have lost the power to explain and shape our lives, to comfort, frighten, or control. What remains is nature, but nature is a blank, and not, as Emerson thought, a blank in the eye of the beholder but a blank indeed. It adumbrates nothing at all:

> There are no shadows in our sun,
> Day is desire and night is sleep.
> There are no shadows anywhere.
>
> The earth, for us, is flat and bare.
> There are no shadows.

The old poetries are thus undone. Still, poetry is what is called for, a new poetry, not of heaven and hell but of earth: "Poetry / / Exceeding music must take the place / Of empty heaven and its hymns." The public sets the poet's task: "play, you must, / A tune beyond us, yet ourselves." This is the burden of all of Stevens's later work, to describe and perhaps to write a transfiguring poetry that is also wholly of Oxidia, this place and time, a poetry that is neither materialistic, solipsistic, nor transcendent, or that is all and none of them at once. In "The Man with the Blue Guitar," the guitarist-poet makes a number of attempts. He corrects and instructs himself as he does so, and is corrected and instructed by his demanding public. None of his attempts is definitive; together they present a list of options Stevens does not so much choose among as exercise in sequence and at once.

In describing the characteristic patterns of the long poems of Stevens's late but not final phase—from *The Man with the Blue Guitar* (1937)through *Parts of a World* (1942), *Transport to Summer* (1947), and *The Auroras of Autumn* (1950)—Helen Vendler outlines "three large manners." One, "despairingly and in tones of apathy, anatomizes a stale and withered life." Another, "in an ecstatic idiom, proclaims, sometimes defiantly, the pure good of being. . . ." "The third and most characteristic form is a tentative, diffident, and reluctant search for a middle route between ecstasy and apathy, a sensible ecstasy of pauvred color, to use Stevens' own phrase."[61]

To some extent, those three manners can be distinguished from one another in the poems of this period. In "The Man with the Blue Guitar," for instance, the first extreme is expressed in images of a materialism so thoroughgoing that human beings become "Mechanical beetles never quite warm." This chills the creative urge: "The strings are cold on the blue guitar." A similar naturalistic chill is the root circumstance of "The Auroras of Autumn" and "An Ordinary Evening in New Haven," and it threatens to overwhelm the speaker of "Esthétique du Mal." That poem discovers yet again the sublime totality of nature's blank indifference to human concerns: "Except for us, Vesuvius might consume / In solid fire the utmost earth and know / No pain." One result is dejection, as in this passage, where a surreal transition from the horrors of World War II to a dull suburban peace collapses every state of life into a uniformly murderous and quotidian reality:

> Life is a bitter aspic. We are not
> At the centre of a diamond. At dawn,
> The paratroopers fall and as they fall
> They mow the lawn.

Related distresses occur frequently in *Parts of a World*. In "The Dwarf," fall and winter all but defeat the poet, who is left beside his lamp, "there citron to nibble / And coffee dribble. . . ." "Add This to Rhetoric" contrasts poetry and nature: "It is posed and it is posed. / But in nature it merely grows."

With no absolute to guarantee poetry's access through nature to the truth, words have no permanent relation to the world. The result is predictable; we live bleak lives in a blank place:

> To-morrow when the sun,
> For all your images,
> Comes up as the sun, bull fire,
> Your images will have left
> No shadow of themselves.

Elsewhere in the poems of this period, the loss of absolutes has the opposite effect. Instead of inducing apathy or dejection, it frees the poet for creativity and pleasure. In "The Man with the Blue Guitar," speech is refreshed with nonsense. A poet goes on a solipsist's spree; he makes nature a tractable toy, like a seal or a magus:

> He held the world upon his nose
> And this-a-way he gave a fling.
>
> His robes and symbols, ai-yi-yi—
> And that-a-way he twirled the thing.

The whoop and the rhymes express a Hoonish confidence in creative energy and control. Such moments are rare in the later poems. More often, the extreme of ecstasy now appears in passages of intense calm where the exercise of imaginative power, especially in its decreative form, invents the sense that nature is "enough" and allows the poet to experience the pure good of being. Such passages occur repeatedly in *Parts of a World*, where decreations of the absolute permit the world to ripen, as in these lines from "On the Road Home":

> It was when I said,
> "There is no such thing as the truth,"
> That the grapes seemed fatter.
> The fox ran out of his hole.

Nature reveals itself to the nonmetaphysical voice and eye in "The Latest Freed Man" as well. "Tired of the old descriptions of the world," the man has "just / Escaped from the truth" and learned "To be without a description of to be." For him, the morning now "is color and mist, / Which is enough: the moment's rain and sea, / The moment's sun." When "Everything is shed," as in "The Man on the Dump," "the moon comes up as the moon." "The Sense of the Sleight-of-Hand Man" puts it this way:

> It may be that the ignorant man, alone,
> Has any chance to mate his life with life
> That is the sensual, pearly spouse, the life
> That is fluent in even the wintriest bronze.

The long poems of this period also describe moments when nature seems sufficient. "Notes Toward a Supreme Fiction" exhorts the poet-in-training, the ephebe, to "become an ignorant man" and "see the sun . . . with an ignorant eye," then praises the promised result:

> How clean the sun when seen in its idea,
> Washed in the remotest cleanliness of a heaven
> That has expelled us and our images. . . .

"Esthétique du Mal" imagines as "The reverberating psalm, the right chorale," a conception of ourselves as "a race / Completely physical in a physical world" and claims that, compared to our intense experience of earth, the experience of "non-physical people, in paradise," would seem merely "The minor of what we feel." "Credences of Summer," recalling a day from Stevens's youthful visits to the eastern Pennsylvania countryside, also describes a moment of natural sufficiency:

> One of the limits of reality
> Presents itself in Oley when the hay,
> Baked through long days, is piled in mows. It is
> A land too ripe for enigmas, too serene.

It will already be obvious to many readers that the examples I have given of Stevens's extreme positions of apathy or ecstasy in the poems of this phase are too "impure" for the purpose. For instance, the image of the sun as a bull, in the passage from "Add This to Rhetoric," enlivens the imageless dullness the lines supposedly describe, while the assertion of blankness cleans the slate for new rhetorical additions. Despite the erasures of winter, the midget-poet of "The Dwarf" still has his writing lamp and the summer pleasure of eating citron. As to the bitter lines from "Esthétique du Mal," aspics are aspects and have their clarities. Passages offering ecstasy or contentment are often similarly qualified by the presence in them of opposite moods. In the celebratory lines from "The Man with the Blue Guitar," the expression "Ai-yi-yi" conveys distress and bemused resignation as well as enthusiasm for the solipsist's costumes and props. In "On the Road Home" the grapes only "seemed" to grow "fatter" in the absence of the truth. The ambiguous word "ignorant," used in several passages, inserts a similar qualification. The word "expelled," in the lines from "Notes Toward a Supreme Fiction," connotes paradise lost as much as successful decreation. And the "reverberating psalm" of "Esthétique du Mal," although "scrivened in delight," is a "thesis," not a law. More generally, in all of the longer poems the decreative cleansing of reality from preconceptions is presented not as an end in itself (the process is endless, since reality is always being reconceived and re-presented), but as a preliminary stage in a continuous process. In the words of "An Ordinary Evening in New Haven," "Reality is the beginning not the end." Furthermore, for all their subjective satisfactions, the contentments those passages describe are imposed by language on an indifferent natural world, a matter Stevens is of several minds about. A final example: The moment of perfection evoked in the lines from "Credences of Summer" is only available in a poem in which "the mind lays by its troubles." The studied deliberateness of that conditioning act restores the threats it holds in abeyance. The phrase "*One* of the limits of reality," the implications of excess in the repeated word "too" ("too ripe," "too serene"), the evocation of a fruitfulness about to rot, the suggestion of actual enigmas carelessly ignored—those unsettle the tone of contentment they set forth.

To put it another way, Vendler's third "manner," the search for a "sensible [that is, a felt *and* tempered] ecstasy," typically impinges on supposedly pure extremes of apathy and ecstasy alike. The result is not a "diapason of synthesis" but something a good deal more "astringent." The most important development in the poems of this period is the evolution of formal and stylistic devices that present Stevens's familiar themes in a new key. In poems from *The Man with the Blue Guitar* through *The Auroras of Autumn*, he evolves a provisional style to express his provisional fictions. Such a style is necessary because Stevens's central issue has become the problem of how to create credible meanings ("a larger poem for a larger audience") without solipsistically ignoring the naturalistic facts of reality—how to create fictions that provide the experience of belief and yet remain provisional enough to recognize and include the limitations they struggle to surpass; how to make invention feel like the equivalent of both discovery and creative imposition at once.

The most obvious aspect of Stevens's development of a provisional style in these years is his increasing use of long, nonnarrative, loosely organized meditative sequences. Hinted at as early as "Thirteen Ways of Looking at a Blackbird" in *Harmonium*, and expanded in "Like Decorations in a Nigger Cemetery" in *Ideas of Order*, the provisional sequence becomes Stevens's normative mode in the long poems of this period, among them "The Man with the Blue Guitar," "Esthétique du Mal," "Credences of Summer," "Notes Toward a Supreme Fiction," "The Auroras of Autumn," and "An Ordinary Evening in New Haven." It is a style in which the orderliness of beginnings, middles, and ends is replaced by contemplative expansions and contractions; in which linear development is replaced by endless circlings of adjustment and readjustment; in which single narratives, patterns of imagery, metaphors, characters, or myths are replaced by prodigiously plural inventions; in which closure is replaced by open-endedness; and in which certitude and statement are replaced by an implicitly infinite state of indeterminate reconsideration. This produces a poetry of possible meanings rather than of meaning in the usual sense.

Stevens's development of provisional forms in this period has counter-
parts in his new handling of language and metaphor. It is conventional to
ascribe Stevens's later style to the abandonment of his richest, most foppish
rhetoric after the failed experiment of *Owl's Clover*. And Stevens did exhort
himself to "get rid of the hieratic in everything."[62] But the sparer usage of
Stevens's later poems has a rhetoric of its own. In *On Extended Wings*, Helen
Vendler provides a nearly exhaustive catalogue of the new style in which the
poet employs a range of semantic and syntactic devices for joining assertion
and doubt, for creating a provisional speech that will satisfy without insist-
ing on adherence. For example, Stevens typically uses such words as "may,"
"might," "must," "could," "should," and "would" to resolve his poems. Of
course, "resolve" is hardly the word. That device, and such related ones as
the use of questions in place of or as statements, a tendency to follow
conditionals with the indicative mood, the repeated use of "seems" where
"is" is expected, the employment of such words as "when," "until," and "if"
to create and to undermine the appearance of one or another stable pres-
ence, the use of ellipses at critical junctures, and a reliance on the optative:
the placement of every possible perfection in a deliberately mythical or
otherwise unstable future, all have the double effect of making us forget *and*
recall the conditional aspect of Stevens's "conditional propositions," so that
we join him in assenting to and resisting them at once.[63] Thus we find
satisfaction in the fictive while recognizing it for what it is and discovering in
it the circumstances for its own inevitable collapse and eventual replace-
ment. That response permits us the pleasure of closure without the life-
denying finality and illusion of permanence that are its usual companions.

Stevens's use of metaphor in these poems has a similar effect. As we have
seen, he came to insist on metaphor's capacity for defining resemblance
rather than identity, and in such a way that his own metaphors emphasize
difference as much as likeness. In this, he is nearer the use of simile than
metaphor in the usual sense, and he is never far from a metonymic sense of
likeness as juxtapositional rather than guaranteed by any metaphysical
realm of symbolic correspondences beyond. Those issues are most clear in
the details of actual poems, but they can be seen in what Vendler calls the
ease with which Stevens's language "modulates from 'reality' to 'as if' . . . ,
making the two almost interchangeable at times." Stevens uses the "as if"
construction without the subjunctive it requires in order to create the ap-
pearance (or "elusion") of identity typical of romantic uses of metaphor, but
he does so in such a way that, at the very moment of assertion, identity is
called into question by semantic disjunction.

The most significant stylistic development of this period is harder to de-
fine. It has to do with Stevens's beliefs that "everything must go on at once"
and that "[e]verything needs expounding all the time." In the earlier poems
the combination of inclusiveness and self-interrogation such views imply

typically occur in separate poems or sections of poems, as in the way the reductions of "The Snow Man" are left to conflict with, correct, or be corrected by the self-expansions of "Tea at the Palaz of Hoon." But in the later poems, Stevens's many conflicting responses to the collapse of transcendent or metaphysical absolutes collide and collude in ways that produce neither the containing tensions extolled by the New Critics nor any resolving synthesis. J. Hillis Miller comes closest to describing the nature and effect of Stevens's stylistic devices in the later poems (especially the sequences) when he says that in them Stevens tries to "move so fast from one season [or mood] to another that all the extreme postures of the spirit are present in a single moment. If he can do this he will never pause long enough at any extreme for it to freeze into dead fixity, and he will appease at last his longing to have both imagination and reality at once."[64] Part of the effect is that this unity dissolves as it is achieved. It remains conditional and prospective ("If he can . . . , he will . . .") even as it appears to occur. This is an illusion, a kind of trick, but a trick that avoids being mere "elusion" by including whatever resists it and by exposing its magical devices to its own and the reader's scrutiny. Stevens's marriages are harmonious and skeptical at once, their consecrating copula "as if," not "is."

The blurring but not quite obliterating speed that Miller describes is essential to what Vendler calls Stevens's third "manner," the search for a "sensible ecstasy." This process and its results are hinted at in the ways that even the more extreme passages of apathy or ecstasy in these poems include their own opposition. It is especially apparent in passages that attempt to define the ideal poet or poem. Of course, especially in the longer poems, Stevens's effects occur on a large scale, and his rapid shiftings of thought and mood and his provisional perfectings are best experienced in sweeping vistas. Here, however, close-ups will have to do.

Most of the poems of this period respond to the same facts of lost absolutes, stony nature, and secular disorder (now including World War II) that are felt in "The Man with the Blue Guitar." They also share that poem's extreme states of desolation and contentment, and its effort to join them in a "sensible ecstasy." That attempt finds its most characteristic form in projected images of the ideal poet and poem. Responding to the demands of his audience, the poet-guitarist of "The Man with the Blue Guitar" admits that he "cannot bring the world quite round," yet he claims the ability to "patch it as [he] can." The assertion already contains a qualification. Still the poet patches the world in part by imagining a hero:

> I sing a hero's head, large eye
> And bearded bronze, but not a man,

> Although I patch him as I can
> And reach through him almost to man.

"[A]lmost" is the crucial word. Susan Weston has spoken of Stevens's "'almosting' it,"[65] and Stevens's response to the poet's task often involves not only a projection of his possible song but also an interrogation of it. Here, for instance, the guitarist-poet worries that in reaching through his hero "almost to man," his song may "miss . . . things as they are"; that is, he fears the imagination may evade the real in the very act of abstraction it is fated to use to approach it. This is Stevens's invariable condition. And an opposite or materialistic approach offers the poet no escape; we murder man to dissect him, "drive the dagger in his heart," "lay his brain upon the board," "nail his thought across the door."

"The Man with the Blue Guitar" has other blurrings of contentment and distress, but finally the poem moves toward an optative definition of what the ideal poet (a figure sometimes conceived of as "anyone," sometimes as a hero) might be able to achieve. As usual, this requires first a decreation: the ethereal "lark" is deposed from the "museum of the sky" and mind; it is replaced by the earthy "shriek" of a cock-pheasant. Then the guitarist's voice shifts from description to instruction, as he tells the ideal poet what to do: "Throw away the lights, the definitions," he says; "do not use the rotted names." Replace the old terms with new and create the bread and stone of a secular communion. As that surprising and strangely telescoped pairing indicates (is wine diverted into pine?), this is a communion that will both satisfy and starve. It will starve because, when the new definitions harden, they will become identical in effect with the old and return us to the stale world of sleep and forgetting. But in the *moment* of making, when nature and the imagination join in an act of creation, we are refreshed and "saved."

> The bread
> Will be our bread, the stone will be
>
> Our bed and we shall sleep by night.
> We shall forget by day, except
>
> The moments when we choose to play
> The imagined pine, the imagined jay.

There is ecstasy in this, but it is a "sensible ecstasy," cast in the future tense and tempered by the recognition that ecstasy will wither and apathy return. It is typical of Stevens in this mode that another counternotion is present as well: the sleep and forgetting that undo our satisfactions also encourage decreation, that is, they enable as well as require the creation of new satisfactions.

"Esthétique du Mal" is more concerned with malady, suffering, or pain than with evil in the usual sense, or perhaps it is concerned with our feeling that, even though Satan is dead, evil still seems palpable and present. What makes the death of Satan "a tragedy / For the imagination" as well as a liberation of it is that the explanation for suffering is gone while the experience of suffering remains. The pattern is familiar; it is with devils as with gods: we are "Free from their majesty and yet in need / Of majesty." Just as Stevens ascribes our longing for divinity or transcendence to nature's grandeurs, the sublime, so he attributes our sense of evil to an aspect of that sublime:

> Except for us, Vesuvius might consume
> In solid fire the utmost earth and know
> No pain (ignoring the cocks that crow us up
> To die). This is a part of the sublime
> From which we shrink. And yet, except for us,
> The total past felt nothing when destroyed.

This passage is typical of Stevens's later style in the way it uses opposed statements in an additive rather than contradictory or corrective manner. Both nature's utter indifference ("Vesuvius might consume . . . the utmost earth and know / No pain"; "The total past felt nothing when destroyed") and our biblical and "instinctive" or superstitious sense of nature as responsive to our lives ("the cocks that crow us up to die") are part of the world as it is, as the repeated phrase "except for us" insists.

Stevens is not content to leave it there. He hopes to find some way to salve our suffering. In one section of the poem he suggests that our invention of "an over-human god"—whose sympathy and compassion are excessive for the facts of life as lived—is responsible for the false expectation that nature will sympathize with us, and thus responsible as well for the suffering we feel when it does not. Therefore, it may be that a vision of nature freed from such expectations and inventions, that is, a vision of nature as wholly indifferent, could provide sufficient comfort:

> It seems
> As if the health of the world might be enough.
>
> It seems as if the honey of common summer
> Might be enough, as if the golden combs
> Were part of a sustenance itself enough,
>
> As if hell, so modified, had disappeared,
> As if pain, no longer satanic mimicry,
> Could be borne, as if we were sure to find our way.

On the one hand, "sustenance," "health," the summer's honey in "golden combs," and the certainty that we will "find our way." On the other, "hell" and "pain." And "asserting" the ascendency of comfort over suffering, these few dubious words: "seems" and "might" and "could," "as if," "as if," "as if."

The poem's rapid intertwinings of hope and doubt, of affirmation and exhaustion are also created in other ways. As in the other sequences, the fertile presentation of variations on a theme from section to section of "Esthétique du Mal" suggests the possibility of infinite variations. This, too, has its double implication: the impossibility of ever reaching resolution, a final, stable answer, is cause for desolation; it is cause for ecstasy as well, since the absence of conclusions keeps life open to creativity and change and free from final evil. It is Stevens's achievement to make us feel both of those things at once and as something other than simple contradiction.

In the last section of the poem, Stevens celebrates achievement while lamenting limits: "Speech found the ear, for all the evil sound, / But the dark italics it could not propound." Those lines shift from elation to apathy with a speed that creates a "sensible ecstasy," a satisfaction that does not ignore the facts that chasten it:

> who could have thought to make
> So many selves, so many sensuous worlds,
> As if the air, the mid-day air, was swarming
> With the metaphysical changes that occur,
> Merely in living as and where we live.

This marries metaphysical and physical realms. It is partly an "elusion": "as if" demands the subjunctive that conditions possibility with doubt; Stevens uses the simple past. Thus he makes the merely possible seem real. But he does so in a way that exposes the artifice involved, so that malign elusion becomes "benign illusion." Language betrays and "saves."

"Credences of Summer" is an "esthétique" of good. It makes actual the sort of world our needs demand, a natural realm in tune with our desires. The poem is similar to Frost's "Directive." Like it, and like much of Stevens's work in this period, it is filled with self-reflexive echoes of earlier poems; it presents a timeless place where we might "be whole again beyond confusion" in a way that reveals the place as artificial while still avowing its power to refresh if not redeem us. A single passage can serve to make the point:

> Now in midsummer come and all fools slaughtered
> And spring's infuriations over and a long way
> To the first autumnal inhalations, young broods
> Are in the grass, the roses are heavy with a weight
> Of fragrance and the mind lays by its trouble.

The use of seasonal cycles to indicate a moment out of time ("this is the centre that I seek. / Fix it in an eternal foliage / / And fill the foliage with arrested peace") keeps time present with all its natural enigmas intact: slaughters, rages, fulfillments, and drawings back.

Stevens's superlative poem of this sort is "Notes Toward a Supreme Fiction." The title makes the argument. The supreme fiction is Stevens's name for the ultimate poem that would replace all the failed religious, philosophical, and poetic systems of the past, and do so in a way that would wholly satisfy both our naturalistic knowledge (it would be a "fiction") and our need for the sublime (it would be "supreme"). But such a poem cannot be realized. If it were, it would be in words. Then, like Phoebus, it would be "A name for something that never could be named" and meet in its turn the fate of every fiction that once had reigned supreme: "The death of one god is the death of all." And so Stevens shifts the poet's role from the creation of replacement objects to the act of replacement itself, and to the interrogation of that act. Thus, the poet and the poem offer "notes" "toward" the supreme fiction. We cannot have the perfection we desire; this is Stevens's version of the Fall. It is also his version of grace and resurrection; perfection's elusiveness keeps us striving and alive.

"Notes Toward a Supreme Fiction" rehearses most of Stevens's themes and moods in an astonishing, even profligate series of inventions, and in the provisional style characteristic of the sequences of this penultimate phase. We are told, for instance, that poetry "refreshes life" by decreating preconceptions and allowing us contact with nature in "the first idea." This stimulating poverty turns out to have its own "ennui" and encourages us to create new conceptions of our own. But when those conceptions become preconceptions, they, too, will be "fatal." Thus the supreme fiction is not to be written. At the same time, and knowing that, one must try to write it down. The poem offers many possible models, all of them undone as they are uttered: "the MacCullough," major man, sufficient nature, "times of inherent excellence . . . not balances / That we achieve but balances that happen." None will do; each is a "False flick, false form." But each is also a "falseness close to kin." Even when "Notes" seems to have found a formula beyond falseness, a model for inclusion so complete as to contain every conceivable season, extreme, or mood, the apparent perfection unravels. These lines seem a summary of what Stevens's later style has attempted to achieve:

> He had to choose. But it was not a choice
> Between excluding things. It was not a choice
>
> Between, but of. He chose to include the things
> That in each other are included, the whole,
> The complicate, the amassing harmony.

For all the breadth of their embrace, however, those words, spoken by the Canon Aspirin (his name implies a genius both for aspiration and sedation),[66] exemplify Charles Berger's statement that "Stevens is deeply seductive when using inspired rhetoric to purvey false cures."[67] The Canon made a brave choice, but in choosing he thought to come to conclude. As Canons (and canons) will, he denied the continuity of change and succumbed to premature closure. This suggests the challenge the poem presents. It asks us to enjoy such "notes" as it and the Canon make, for they are "close to kin" of the "supreme fiction" we seek. It asks us, too, to refuse them our ultimate allegiance, for they, like every form, are "false."

This is especially clear in the poem's conclusion. "Notes Toward a Supreme Fiction" ends with a splendid image in which language makes the opacity of nature brilliantly translucent. Transformed by the poetic act of naming, the "fluent mundo" will have become a poem; the world "will have stopped revolving except in crystal." Stevens's usual qualifications are all in place—the word "until" introduces the passage, putting off the presence about to be described; the phrase "will have stopped" keeps prospective what sounds as though it had already been accomplished; "except" includes restrictions; and "crystal" implies not only many-faceted beauty but fragile hardness and artificiality. Yet here even those restraints are not enough. As the poem's other marriages collapsed—those of reality and imagination, of the "great captain and the maiden Bawda," of the Canon's widowed sister, and of the Canon's own "amassing harmony"—so the final marriage in which poetry and the natural world unite in crystal is decreated, too. A coda reopens every issue, returning the poem to the daily world where ordinary soldiers fight and die and where the "war between the mind / and sky," between the human need for order and nature's fecund beauty and indifference, goes on and "never ends." The enjambment enforces separation. It is the jar and Tennessee again. And yet ("and yet, and yet, and yet"):

> The two are one.
> They are a plural, a right and left, a pair,
> Two parallels that meet. . . .

We know, of course, what parallels do not do. The next words are "if only," and the war goes on.

In one of the "never-ending meditation[s]" of "An Ordinary Evening in New Haven," Stevens describes our "permanence" as "composed of impermanence." This is difficult poetry; Stevens's remarks on language illuminate it. Transcendentalism promised that speech transforms the world, dissolving nature to reveal the truth it harbors and conceals. In "On the Road Home," speech alters reality, or seems to: "It was when I said, / 'There is no such thing as the truth,' / That the grapes seemed fatter." But nature does not dissolve; it ripens. Language discovers the world of our desires in the world. This satisfies, but only insofar as it admits that the world is known not as it is but as it seems, that there is no truth to find. And insofar as it does that, we cannot be consoled. In section XII of "An Ordinary Evening in New Haven," the act of speech marries words to the world: "The poem is the cry of its occasion, / Part of the res itself and not about it." In section XVII, words and world divorce: "A blank underlies the trials of device." Elation and desolation, the sublime and the naturalistic, our desires expressed in words and wordless nature, they marry and divorce, detach and intertwine: it is "as if . . . words of the world are the life of the world." "As if" and "are." As if.

Stevens's last poems, printed in "The Rock" section of *The Collected Poems* and in *Opus Posthumous*, continue to explore his central theme: how, in a world without absolutes, to satisfy our naturalistic knowledge and our need for the sublime. In a sense, Stevens's subject never changed from the time he discovered that God and transcendental nature had died. But the style of his attention to it altered as his possible responses multiplied and resisted resolution. In the last poems, Stevens achieves a new inclusion, not by speed or prodigal invention but by an almost preternatural calm. He keeps his claims and disavowals, but yields the grander gestures, the mythy stuff of supreme fictions and major men. He accepts the world as having two dimensions that no third term will come to synthesize, no superman or supernatural absolute will merge as one. The "war" that "never ends" goes on. But in his last poems, Stevens somehow moves beyond the war of mind and sky. He accepts the gulf between the human need for transcendence and nature's blank indifference as the way things are. He achieves no resolution, yet he does not despair or surrender his desires. He lives in the world of his poems; he lives in the world outside. He writes. Language is his bridge between self and world: it sustains us and falls apart.

"The Plain Sense of Things" describes a world—Elizabeth Park, or Stevens's poems—in a season of decreation and decline. A stripped place "After the leaves have fallen," without sources outside ourselves for what we feel, it is nearly beyond words: "It is difficult even to choose the adjective / For this blank cold." And yet the desolation stirs, the search for the adjective goes on. An observer appears and is observed. The silence rustles. Natural almost as nature, the imagination does its necessary work, imagining "the absence of . . . imagination," reflecting "without reflections" on the world.

Other poems find warmer tones, but theirs, too, are muted satisfactions, defining art as our nature out of tune with nature yet intact. In "A Quiet, Normal Life," "There was no fury in transcendent forms. / But [the poet's] actual candle blazed with artifice." In "The Planet on the Table," "Ariel was glad he had written his poems," not because they achieved transcendent truth or found a substitute for immortality in fame, but because he hoped

> that they should bear
> Some lineament or character,
>
> Some affluence, if only half-perceived,
> In the poverty of their words,
> Of the planet of which they were part.

Having made his book, the poet lets it go, leaving it to endure the decreations that will come.

Stevens still makes claims for his poems, but the anxiety of influence, the burden of the past that had beset him since his Harvard days, when it had seemed "that all the poetry had been written,"[68] is calmed. So, too, is the poet's passion that his poems explain the world, replacing holy writ, and even his passion that his poems should survive his life. The claims Stevens makes for poetry now are the quiet ones that a knowledge of art as fictive process rather than the creation of truthful objects requires. In "The Poem That Took the Place of a Mountain," the title's ambitions are both realized and undone. His book, where "he had recomposed the pines" to find at last "the outlook that would be right," has become the place where he perhaps might "Recognize his unique and solitary home." This gives and takes away at once; the poet's task is "not to console / Nor sanctify, but plainly to propound."

And still things go around. In "Of Mere Being" Stevens once more makes an image for the imageless desire that makes us yearn in vision and in vain for the sublime. In the "palm at the end of the mind," a golden bird sings "without human meaning, / Without human feeling." Illusion or elusion, fact and artifact, "false flick" but "close to kin," somewhere beyond us the palm and the bird exist:

> The palm stands on the edge of space.
> The wind moves slowly in the branches.
> The bird's fire-fangled feathers dangle down.[69]

Those fangled feathers dazzle and betray.

There is no finality in Stevens. Still, for me, Stevens's final words are the ones he chose himself to conclude *The Collected Poems*. In "Not Ideas about the Thing but the Thing Itself," Stevens once again revises and revives the transcendental confidence that spring is the sign of the resurrection of poetry and of life. Indoors at "the earliest end of winter," the aged poet hears the "scrawny cry" of an unseen bird predicting the season to arrive. It "Seemed like a sound in his mind." The old need to define and redefine, to assert and disavow, to compose and decreate in order to find not a "false flick" but "the outlook that would be right" is still at work. The self within and the world outside marry, divorce, entwine. But elation and despair have been replaced by something else, not the inhuman more of the transcendental sublime, not the inhuman less of the materialist's empty world or the solipsist's overflowing mind, but a "sensible ecstasy" instead. The "scrawny cry" outside and the "scrawny cry" within might "seem" alike, but the cry was as actual as imagined, actual and heard: "It was like / A new knowledge of reality." And that was all.

Harold Bloom has said that for Stevens "discovery" is "one of the strongest of words."[70] It is. Not because Stevens is confident that nature contains transcendent truths for us to find. There is no final truth, as all his decreations show. The imagination rises nobly to resist. But its imposing impositions never wholly satisfy our knowledge or our needs. As in these lines from "Notes Toward a Supreme Fiction," the idea of discovery requites and resists our desires all at once. It measures what Stevens lost and found:

> to impose is not
> To discover. To discover an order as of
> A season, to discover summer and know it,
>
> To discover winter and know it well, to find,
> Not to impose, not to have reasoned at all,
> Out of nothing to have come on major weather,
>
> It is possible, possible, possible. It must
> Be possible.

Like curtains in the house of the metaphysician, our need for knowledge fills and fails and swells. In our "old chaos of the sun," the absence of absolutes lays us low and lifts us up. In *The Necessary Angel*, Stevens wrote, "Modern reality is a reality of decreation, in which our revelations are not the revelations of belief, but the precious portents of our own powers."[71] For Stevens the portents stayed just that and their revelations precious thus.

CHAPTER FOUR

MARIANNE MOORE

*As if, as if, it is all ifs; we are at
much unease.*

MARIANNE MOORE'S poems "trek . . . through knowledge to acknowl-
edgment."[1] Robert Pinsky's phrase is lucid and cryptic; Moore might have
approved.[2] The trek Moore's poems inscribe is not a pilgrimage, not ex-
plicitly religious, but it has a religious dimension. Its course is convoluted.
Margaret Holley writes that "Moore did not enter the modernist stream
through its challenge to the old spiritual order," but "joined and advanced it
through a radically new prosody."[3] John Slatin remarks upon the difficulty
Moore faced in reconciling her interest in innovative writing with the
gentility—including a conventional Protestant piety—"which was and re-
mained a fundamental aspect of her sensibility."[4] Many critics chronicle
Moore's religious background and practice, usually in order to notice the
relationship of Christian ethics to her esthetic and thematic values, and in
order to distinguish any metaphysical claims her faith might seem to imply
from the generally earthbound realm of her poems.

Moore was raised a Presbyterian. Her maternal grandfather, with whom
she lived as a child, was a Presbyterian minister, as was her brother, Warner.
She and her brother remained close; she offered him ideas for sermons, and
for a time she and her mother kept house in his parsonage in Chatham, New
Jersey. Moore lived with her mother until the latter's death in 1947, and she
typically acquiesced to Mary Warner Moore's judgments. Mrs. Moore's for-
midable piety is indicated by Elizabeth Bishop's recollection that on each of
her leave-takings after visits to the Moore household Mrs. Moore followed
her out into the hall, held her hands, and said a short prayer.[5] As a student
at Bryn Mawr, Moore herself, "unlike her classmates, refrained from work
on the sabbath" (a fact lent nuance by her admission that the source of her

"zeal to be present" at morning chapel "was not devoutness" but the "unpredictable originality" of the remarks delivered by M. Carey Thomas, the college president[6]). Moore continued to be a practicing Christian throughout her life. Writing two years before Moore's death in 1972, Donald Hall reported that she had attended services "every Sunday of her life" and had taken an "interested and active part" in church affairs.[7]

In 1953, in a piece called "Conscience," Moore affirmed her faith: "Choice is inescapable; and with the aid of humility in subordinating self-will to God's will—to the voice of the ages alive in us through Christ—the spirit attains *true* freedom, in which it continues to live and not die."[8] The passage is a rarity in Moore's published work. It was most unusual for her to speak so clearly of supernatural matters; in fact, she scarcely addresses such metaphysical issues as the existence of God, the soul, or eternity at all. Perhaps her explicitness in this case reflects the conventions of her occasion: she wrote "Conscience" for the *Church of the Epiphany Bulletin*. Usually Moore was reticent, preferring reserve to assertion in such matters. She admired Landor, who, when "considering . . . infinity and eternity," "could only say, 'I'll / talk about them when I understand them.'" While she felt that Reuben Brower belabored Frost's "resistance to being thought 'religious,'" she endorsed the poet's habitual restraint in that regard, saying, "A 'sober preference for not knowing too much' was basic in him but did he not affirm the only wholesome thing? 'The strong are saying nothing till they see.'"[9] The skeptical nature of Frost's so-called affirmation is often matched in statements by Moore. Even when confirming her belief in prayer, she contrived to be indefinite: "Yes, I believe in prayer—as a mystery which can endow one with more power perhaps than any other spiritual mystery, yet a mystery which cannot be exposited to the point where it is not a mystery."[10]

Moore's religious outlook is intricate and subtle. Both of the "spiritual" comments quoted above appeared when she was in her sixties, at a time when the war, the death of her mother, her personal fame, and her own aging had urged her toward a more open and communitarian advocacy of values that she had earlier interrogated as well as enacted or implied. Moore was capable of bringing to religious questions the same empirical rigor she applied elsewhere, as when she wrote, "The lurking sense of an adhered-to attitude on the part of those who regard themselves as religious, stands in the way of what they might do for one." Whatever metaphysical doubts she may have had, however, Moore was as reticent about them as she was about her faith. She did write these admiring words about Emily Dickinson: "She saw no comfort in refusing to question that about which she wished most to be sure. 'Are you certain there is another life? When overwhelmed to know,' she said, 'I fear that few are sure.'" Perhaps those sentences verify Moore's remark that "it is a curiosity of literature how often what one says of another seems descriptive of one's self." Moore often maintained opposed or mixed viewpoints. She described a "skepticism that 'doubts in order to believe.'" And she cites with approval Kenneth Burke's statement that the artist "must recognize the validity of contraries," praising Burke in her usual palimpsest-like way by quoting his quotation of Emerson's maxim that "[o]ur moods do not believe in each other." She enacts and illustrates the axiom when she says of M. Carey Thomas, "A rebel against ambiguous morality, she deplored over-concreteness in religion." Moore thought "paradox at its compactest" a "crowning attraction," admired "undogmatic decisiveness," and, in considering writers' dogma, found Hardy's "tenacious incredulity" and Robinson's "tentative credulity" to be "obversely helpful."[11]

Still, the fact of Moore's faith remains, and the nature and degree of its importance to her "uncollected poetics," to her belief that "[t]he power of the visible / is the invisible," reward attention.[12] Again, the usual critical approach to this matter is to describe Moore's Presbyterian context and to note the presence of ethical and the absence of doctrinal Christianity in her poems.[13] This is accurate as far as it goes, but it underestimates the way in which Moore's religious background contributed the particular forms of natural supernaturalism that shape her epistemological and esthetic attitudes. Geoffrey Hartman suggests a possible approach.

In his notes for the sleeve of the recording Moore made for the Yale Series of Recorded Poets, Hartman writes that Moore's poems show the "clear identifying mark of the Puritan." (This has little to do with her supposed "puritanical" streak; if Moore could censure another poet's deployment of the term "water closet" in a poem, or justify her own use of the word "rump" in conversation only because she was sure her mother would recognize the allusion to Cowper's pet hare, she also said, "prudery in itself is a kind of obscenity.")[14] What Hartman recognizes as the badge of the Puritan in Moore is her "extreme reverence for created things coupled with an extreme distrust of the self." The Puritan reverence for created things has its source in the notion that nature is God's second book. A companion volume to the Bible (which guarantees the correspondence between visible and invisible things), nature is inscribed with truth and is therefore a potential source of knowledge. Puritan distrust of the self stems from the belief that humanity is fallen, from which it follows, among other things, that the human facility for interpreting nature and discovering its truth is radically limited, subject to error, and profoundly to be mistrusted. As Hartman suggests, Moore shares those views, but she does so with significant differences.

For the Puritans, the likelihood of human error in interpreting nature is intensified by the belief that nature itself is fallen, has lost its transparent legibility, and threatens to be a sensual snare for the lapsed sensibilities of humans. The Puritan "solution" to the dilemma of having a vitally significant "natural" text, but one with a blighted provenance and a flawed readership, is an uneasy mating of the reverence for created things to its opposite, *contemptus mundi*. One offspring is a powerfully controlled system of interpretation in which authority is reserved to regenerate souls, especially the clergy, and in which the range of possible meanings for natural facts and events is sharply restricted to established biblical patterns, as in Winthrop's "reading" of the snake behind the pulpit. Nature's meanings, insofar as they are properly perceived or discovered, are unequivocal—singular, predictable, and certain. The role of poetry in such a system is small, limited in theory if not always in practice to the memorable and attractive conveyance of known truths.

Moore's distrust of the interpreting self is great, as is her reverence for created things. In those matters she seems a Puritan indeed. But Moore's reverence for nature is not curtailed by the Puritan sense of it as fallen. She admires nature in its own right as well as in its potential as a source for meaning. At times, she seems to regard nature with the romantic or transcendentalist confidence that it provides an unblemished corrective model for compromised human consciousness. Yet while Moore's poems seek and sometimes seem to find in nature the translucence that is transparency's trace, they certify that nature's original transparency is lost to human sight. Moore always maintains a Puritan sense of the permanent gulf between human and natural spheres, and she has extreme doubts about the human capacity to know the truth of nature either in itself or as it points beyond. Similarly, while even Moore's most thoroughly descriptive nature poems retain an interest in the discovery of meaning that aligns her with Puritan concerns (and with a more modern emphasis on how meaning is generated, on the meaning of meaning), she never follows the Puritans in twisting her natural details into conformity with interpretative expectations or traditions. Quite the opposite, in fact, since the (Protestant) tendency to distrust all institutionalized authority and truth in favor of individual reexaminations of every fact and value is especially strong in her. Where the priority of doctrine caused the Puritans to reduce natural facts to singular and certain correspondences with scriptural truth, Moore allows both nature and interpretation their eccentric variety. Except in her earliest work, her readings of nature are typically equivocal and polysemous; they are not guided by any single authoritative source. While Moore does employ such Puritan devices as allegory, emblems, mottoes, and epigrams, she usually qualifies and questions them, sharply limiting their application. Yet if Moore lacks the surety of Puritan biblical and clerical guides to exegesis, preferring current and empirical explorations, she also lacks the faith that lends certainty to the individual interpretations which result—that is, the transcendentalist's faith in the visionary self and its guaranteed access to absolutes. Moore distrusts authoritative "readings"; she also doubts her own. Margaret Holley has tracked the disappearance from Moore's poems of the pronoun "I" in its privileged role of knowing witness,[15] a development in keeping with her Puritan (and postmodern) distrust of the self.

While Moore evades the Puritan relegation of the poet to mere ornamenter, she also deviates from the romantic sense of the poet as an especially visionary or insightful figure, the inventor of or creative contributor to meaning and truth. When Hall asked her at what point poetry became "world-shaking" for her, she replied, in something like thunder, "Never!"[16] Moore repeatedly rejected the (blasphemous) notion of the poet as creator. Her epistemological and esthetic model remained the Puritan one of discovery, however constrained it was in its workings and however compromised it was by her pointed awareness of radical subjectivity. Moore's empirical emphasis grounds her belief that poetry and science are parallel activities, and includes her modernist insistence that neither poetic nor scientific discovery is permanent or final; each is a matter of process: "it's not established once and for all; it's evolving." (She says something similar about spiritual life when she calls "'the journey from sin to redemption, perpetual'").[17] Rejecting the romantic myth of the poet as creator, hopeful to discover truth yet aware that the search is endless, fearful that we only invent what we seem to find, Moore also denies the Emersonian hope that words and things might be reunited so as to restore or to imitate the original Logos of creation. For her, language is fallen; words are suspected instruments: at their best they *approximate* identity with what they would represent. In this, as in other matters, Moore is aligned with neoclassical and modernist notions of the poet as a craftsmanlike maker, so much so that her poetry comes to emphasize consolation over salvation, a view incompatible with Puritan or romantic transcendental traditions. In fact, much of Moore's work so strongly emphasizes the arbitrary and "textual" aspects of human assertions and expressions of significance as to seem postmodernist.

If those issues—and the implication of Moore in classic, romantic, modern, and postmodern, as well as Puritan, versions of epistemology and esthetics—seem remarkably tangled and indistinct, that is as it should be. Moore's decisiveness is undogmatic. Her poetry does not stem from answers or solutions but from the questions and problems raised by competing points of view about how and how much we know and about the limitations and powers of poetry to discover or create meaning. She described her situation clearly in a passage partially quoted above: "The lurking sense of an adhered-to attitude on the part of those who regard themselves as religious, stands in the way of what they might do for one. When we get away from the mystical, however, we put ourselves under the power of nature and nature is cruel."[18] Caught between habitual fraud and instinctual cruelty,

Moore maintains her interest in the "mystical," her word here for the absolute or transcendent. But she is frank about her doubts with regard to its existence and about the implications and ramifications of those doubts. In the twenties, Moore spoke of the "universal need for something which transcends the literal."[19] She did not specify if anything answers the need, or whether the something required must be transcendental or might be merely figurative. Late in her career she adopted the consolatory view that we live by fictions that we choose and defend, recognizing them for what they are, yet giving them the credence of absolutes. As she says in "Armor's Undermining Modesty," "What is more precise than precision? Illusion." But that view obtains only after a long and fascinating exploration of epistemological and esthetic issues, often undertaken in the context of nature. Moore's acknowledgment of "illusion" comes only after a trek through knowledge, through a world of "modified illusions" where "Unconfusion submits / its confusion to proof."[20]

The religious doctrine that conditions Moore's particular form of natural supernaturalism is the Fall, including its paradoxical element of *felix culpa*. Judeo-Christian paradoxes provide Moore with many of her themes: freedom in constraint, humility as strength, relinquishment as possession, armor as a weapon; Bible commentaries were an important source for her work, including the illogical logic of her sometime notion of poetry as "'prose / with a sort of heightened consciousness.'" Prelapsarian and postlapsarian categories, and a conception of the Fall as both primal disaster and happy fault, are fundamental to Moore's epistemological and esthetic attitudes. Bonnie Costello and John Slatin have noticed this quality in Moore's thought.[21] It appears not so much in her prose as in those poems that define her poetics, especially "Poetry" and "In the Days of Prismatic Color."

For Moore, poetry is two things: an ideal unattainable by even the finest efforts of fallen humanity (this is one reason why she frequently insists that what she writes is not poetry at all), and an actual, if fallen, practice that succeeds or fails in achieving our nearest approximation to the ideal. In "Poetry," her most explicit attempt at an *ars poetica*, each of those kinds appears. There is ideal poetry, which Moore presents as absence, employing a kind of negative version of the optative mode. Ideal poetry can be imagined but not written; its conditions can be laid down but they cannot be met; no example is given because none exists:

> nor till the poets among us can be
>   "literalists of
>   the imagination"—above
>   insolence and triviality and can present

for inspection, "imaginary gardens with real toads in them,"

                                                  shall we have

it.[22]

"It" is, of course, poetry; here, ideal poetry, the kind that fallen human beings apparently cannot write. Even at their best, actual poets do not achieve poetry. In the seemingly perpetual "meantime" between present practice and an imagined and indefinite future perfection ("till"), they can only hope to demonstrate that they "are interested in poetry," a position at some remove from producing it.

Moore's poem also defines the poetry of actual practice. This is of two sorts. There is the kind of poetry Moore famously dislikes ("I, too, dislike it," she writes, embracing and coercing the reader at once). This is the poetry of "fiddle" and "high-sounding interpretation." "[D]erivative" and "unintelligible," it is "not poetry" at all when seen from the perspective of ideal poetry. Seen from the vantage of actual practice it is failed poetry, inauthentic in feeling, thought, and expression. There is, though, another kind of actual poetry that has "in / it after all, a place for the genuine." Although hardly ideal, this poetry is attainable and can be exemplified in the poem as ideal poetry could not be; it is enacted here in catalogues depicting the excited potency of creatures and persons in action or prepared for action— actions which are natural and "useful," as authentic poetry must be.

In the sequence of Moore's poem, authentic and inauthentic actual poetry appear first and are judged against one another; they are then placed in contrast to ideal poetry. This enacts the pride that goes before and the fall that comes after. It indicates the radical limits of even our best achievements. The source of those limits, to say it again, is our fallen condition, whether we have fallen into consciousness or sin. We can apprehend the genuine and admire its energy, but we cannot perceive it transparently and so see through it to the truth it literally stands for. Our response to this circumstance is what allows us the authentic poetry we have (this is the "fortunate" aspect of *felix culpa*), but—in keeping with the paradox—it is the source of inauthenticity and failure as well. In attempting to grasp the transparency we cannot see, we tame (or "cook") "the raw material of poetry," using the implements of reason, order, and form to discover its meaning or truth. In the process we lose what we would gain, imposing on (and as) the genuine the "high-sounding" and "derivative" interpretations we seek to avoid. In Moore's presentation of these matters, the supposedly separate categories of the "genuine" and the "raw" are deliberately confused (the act of making distinctions blurs as well as clarifies difference). In the same way, her apparently "natural" form involves the exercise of syllabic artifice—and resistance to it. In an unfallen world, the genuine and raw, the natural and artificial would be one. We see only what we think are hints of that lost unity, reflections of transparency in moments of ecstatic response. Those occasions cause us to strive for "something which transcends the literal." The effort ennobles and undoes us.

Moore states her perception of the poet's happily flawed circumstance directly in an epigram from the 1915 poem originally called "*So far as the future is concerned . . .*" and later retitled "The Past is the Present." There she writes, "Ecstasy affords / the occasion and expediency determines the form." This suggests a self-limiting pragmatics of the sublime, in which the generous gift of miraculously intense experience, afforded as a kind of grace, becomes the source for a poetry that preserves and loses the intensity it would express because its only recourse is to the useful but makeshift and self-interested means of language and form, determining means that we lack the freedom to surpass.

For Moore, in a phrase from one of her essays, the fallen world has become "Nature's hieroglyphics of the visibly significant." Inscribed with writing that is both sacred and obscure, nature retains the signs of truth, but they are hard to read. Furthermore, Moore is deliberately inexact (it is one of her modes of precision) about whether the surfaces of the world potentially reveal only its own depths or signal the existence of an absolute spiritual realm that informs and transcends this one. The former view implies an empirical method of discovery that reveals secular depths by precisely observing and anatomizing surfaces (Moore took great interest in the adaptive forces underlying animal structures and behaviors, for instance; as Helen Vendler says, the essential biographical fact about Moore is that she spent her years at Bryn Mawr as a biology student). The latter view suggests a spiritual method of discovery that reveals sacred depths by reading the world's inscribed surfaces according to a preexisting code. Of course, those contrasting approaches may only be "opposed each to the other, not to unity." Moore's poems abound with the interplay of surface and secular depth. In prose, she delights in describing herself as "an American chameleon on an American leaf," cites approvingly Eliot's distinction between "brilliance of surface and mere superficiality," and seconds his claim that in the works of Ben Jonson " 'The superficies *is* the world.' " She is concerned with spiritual depth as well. She asks, "Is the Real Actual?," a metaphysical question charged with Platonic, Puritan, and transcendentalist implications. She gives this "answer," remarkable for its empirical stress and for its blend of tentative assertion: "The realm of the spirit is the only realm in which experience is able to corroborate the fact that the real can also be the actual." Whether or not experience has access to that realm is left unstated.[23]

Those possibilities, attitudes, and remarks bear on Moore's claim that "[t]he power of the visible / is the invisible." They do so without expositing it "to the point where it is not a mystery." Moore once said, "when I am as complete as I like to be, I seem unable to get an effect plain enough." She makes the same point more affirmatively when, in "The Mind is an Enchanting Thing," she praises "conscientious inconsistency." As she said in one of her earliest poems, "A Jelly-Fish," published in 1909, the "fluctuating charm" of the "Visible, invisible" can be apprehended only if "you abandon your intent" "to catch it." Moore's circumspection and inclusiveness are concomitants of her sense of the epistemological and esthetic possibilities and limits characteristic of fallen human nature, whether that condition is factual or figurative. "Conscientious inconsistency" represents an undogmatic and decisive attitude in which the poet maintains her openness to the possibility of knowing by resisting any final or certain knowledge. Moore puts the matter in religious terms when she recommends that doubters assume the listener's stance: "[I]s it not true that 'God is messageless' unless one listens?"; "One should above all, learn to be silent . . . ; to make possible promptings from on high." She never says for certain that "promptings" arrive, but in secular terms, too, Moore urges the receptive posture of an intensely disinterested observer, as when she sanctions "the Montaigne library-motto": "I do not understand; I pause; I examine."[24]

The lapsarian paradoxes of Moore's ways of thinking have extensive implications. Pamela White Hadas suggests their range when she discusses Moore's simultaneous embrace and rejection of two views of the nature of things that seem to be mutually exclusive. In one view, the world has a "secret center" to which its surfaces lead, a center that gives those surfaces their meaning and purpose and that our readings of surfaces more or less successfully approximate. The secret at the core of things might be the "really Real" of Platonic idealism, God's originary Word, entropy, or some other transcendent or empirical absolute. In the other view, the world is layer upon layer of appearance. It has no center to validate any one layer as more true than any other, and no "truth" by which we might evaluate whatever layers of meaning we add to the world as we read it. Hadas concludes that Moore does not choose between those views but "says both yes and no" to each, "meaning both most sincerely and consciously."[25] It is so with her sense of surfaces and secular and sacred depths as well. The likelihood of a "secret center" is kept open in her poems by her refusal to insist derivatively upon one. The refusal permits even the possibility that the Fall itself is only an analogue of our yearning for a knowledge and perfection we cannot have, the possibility that truth is an "illusion created out of the artist's superfluous desire."[26] What Moore said of Dürer can be said of her—her "many sagacities seem . . . not to starve one another."[27]

The lapsarian vocabulary I have been using to discuss Moore's epistemological and esthetic positions does not occur in "Poetry," although the poem does record a brisk descent from the ideal. Details of the Eden story *are* conspicuous in several poems roughly contemporaneous with "Poetry": in "When I Buy Pictures," published in 1921; in "Marriage" and "An Octopus," which appeared in 1923 and 1924, respectively; and in Moore's most explicitly Edenic poem, "In the Days of Prismatic Color," published in 1919, the same year "Poetry" appeared. The paradigm of the Fall was much on Moore's mind in the years when she formulated her mature poetics.

"In the Days of Prismatic Color" is explicitly epistemological and esthetic, concerned with primary and secondary modes of perception and understanding, and with matters of expression, of form and "feet." It begins at or near the beginning, with an almost nostalgic account of nearly primal perfection; then, with precipitous brevity, it reports the Fall:

IN THE DAYS OF PRISMATIC COLOR

not in the days of Adam and Eve, but when Adam
   was alone; when there was no smoke and color was
fine, not with the refinement
   of early civilization art, but because
of its originality; with nothing to modify it but the

mist that went up, obliqueness was a variation
   of the perpendicular, plain to see and
to account for: it is no
   longer that. . . .

In an attempt to reach an original moment, Moore has pushed back before the creation of Eve, before perception was tainted by the need for communication, to a time when Adam's pristine solitude assured an apprehension of color unblemished by the obscurations of civilization and art, activities that are essential to fallen humanity but that paradoxically dim as they refine. Yet even in this thoroughly prelapsarian state, Adam already seems fallen.

The color Adam perceived was prismatic; he did not see primeval white, nor the primary colors of "the blue-red-yellow band" either; instead he saw the seven colors of the spectrum produced when light passes through a prism. If Edenic color was unmarred by such "civilized" products as smoke, it was modified by mist, a natural but still obscuring substance. The word "days" in the title puns on "daze." Furthermore, even when he was alone, Adam was already characterized by "obliqueness" in relation to the perpendicular (a kind of geometric parallel to pure white light). But Adam's obliqueness, unlike ours, was "a variation / of"—not from—"the perpendicular, plain to see and / to account for," if impossible to correct. Adam's relative perfection of perception was real enough, and certainly preferable to our more drastically lapsed and "unaccountable" condition, but it was already at a remove from absolute perfection. The situation is something like that in "Poetry." Various degrees of authentic and inauthentic human perception—and, for those who come after Adam, expression—are compared both to one another and to an unattainable ideal.

As a feminist, Moore redistributes the burden usually reserved for Eve, and we inherit from Adam an instensified "obliqueness" in matters of seeing and saying. Our fall has its happy aspects—perhaps because it affords us a pleasantly dizzying wealth of shadings and hues (in "When I Buy Pictures," Moore admires "an artichoke in six varieties of blue"); certainly because it affords us the potential ecstasy of attempted returns to primal plainness. However, the tools we have for the attempt, the determined and determining expedients of civilization and art, while they are necessary and useful, are also a "pestilence," as likely to conduce to obscurity as to clarity. They add "smoke" to "mist." Still, those expedients are our only instruments; if we use them with care, admitting the dangers, "complexity is not a crime." Too often, though, we carry complexity "to the point of murkiness / and nothing is plain." Making complexity an end in itself, we are "committed to darkness," as if we mix what clear colors we have into some sooty, outlaw infusion. In part, Moore is criticizing herself. As she said elsewhere, "Always in whatever I wrote . . . I have had a burning desire to be explicit; beset always, however carefully I had written, by the charge of obscurity."[28] But Moore's harshest criticism is reserved for those who make of obscurity a self-regarding esthetic law,

> . . . as if to bewilder us with the dismal
> fallacy that insistence
>   is the measure of achievement and that all
> truth must be dark.

Her summary judgment is damning and direct: "Principally throat, sophistication is as it al- / / ways has been—at the antipodes from the init- / ial great truths."

Throatily gorgeous, gorging, and sophistical, those who promote complexity as a criterion of excellence devour light. Moore illustrates the principle of obscurity in action by borrowing a description from the *Greek Anthology*; it stresses the monstrousness of such a view: " 'Part of it was crawling, part of it / was about to crawl, the rest / was torpid in its lair.' " As in the earlier passage, Moore's line breaks emphasize an essential disorganization. The judgmental force of the passage can be felt by contrasting it with Moore's illustration of an esthetic principle she endorses: "Imagination implies energy and imagination of the finest type involves an energy which results in order 'as the motion of a snake's body goes through all parts at once, and its violation acts at the same instant in coils that go contrary ways.'"[29] Moore's attack on complexity as principle rather than expedient is clear enough. Still, expedients—obliqueness in perception, indirectness in expression—are the inevitable lot of fallen creatures.

Moore's own obligations to complexity appear in the turn to the poem's conclusion, where the word "classic," virtually suspended between stanzas, shifts from a term of approbation to one of blame. This is a shock at first. The classical emphasis on clarity, on the ideal, on a "perpendicular" purity of line, would seem the perfect antidote to "dismal" obfuscation and its "gurgling," "fitful advance." Perfection is precisely the problem; it is as much a "pestilence" as willful complexity is. From Moore's postlapsarian perspective, classical art seems to ignore too easily or repress too calmly the limitations and complexities of actual experience. In assuming that it has achieved the ideal, it is smug or blind—especially when "experts" make it an icon or model to be permanently admired and endlessly repeated. This is the source of Moore's audacious and abrupt attack: "Truth is no Apollo / Belvedere, no formal thing." The "verbal physics"[30] of her lineation assaults the god *and* his statue (as well as the "monumentality" implied by both). The passage is a marvel of concision. "Belvedere" (the statue is named for its location in the Belvedere gallery of the Vatican palace) means "beautiful view"; the word recalls the poem's interest in perception, just as the word "formal" recalls its interest in expression. "Apollo"—the god of original, preprismatic light, and of poetry, by which we attempt to get back to it—recalls them both. What he represents is not to be comprehended in any work of art; his name implies "destruction."

Moore's choice of the Apollo Belvedere for attack has particular application to her own esthetics. As a Roman copy of a lost Greek original, the statue is in a sense already fallen. Nonetheless, it was enormously popular in the eighteenth and nineteenth centuries. As H. W. Janson writes, "Winckelmann, Goethe, and other champions of the Greek Revival thought it the perfect exemplar of classic beauty; plaster casts or reproductions of it were considered indispensable for all museums, art academies, or liberal arts colleges, and generations of students grew up in the belief that it embodied the essence of the Greek spirit."[31] Moore attacks not only the statue but also the process that made it a cultural shibboleth. Recommending work that seeks perfection while including the limitations and complications that (however happily) impair it, and while avoiding the "'ready made,'"[32] Moore rejects an art that combines pretensions to originary perception and expression with an authoritarian esthetics of imitation and replication.

However obliquely, Moore is bold. She offers her own work as more difficult than either classical clarity or modern obscurity. Her poem is like the snake, an order of energy moving in contrary directions. In its alternation of justified left-hand margins and indentations, the verse snakes down the page, but Moore distrusts the shapeliness of formal imitation. Rejecting symmetry, she truncates the poem's last stanza and all but silences the expected rhyme (where we have had such full, if "Unemphasized," echoes as "was"–"because," "and"–"band," "dismal"–"al-," and "it"–"fit," we now hear "likes" and "by"). Moore's poem accepts its own "obliqueness." Winding from an extreme of false complexity to one of false clarity (extremes united by having sources "in the Greek"), the poem casts its symmetry as a snake casts its skin. Having rendered the model of classical beauty as monstrous as darkly willed complexity is, her poem partakes of both without succumbing to either.

The conclusion of "In the Days of Prismatic Color" is appropriately epigrammatic and enigmatic both:

> Truth is no Apollo
> Belvedere, no formal thing. The wave may go over it if it likes.
> Know that it will be there when it says,
> "I shall be there when the wave is gone by."

The wave may represent either chaos or form. Neither by carrying complexity "to the point of murkiness," where it becomes a crime, nor by steamroller-like strategies of formal compression, can we hope to conquer or capture "Truth." As an alternate course, Moore offers her own way of using energy to produce an order that includes complexity. But she also admits that her method, if less a crime or a falsehood than the others, is also a "pestilence"; the perpendicular truth remains beyond *its* reach as well. Moore's rigorous and inclusive vision is the legacy of the fortunate fall. As she says in "Smooth Gnarled Crape Myrtle," "An aspect may deceive"; "Art is unfortunate." Still, it is what we have, the source of a precise and perceptive energy of response that permits us to move in a singular way while expediency's "violations" force us in many directions at once. Those notions motivate Moore's "conscientious inconsistency," her "contrary ways."

In the poem "Tell Me, Tell Me," Moore appraises Henry James as one

> who "breathed inconsistency and drank
> contradiction," dazzled
>   not by the sun but by "shadowy
>   possibility."

She might have said it of herself. Perhaps she did, since she maintained that "appraisal is chiefly useful as appraisal of the appraiser."[33] Moore's poems are "'polished garlands' of agreeing difference"; they mix art and nature, unity and diversity. The quoted phrase is from "Sea Unicorns and Land Unicorns," a title that reflects Moore's interest in amphibious things, in creatures or objects adapted to inhabit dual realms: land and sea, fact and fantasy, reason and unreason.[34] The contrarieties of Moore's poetics follow patterns set by her contrasting and sometimes contradictory attitudes about the relationship of the visible to the invisible and by her emphasis on the Fall and the paradox of *felix culpa*. Among those contrarieties are her amphibious notions about the artist's originality and belatedness.

The materials of Moore's poems are rarely drawn straight from nature or direct experience. Usually, her subjects have been subjects before and trail a digest of sources: newspapers and magazines; anecdotes, biographies, and memoirs; encyclopedias and handbooks; books on fashion; histories and natural histories; sermons, collections of letters, and traveller's tales; drawings and photographs; nature films; museum exhibits and catalogues; even works of literary criticism. Moore represents the represented. Her emphasis on materials previously interpreted, depicted, and described accents our separation from the original and asserts the secondary and belated aspects of writing. Moore's re-representations foreground interpretative issues as problematical, and they indicate the intertextuality of a fallen world in which prior texts are inescapable determinants of current ones. In this way she questions the concepts of creativity and originality, of authorial "ownership," and of authority itself. This has a postmodern ring, but Moore's response to the implications of intertextuality is diverse.

By stressing the cobbled nature of her effects, Moore participates in that disruptive aspect of collage that exposes the duplicity of art.[35] Collage places under erasure conceptions of the artist as a creator ex nihilo or from the recesses of a singular self, as it does conceptions of works of art as self-generated, independent creations. But in Moore's version at least, the erasure is incomplete; the smudge of originality remains. In the term Holley borrows from Lévi-Strauss, Moore is a *bricoleur*. She does not create "wholly anew." Rather, she makes things out of " 'odds and ends left over,'" building "'structured sets . . . by using the remains and debris of events.'"[36] But at the same time Moore's poems are unmistakably hers. Her techniques emphasize the power of the artist who wrenches materials from their original contexts and orders them in new patterns with new, if not quite original, significations. The materials of Moore's poems trail their already represented pasts, but they are not wholly bound by them: tracking the "Notes" often shows what liberties Moore took with her supposedly determining sources. For all her polite citations, she pirates material with the rough insouciance she liked in Samuel Butler's boast: if something "is appropriate, I appropriate it."[37]

The most prominent site of the contest between originality and belatedness in Moore is her famous use of quotations. This is an intricate matter: sometimes Moore's quotations are exact, sometimes not; occasionally she places original material in quotation marks or quotes borrowed material without the sanction of punctuation; often her quotations are lifted so completely out of context that they retain only tenuous links to their original intent—a matter Moore's seemingly scrupulous notes conceal as well as expose. R. P. Blackmur makes the summary point: Moore uses quotation marks for "all the values of setting matter off, whether in eulogy or denigration."[38] Exactly. Moore's quotation marks bow humbly to authority or express admiration, but at least as often they question, make ironic, or mock the matter they enclose. Frequently her authorities are not authorities at all in the usual sense, but a child's drawing, perhaps, or the *Illustrated London News*. That can indicate both the power of quotidian reality over her texts and the power of her texts to reform the ordinary.

Moore's quotations surrender her own authority to the multiple perspectives of other voices and views. Her orchestration of those voices and views into original textures manifests her authority over them. Moore's habit of allowing others' words to interrupt her own has the same double effect as her use of pre-represented material. It reminds us of the problematic status of the poem and undercuts the primacy of the author and the text; it asserts the author's power to choose and evaluate, to control and contain. Whether borrowed or thrust upon her, Moore's quoted material is neither wholly unassimilated nor wholly taken in. As Slatin says, it threatens the poem's original, independent, and self-possessed existence without entirely defeating it.[39] Moore's practice of revision raises similar issues, whether it involves revision within poems—as in the characteristic self-correction of "Silence": "'The deepest feeling always shows itself in silence; / not in silence, but restraint'"—or between versions of poems, as in the notorious case of "Poetry." Expressing "an essential ambivalence about poetry's capacity to assert and form a multifaceted world,"[40] it both checks and extends the poet's authority over her work.

Moore's ambivalence about originality and belatedness is revealed in a number of comments about the subject. The following are an epitome: "We look at imitation askance; but like the shell which the hermit-crab selects for itself, it has value—the avowed humility, and the protection"; "We cannot ever be wholly original. . . . Nevertheless an indebted thing does not interest us unless there is originality underneath it."[41] Moore's amphibian position with regard to indebtedness helps explain her mixed feelings about poetry. Her attitude toward both literary tradition and her own work is conservative and progressive at once; she is interested both in "preservation" and in "dismantling and renewal."[42] In Moore's own words, although "genius" is "always in revolt" and the artist "riotous" in "attitude toward the existing body of art, in so far as a thing is really a work of art it confirms other works of art."[43]

Moore's sense that originality is ultimately to be desired and impossible to attain also shapes her ideas about language. Her view of the writer's circumstance is contained in this fact: when she avowed that "'the imperiousness of all art'" causes it vigorously to reject the company of the "'ready made,'" she was quoting someone else's words. Moore is imperious herself in disliking the "compulsory connective, stock speech of any kind"; her language is notably innovative. Yet her poems teem with such items of definitively "stock speech" as emblems, epigrams, and mottoes. Those derivative presences are explained in part by her rhetorical assertion: "When a thing has been said so well that it could not be said better, why paraphrase it?" But stock materials are often on display in her poems in order to be questioned, revised, and contested. When she called aphorism "one of the kindlier phases of poetic autocracy,"[44] she compromised the compliment. Hadas suggests that Moore uses mottoes and proverbs as a scientist uses scientific paradigms.[45] Her condensed versions of traditional wisdom are often chosen not because they contain the truth and conclude exploration, but because they designate areas for renewed experimentation or mark out boundaries whose ability to comprehend new evidence requires proof. "'Science is never finished,'" she writes in "The Student," quoting Einstein's adage.

Moore's faith that we pursue the ideal with fallen means stimulates other contrarieties in her work: for instance, her ambivalent attitudes about the categories of the natural and the artificial. Regarding style, Moore said, "Unemphasized rhymes, a flattened rhetoric, and retreating verse patterns are likely to be sincerer than is convenient to the reader." That statement is glossed by this one: "My own fondness for the unaccented rhyme derives, I think, from an instinctive effort to ensure naturalness." The oddity of the phrase "effort to ensure naturalness" is of the essence. In the poem "England," Moore speaks of "modified illusions." In a review, she wrote, "Science's method of attaining to originality by way of veracity is pleasing."[46] In each case, the ideal—which in Moore is to be understood as an unhindered natural and "visionary" knowledge of "original" truth—is obscured by the means required to seek it, means estimable as the best we have but compromised by the artificiality that defines them: effort, modification, method. To *attain* naturalness is a paradox indeed. It configures Moore's mixture of natural and highly artificial effects, her combination of formal and colloquial diction, her syncopated rhythms, her alternations of exposure and concealment, her interest in both wild animals and highly finished works of art, and her varying practice of rhymed and unrhymed, syllabic and free verse, each infused with prose, each with its competing implications. Moore's poems evoke the reality of nature by means of their great referential precision. By means of their "oddity and difficulty,"[47] they stress the artifice of composition.

The dual emphasis on nature and artifice in Moore points to still other contrasting aspects of her work. Hugh Kenner locates Moore in "a world that does not speak and seems to want *describing*." He praises her attention to the surfaces of language and the world and congratulates her on avoiding "the supreme insult we can offer to the other," having, "on too little acquaintance, something to say 'about' it." The applause is apt: Moore refuses closure; she puts off as if forever conclusive interpretation; she grants its "proper plenitude" to fact.[48] But Kenner underestimates the extent to which Moore, however reserved, has things, however restrained, to say "about" the world. Moore was persistently interested not only in facts but in the relationship between fact and value, fact and meaning, fact and concept. Perhaps that is why she defined poetry as "fact plus imagination."[49] George Nitchie concentrates the matter when he writes that Moore's impulse "to note particularities despite, or even because of, their refusal to lend themselves to application" is "constantly involved with the counterimpulse" "to generalize, to reduce particularities in the interest" of meaning, abstraction, and truth. Costello puts it this way: "Moore's best poems express a conflict between her desire to form and delimit thought and experience and her alertness to unassimilable detail."[50]

The invigorating tension between detail and doctrine in Moore's poems yields such related contrarieties as her dual attitudes about explicitness and obscurity and concision and expansiveness. In a late poem ("Values in Use"), Moore asked "Am I still abstruse?" Given her ideal of original clarity, it is not surprising that she worried about the obscurity she was often charged with and that she knew was an essential and energizing if unfortunate aspect of verse—her chosen means to whatever modified clarity humans might attain. Moore strongly disliked clarities of the wrong kind, self-deceiving certainties or "the tawdriness of unnecessary explanation." She praised Louise Bogan for a quality her own poems share, titles "with no subserviences for torpid minds to catch at." Moore said more than once that deep feeling "tends to be inarticulate" and, when articulate, to seem enigmatic. That was praise. Yet she concurred with Voltaire's objection to enigmas and deplored "an inadvertent ambiguity." She also confessed "a very special fondness for writing that is obscure . . . because of the author's intuitive restraint." She thought that "we must have the courage of our peculiarities." Her favored conclusions about these matters shade toward enigma themselves: "How obscure may one be? . . . I suppose one should not be consciously obscure at all"; "we must be as clear as our natural reticence allows us to be."[51] Moore's best poems are "lucid without sacrificing implication,"[52] obscure in striving to be explicit.

Moore's views on concision and expansion are similarly rich. She says, "a poem is a concentrate." She considers "terseness . . . synonymous with a hatred of sham" and believes that "[o]ne of the most eloquent phases of savage resourcefulness is thrift." Moore could be savagely frugal herself, concentrating poems to a denseness that nears opacity. And she praises writers for "repudiating miscellany." But Moore admires writers who are "reckless," too, saying, "if you can't be that, what's the point of the whole thing." She used these statements by William James to curb her own predilections for the formal, rational, and condensed: "[m]an's chief difference from the brutes lies in the exuberant excess of his subjective propensities. Prune his extravagance, sober him, and you undo him." Commenting on an exhibition of artwork by children, Moore wrote, "The tendency to multiply detail is instinctive."[53] She could be savage in that way too. Her poems sometimes overflow in seemingly artless profusions of specifics. Moore, who often used double negatives to achieve an expansive concision in which a thing's direct opposite is both precisely denied and brought to bear, might be called a not injudicious gardener: she prunes *and* nurtures sprawl, liking abundance as much as pattern, disliking too much of either one.

All the stylistic and conceptual contrasts I have been discussing stem from a perception of the human condition that is rooted in the paradigm of the Fall. Desiring a seemingly lost and unattainable ideal, we work with tools that permit us "'piercing glances'" at perfection yet obscure what they unveil. Thus Moore's essential questions remain perpetually open. Perhaps the world is inscribed with God's originating Word. Then our task is logocentric, to strip away appearances in an effort to discover the world's core, its single truth. We act without hope of any final, earthly confirmation of our discoveries. Nonetheless, while using traditional and artificial means, we strive for an original naturalness of expression in which detail and doctrine would be one, in which language would be condensed in the service not of obscurity but of a clarity utterly explicit—like an ultimate formula capable of comprehending every fact. Moore considers other possibilities, too. Perhaps the world is a coreless tissue of appearances, all "as ifs" and "ifs," an endless sequence of layers that we invent and impose while we think that we strip them away. Or perhaps the world—including the presence, perceptions, and expressions of others, human or not—is a plenum of pleasurable differences, differences that at moments let us live and write with an intensity or "gusto" approximating, if it cannot quite recapture, primal bliss. As to the powers of poetry and the poet, Moore describes one of her own poems ("In the Public Garden") as "a grateful tale— / without that radiance which poets / are supposed to have." "Supposed" is a knot. It chides the work at hand for lacking the visionary power that poetry—including her own— should have, and usually does; it also suggests that the entire notion of poetry as an especially insightful kind of visionary seeing is only a supposition. However unsure she may have been, Moore goes on faith, the scientific and religious faith that the world may carry meaning and that we must try to find and know it—know it without claiming for certain that we do, and while acknowledging that we may invent or inscribe what we think we discover. Moore liked Yeats's story of "being told as a boy, that he had reined his pony in at the same time he had struck it with the whip."[54] It had application.

Moore's early poems interrogate "truths," sorting information, bad and good. Bad information often comes from "good" sources: authorities, idioms, truisms. Good information comes from attention and experiment, from willing disbelief. As an investigator, Moore's goal is knowledge, but also judgment, even justice. In the late 1960s she said, "To me, growing up means being able to change from a fixed opinion."[55] Moore grew up to challenge the fixed opinions of conventional wisdom. In the 1909 poem "Progress" (later retitled "I May, I Might, I Must"), Moore offers a bargain: to explain her confidence that she can cross an impassable fen in exchange for information about "why the fen / appears impassable." Information, explanation, and exchange, often confrontational exchange, motivate many poems from the years when Moore began to publish beyond the confines of Bryn Mawr's literary magazine: the period from 1915 to 1917, when her poems appeared in *Poetry*, *The Egoist*, and *Others*.

In her first years at college, Moore's grades prevented her from enrolling in advanced English courses. She majored in "History, Economics and Politics" and minored in biology. Several decades later, Moore discussed the importance of scientific study to her poems: "I found the biology courses . . . exhilarating. . . . Precision, economy of statement, logic employed to ends that are disinterested, drawing and identifying, liberate—at least have some bearing on—the imagination, it seems to me." The phrases "at least" and "it seems to me" introduce qualifications into an assured assertion; the dash, Moore said, signifies "prudence."[56] But Moore's early poems are bold; they often place all but unqualified faith in empiricism as the way to knowledge. In turning to nature as a potential source of value and truth, Moore concurs in an important aspect of the genteel tradition ascendant during her youth. But where genteel writers treated nature as a vast abstraction, and trusted to inspiration, sublimity, and generalization, and to the cautious replication of conventional subjects and forms, Moore's empiricist emphasis treated the actual details of nature and rendered any subject fit for study. Her scientific outlook encouraged the accurate observation of facts and the concise expression of results. It discouraged unfounded generalizations, and it demanded the rejection of conventions for convention's sake while nonetheless requiring that experimentation occur within rigorously disciplined methods and forms. Empiricism helped Moore to dispel the genteel vapors stifling American verse. In her early poems, received truths are repeated, not reverentially, but as hypotheses to be tested, and discarded if unconfirmed.

In her later poems, Moore became less confident in the ability of precise observation to discover "the truth underlying appearances," even doubtful that truth can be discovered or known at all. Hints of those doubts sometimes appear in early poems. But most of Moore's early work "bristles with accuracies." Barbed with "that one integrity: antipathy to falsity," her verse is quilled to repel dogmatists who declaim in the absence of proof. Characteristically terse and judgmental, Moore's early poems often employ direct address: a speaking "I" confronts a subject designated "you." The sometimes caustic self-assurance of this work stems from Moore's empiricist belief that clear seeing uncovers the truth. She quotes Ruskin: "Thousands of people can talk for one who can think; but thousands can think for one who can see. To see clearly is poetry, prophecy, and religion all in one."[57] In her early years Moore shared Ruskin's empirically transcendental faith that vision is visionary. If she later came to think that illusion is more precise than precision, her early poems puncture the illusions of false precision, accosting certainties that are assumed or otherwise unearned.

Among the "certainties" Moore combats in the poems of this period, several have to do with human interpretations of natural facts, particularly those symbolic interpretations that seem arbitrary and absurd from an empiricist point of view. "Injudicious Gardening" provides an example. Moore's note to the poem quotes passages of two letters from Robert to Elizabeth Barrett Browning, passages in which he equates yellow roses with infidelity, accepting the symbolic meaning attributed to them by a dictionary of flowers. Although Moore apologizes for her "effrontery" in judging a private communication, she is annoyed by Browning's assumption and rises to respond. (One of Moore's habits in quoting written material is to treat it as speech, as a voice to heed and argue with; thus, her "ears" are "offended" by Browning's words.) In the age of Browning societies and other ladylike styles in cultural homage, Moore toys with so reverenced an ideal as fidelity. She implies that her faithfulness is to facts rather than to romantic, poetic, or interpretative traditions, and she criticizes not only a famous poet and a famous love story, but the entire symbol making process as well.

> If yellow betokens infidelity,
>> I am an infidel.
>>> I could not bear a yellow rose ill will
>>> because books said that yellow boded ill,
>> white promised well.

Better a heathen than a fool, Moore seems to say. She may have had a personal stake in the matter: her mother's garden in Carlisle, Pennsylvania, had only yellow flowers.[58] But Moore is less concerned to vindicate yellow roses than to challenge a way of knowing that ascribes meaning by imposition, ignoring or coercing the objects it claims to comprehend. The "books," those dim authorities, are as wrong in elevating white as in debasing yellow roses; the reverse evaluation would equally lack a basis in fact and be no improvement. Moore buttresses this argument with her own rhetorical energy in matching verbs to the kinds of results they predict: "boded ill"; "promised well." Those words are "fit" as arbitrary symbol systems of colors and flowers cannot be, and perhaps the best gloss on "Injudicious Gardening" is Moore's remark that symbolism and representation are essentially incompatible.[59]

Moore distrusts the symbolizing process and prefers description, but she also shares Gertrude Stein's awareness that "description is evaluation."[60] (She shares Stein's alertness to strange and disruptive linguistic effects, too, rhyming "infidel" with "well," "ill" with "will".) Moore's early poems almost always judge as well as depict, and if she exposes the fraud of arbitrary emblems she also composes emblems of her own. In "To a Prize Bird" Moore describes a rooster to characterize George Bernard Shaw; in "To a Steam Roller" she animates that lumbering device to abuse a reductionist critic. In both poems the apparent oddity of the analogue is part of the point and allows for various subtleties of evaluation, but in neither case does Moore permit the demands of comparison to betray the factual nature of her chosen figures. Roosters "strut" with a proper pride that is only a little impudent, a little silly; so does Shaw. In "To a Steam Roller" Moore admits her difficulty in conceiving of a butterfly as companion to a critical mechanism so crushingly indelicate, "but," she says, "to question / the congruence of the complement is vain, if it exists." With those words, Moore deftly dodges any charge of steam rolling against herself and announces her empiricist loyalties once again: if "poetic" butterflies attend upon prosaic machines, the facts as they exist repudiate any theoretical demand for symbolic "congruence." "To a Prize Bird" and "To a Steam Roller" are typical of Moore's early poems in their emphasis on confident judgments and in their use of what Holley calls substantive rather than attributive metaphors,[61] but more important for present purposes, and perhaps for the poet Moore would become, are poems that attack human misappropriations of natural facts. Of those, the most significant is "Masks," which was later revised and retitled "A Fool, A Foul Thing, A Distressful Lunatic."

"Injudicious Gardening" condemns the aristocratic language of flowers; "Masks" condemns a commonplace idiom in which animals are abstracted as synonyms for human attributes, the loon for lunacy, the goose for silliness, the vulture for filth. In another poem from the same year, 1916 ("In This Age of Hard Trying, Nonchalance is Good and"), Moore characterizes such speech as "the haggish, uncompanionable drawl / / of certitude." In

"Masks" her rage at a kind of conceptual slaughter—the plundering of animals, the usurpation of their actual existence in the symbol making process—is remarkably overt, probably too overt for effective poetry. Still, the poem is predictive of issues that become essential in her finest work. "Masks" begins:

> "Loon" . . . . "goose" . . . . and "vulture" . . . .
> Thus, from the kings of water and of air,
> Men pluck three catchwords for their empty lips.
> Mock them in turn, wise, dumb triumvirate!

The quotation marks tweezer words for inspection, previewing the poem's stress on language as the betrayer of facts—especially language that is systematically yet carelessly repeated. The revised version of the poem is less systematic itself, more subtly rhetorical. It better reflects the empirical openness to experience that it recommends:

> With webs of cool
>   Chain mail and his stout heart, is not the gander
>   Mocked, and ignorantly designated yet,
> To play the fool?
>   "Egyptian vultures clean as cherubim,
>   All ivory and jet," are they most foul?
> And nature's child,
>   That most precocious water bird, the loon—why
>   Is he foremost in the madman's alphabet;
> Why is he styled
>   In folly's catalogue, distressful lunatic?[62]

As the words "designated," "alphabet," "styled," "catalogue," and perhaps "'ivory and jet'" all show, Moore's emphasis is still on language, although it is now more on written language than on speech. Her judgment is still harsh: purveyors of clichés may be madmen and fools; their practice folly. But those matters are more tentative than insistent here, as are the poem's suggestions for redefinition, its alternate interpretations—brave goose, angelic vulture, brilliant loon. Moore has her own catalogues, but they are lists of attributes rather than a system of predetermined definitions. The poem's main impact is to question the ways in which meanings are discovered or assigned. As in "Injudicious Gardening" or "To a Steam Roller," Moore stresses that the facts as they exist are superior to arbitrary generalizations. But she also knows that "'Superiority' is at the opposite pole from insight."[63] Even in declaring her preference for empirical attention to facts as a better route to truth than the idiomatic repetition of received "wisdom," Moore is flexible enough to include a quotation from a prior source, one that she regards as accurate, and a rather "poetic" one at that.

Moore's combination in this poem of clear-eyed judgment with a provisional or experimental openness to other possibilities augurs significant developments in her verse. It is reflected in two technical devices emerging in all the poems of these years. The first is an almost invisible yet also quietly assertive syllabic patterning—in this case a design of four- and eleven-syllable lines, artful but (as is the lineation) disrupted just enough to avoid being coercively systematic. The second is a subtle texturing of rhyme—here, the weaving of overt end rhymes, somewhat muffled by enjambment ("cool" and "fool," "child" and "styled"), with less obtrusive rhymes, one of them internal ("yet," "jet," and "alphabet"), and with other effects more modest still (say, the modulation of "fool," "foul," and "folly").

"A Fool, A Foul Thing, A Distressful Lunatic" is an epistemological critique; it carries out the empiricist correction of bias and blindness recommended by implication in "To a Strategist," which asks rhetorically, "But when has prejudice been glad to hold / a lizard in its hand."[64] To some extent, Moore is interested in the goose, the vulture, and the loon for their own sakes, apart from their uneasy relation to predatory human conceptions. However, as in most of her poems that re-present material already represented, Moore's major concern is conceptual. She uses the experimenter's method of close attention to the facts as a means for exposing falsehoods masked as truths, but her interest goes beyond the facts themselves. Moore also shares the experimenter's search for "the truth underlying appearances." She wants to describe the vulture, goose, and loon, and to "deconceptualize" them, but she also wants to reconceptualize them in more accurate terms. Perhaps inevitably, those terms have a human dimension. Moore is as willing to use animals as emblems of human attributes and behavior as are the reductionists she resists or attacks; as "Poetry" and "In the Days of Prismatic Color" imply, she has no other choice. The difference is that Moore also insists on describing the animals accurately. She engages in symbolic and emblematic procedures, but she does so while both shrinking and exposing the gap between the animal or object and its role as signifier.

In a sense, the real enemy of this and Moore's other early poems is not so much interpretation as interpretative absolutism, a way of knowing that takes a thing in hand to prey upon rather than to examine and to know it. "A Fool, A Foul Thing, A Distressful Lunatic" recognizes that its reconceptions involve the same human-centered subjectivity as the misconceptions it deposes, different perhaps in degree but not in kind. Moore reevaluates the poem's creatures in human, even superhuman terms: the goose is a hero, the vulture an angel, the loon a genius. This is partly the result of her desire to punish by poetic justice: those who derogate others are derogated in their turn. But it also raises the issue of how subjectivity invades objectivity in human acts of knowing. Moore's sense of her own implication in the interpretative activities she attacks is a feature in several poems of this period, and it becomes the central subject of many in the next phase of her career.

A few poems of this early period attack epistemological failures at the point where they also become failures of esthetic judgment; their subject is often the act of critical interpretation. In "Critics and Connoisseurs," Moore begins to move away from the brief poems of direct address, with their more or less single voices, arguments, and subjects, and toward longer poems with more varied materials and structures and more intricate evaluations. Moore once defined poetry as "a primal necessity," a kind of nourishment.[65] "Critics and Connoisseurs" uses various images of eating to make and refine its case "That there is a great deal of poetry in unconscious fastidiousness." As examples, Moore offers "Certain Ming / products," such works of art as "imperial floor-coverings," but she prefers actions, simple, "natural" actions without consciously possessive or manipulative designs: for instance, a "mere childish attempt to make an imperfectly bal- / lasted animal stand up" (an attempt reflected in the balancing act required to read across the hyphenated line break), or a "similar determination to make a pup eat his meat from a plate." Those actions have their egocentric elements: to "make" a puppy eat from a "plate" is to tame it, to force it to conform to human standards; we are all fallen from true innocence. But there are degrees of declension, and Moore takes pleasure in approximations, in the most innocent exercise of naturally human proclivities that, if they are apt to become destructive when uncontrolled, also have poetic gusto and charm.

Moore's examples of the poetic nourishment to be found in "unconscious fastidiousness" proceed from artful and artificial products toward more "natural" and living actions (the puppy is more "alive" than the badly ballasted toy). As the examples progress, so, too, does Moore's admiration. She prefers not only natural actions but also things perceived directly. She may have read about or seen pictures of imperial floor-coverings, but she has actually witnessed the childish attempts she describes. The phrase "I have seen" appears five times in "Critics and Connoisseurs"; Moore offers eyewitness testimony to guarantee her judgments.

With a complexity of surface and a range of reference unusual in her early poems, Moore now presents a more distant memory. She recalls a swan she had seen in Oxford (and playfully exposes the artifice of descriptive writing by "re-membering" its feet). The swan is at first a negative example. A critic, it represents *conscious* fastidiousness, an extension of its usual reputation for proud and regal beauty. Moore brings enormous visual acuity to the swan's description: it had "flamingo-colored, maple- / leaflike feet"; "It reconnoitred like a battle- / ship." For the moment her precision is less concerned with rescuing the animal from its representations than with creating a representation of her own. The swan's appearance and behavior illustrate the reaction of certain critics to works of art. Instead of following its instinctive "proclivity" to "appraise" and then take what was given it to eat, the swan resisted, assuming a pose of embattled haughtiness. So, too, one supposes, did critics who refused the nourishing art sent their way by such innovators as Marianne Moore herself. But she is not content with so simple a figure or judgment. The swan's "disinclination to move" was not only the result of a fraudulently "conscious fastidiousness," but also of a quite natural "Disbelief" that the "bits" offered it were the real thing, nutritious stuff to swallow and digest. An equal caution might be proper in a critic. And eventually the swan gave in, as at least some critics also did.

At this point in the poem, Moore brings directly to bear the judgment her title implies: "I have seen this swan and / I have seen you." The poem's twice plural title suggests that no single evaluation of critics or connoisseurs will do. Still, the following clause attacks: "I have seen ambition without / understanding in a variety of forms." The syntax here is flexible enough to accuse the speaker herself of a failure to comprehend, just as some of Moore's poems show certain swanlike tendencies to resist experience. But the major thrust is against those who approach art with appetitive pride instead of natural hunger.

The phrase "a variety of forms" reemphasizes the plurality of subject, attitude, and evaluation typical of the poem. It introduces another creature as negative example, "a fastidious ant" (a type of the connoisseur). Apparently the ant's fastidiousness was neither "unconscious" nor "conscious" but something else, blindly instinctive perhaps. As the swan proved more than its conventional representation in overcoming pride, so the ant seems less than its routine depiction as a paragon of pragmatic, productive labor. Moore's descriptive acuity is again at work, and the ant moves with a familiar appearance of systematic pointlessness and dully mechanical repetition. Here, at least, and for the moment, the appearance is accurate. The ant carried heavy items and labored much, but it abandoned the possibly useful stick in favor of a heavier "particle of whitewash" with no nutritive value at all. This represents the sort of connoisseur who prefers the ponderous in collecting, has an elaborate but pointless system mechanically to repeat, and can do everything but usefully discriminate, the act that matters most. Yet the ant was alive and energetic, and part of a social system with its own methods and its own kind of health. In any case, "Critics and Connoisseurs" does not resolve its many and sometimes contradictory judgments. The poem concludes with a rhetorical question that uses words to interrogate the value of having something "to say," that admires self-defense as a means of resisting flux while condemning it for resisting experience, and that compliments the empirical ability to "prove" experience while doubting the value of doing so.

What is remarkable about the poem, in addition to its open-ended conclusion and intricate judgments about art and art criticism and collecting, is its analysis of its own procedures, its raising without resolving the issue of how nature and human meaning interact. The poem has so many elements of allegory that we are tempted to systematically interpret critics and connoisseurs in terms of the swan and the ant, ignoring differences as irrelevant. But these creatures are presented in details so precise and specific as to give them an independent existence of their own. They are individuals, particularized in a way the plural and generalized critics and connoisseurs are not. The effect is enhanced by Moore's inclusion of facts that undermine any clear allegorical interpretation, by her empirical challenge to the standard abstract representations of swans and ants, and by her use of the conventions of reportorial realism. At times the swan and the ant seem the only subjects the poem has. But only at times. Even the most particularized details about those creatures provide astute commentary on the failures and successes of critics and connoisseurs, and from time to time the poem reminds us of its evaluative intent. Seemingly "natural" descriptive conventions are jarred by the self-conscious artistry of syllabics. The point is this: Moore shrinks *and* expands the gap between creatures and what they are used to signify, allowing us neither the absolute "congruence" of allegory, where human priority and the gulf between nature and arbitrary or absolute meanings are givens, nor the comfort of metaphor, where discovery or creation guarantees the identification of the signifier and the signified. We are kept between the absolute and the contingent, between the abstract and the specific, sight and insight, nature and art. We are at much unease— "imperfectly ballasted"; we are also free to play. Such issues, and Moore's new willingness to leave a poem at something like loose ends, without "neatness of finish," and with a surface as disruptive as it is consistent or continuous, point toward the major development of the poems to come.

In the years from 1918 to 1924, Moore published just under thirty poems, many of them in *The Dial*. These joined her early work to make up *Observations* (1924), the first book Moore saw into print herself (the Egoist Press had published *Poems* without her knowledge in 1921). As a title, *Observations* indicates both Moore's continuing interest in empirical objectivity, or clear seeing, as the way to truth and her equally persistent engagement with the subjective processes by which human beings arrive at and give expression to meaning and knowledge. In the poems of this period, Moore remains an investigator, concerned with verdicts, but now she delivers verdicts less often; she is more likely to present an investigation in progress than to announce its results. That development was hinted at in the early poems. Moore's empiricist epistemology and esthetics, her emphasis on "'exact perception,'" always had the indeterminate as their "silent partner."[66] Now the indeterminate is given voice.

This development of a more tentative and exploratory approach to judgment has a partial source in events in Moore's personal life, as do other changes in the poems of these years: increased length, greater complexity, a wider range of reference. Moore's sense of audience and of the poet's role seems to have expanded as her poems appeared more widely and as her experience grew more varied. In 1915, after a season of secretarial training and four years of teaching "commercial subjects" at the U.S. Indian School in Carlisle, Moore made her first trip to New York, where she met Alfred Kreymborg, visited Stieglitz's famous gallery, "291," and began a period of contact with members of the city's avant-garde. In 1916, she and her mother moved to Chatham, New Jersey, and, in 1918, to "the savage's romance" of New York City. There, Moore worked for several years at a branch of the New York Public Library and was enriched not by the city's "plunder," but by the "'accessibility to experience'" New York could provide. In 1925 Moore took over the editorship of *The Dial*, at that time perhaps the nation's finest periodical of the arts.

"[A]s art grows, it deviates," Moore wrote in a review. It deviates from the perpendicular perhaps, but surely from one or more of its own "'initial merits.'"[67] Moore's early poems use empiricism to demolish presumptuous certitudes. The poems of her next period expose her most trusted procedures to scrutiny as well. Exact perception, empiricism, is able to unseat error because it is armed with an objective method guaranteed to produce demonstrable results that experiment can replicate. The method also involves a thoroughgoing skepticism; it subjects *every* truth to doubt and to further investigation, including those "truths" it arrives at itself. Moore was aware of the latter circumstance in her early poems, and it sometimes comes to the fore in them, as in "Critics and Connoisseurs." In the poems of 1918 to 1924, though, Moore's skepticism is more consistently brought to bear on her own perceptual and evaluative practices, and with greater rigor. In a related development, she becomes increasingly sensitive to anomalies in her poetic application of objective procedures. The triumphant assurance with which she used empirical examinations to silence the "drawl / of certitude" risked being "haggish and uncompanionable" itself, and Moore may have felt Christian qualms about her own proclivity to judge and judge harshly. Perhaps she saw her self-assurance as violating the skepticism that empirical observation demands. Also in these years, Moore became increasingly suspicious that the notion of an objective point of view is a contradiction in terms. Her supposedly impersonal observations and judgments were in fact her own, made from an individual perspective and expressed by a subjective voice, the "I" of her poems, enmeshed in its own web of assumptions, preconceptions, and predilections. Moore shares with many modern poets something of Heisenberg's sense that the investigator's subjectivity inevitably invades her observations.

This is not to say that Moore abandoned objectivity as a method or an ideal. However modified, her trust in exact perception persisted throughout her work. It is everywhere in the poems, and Moore's prose pays tribute to clear seeing from early to late; her "dislike of 'a naturalist with an umbrella'" complements her admiration for this artist's working note: "'Wrinkles go at right angles to muscles.'"[68] In fact, Moore's poems of the 1918 to 1924 period become more, not less, objective. When she recognized her own involvement in dubiously subjective assessments, Moore's response was not to abandon but to intensify her effort to achieve objectivity. The paradoxical and essential result was an enlarged awareness that objectivity is problematical. It was a situation she embraced as well as resisted. The greater length of these poems indicates their more exploratory and less conclusive approach, as does their array of less than fully assimilated details and their use of catalogues and multiple speakers. Moore's imagery is now more often perceptual than conceptual; she is more likely to examine than to defend or assault her increasingly plural subjects. Her own voice, as subjective "I," is typically suppressed. Frequently, Moore incorporates quotations in which other voices contradict, complement, or qualify her own, and she often presents them without overt evaluative comment to guide the reader's judgment. Similarly, these poems often proceed by parataxis and so provide little in the way of obvious hierarchies of organization or value. And Moore retreats still further from traditional poetic techniques of structure and control; even nearly invisible syllabic patterns and all but inaudible rhymes eventually give way to less systematic free verse. Jean Garrigue summarizes the renewed and problematical objectivity of these poems when she says that in them "description becomes a kind of plot and its own drama"[69]—the drama has to do with the degree to which objectivity can be achieved and sustained.

But this is only one side of things. Moore is not undone by subjectivity, nor does she give up the ideal of objective perception. She continues to deflate with brio both fools who seek to evade "inevitable experience" and foolish rationalists who think to comprehend experience without respect for "the beautiful element of unreason under it."[70] Moore demands attention to surfaces but is not content with surfaces alone. Moore's attitude is "close to that of the scientist, where the subject is often an object, and the ultimate objective is the truth."[71] Although she does so now with chastened confidence, Moore continues to seek the truth underlying appearances. The poems of this period are as often abstract as they are objectively concrete. A number of poems focus on issues of esthetic judgment. Among them are "Poetry" and "In the Days of Prismatic Color," discussed above. Others are "England," "Picking and Choosing," "When I Buy Pictures," and "Novices." In those and in other poems of these years, concrete details coexist with abstract speculation, whether in the form of definitions or of prescriptive or proscriptive generalizations. These passages from "When I Buy Pictures" emphasize facts: "the snipe-legged hieroglyphic in three parts"; "the medieval decorated hatbox, / in which there are hounds with waists diminishing like the waist of the hour-glass, / and deer and birds and seated people." This passage from the same poem, a pronouncement about art, is markedly abstract: "Too stern an intellectual emphasis upon this quality or that detracts from one's enjoyment. / It must not wish to disarm anything; nor may the approved triumph easily be honored— / that which is great because something else is small."

To some extent the imaginative quality of Moore's factual descriptions creates a bridge to her rather particularized abstractions, but to a greater extent the connection between the details and the generalizations is neither "natural" nor particularly clear. In all of these poems Moore keeps two interests going at once: the attempt accurately to observe and render independent phenomena and the effort to discover and express abstract truth. In an unfallen world, those realms would coincide. Even to the Puritans, for whom the world was a web of postlapsarian snares, facts could be identical with truth when they were read aright. But for Moore, facts and "truth" often conflict or simply remain apart. She continues to seek their identity, but her increased awareness of subjectivity insists that supposedly objective discoveries may be no more than subjective statements of preference. Statements of preference have value—the gusto of predilection, like the "childish attempt to make an imperfectly bal- / lasted animal stand up." But however energetic they may be, preferences also imply that truth is not objectively discovered but subjectively imposed and thus without a guarantee. Moore's poems of this period work in the gap between conceptions of knowledge as discovered and imposed; they are confident and doubtful at once of the poet's and poetry's power. Blackmur captures the delightful and vertiginous effect when he says that Moore constantly presents "images the most explicit but of a kind containing inexhaustibly the inexplicable."[72]

In an essay for *The Dial*, Moore praises the capacity of Marsden Hartley's "tessellated representations of landscape" to "correct the jocund American tendency to guess rather than to know."[73] The tessellated land- and seascapes in Moore's poems of these years also seek to emend esthetic and epistemological carelessness, and in ways that explore the difficulties involved in achieving both representation and truth. "The Fish," "A Grave," and "An Octopus" turn to nature to consider the possibilities and limitations of knowledge and of art.

"The Fish" (the title is also the first line; the creatures it names are not the poem's subject but one set of tiles in the mosaic it constructs) begins as an exercise in observation. Explicit and implicit analogies do much of the work, describing visual phenomena of motion and appearance. The fish "wade / through black jade," and their slow, almost hindered movement through dark water is vividly conveyed. The words "crow-blue" and "ash heaps" capture the color and arrangement of a colony of mussels. The sheer variety of the life and action described seems a warranty of accurate rendition. There are fish, mussels, barnacles, starfish, jellyfish, crabs, and underwater plants. The fish swim, a mussel opens and shuts its shell, water abrades the cliff, and shafts of sunlight turn the dark sea turquoise, revealing barnacles trying to hide in crevices.

The poem's emphasis seems to be entirely on the straightforward presentation of stable facts. But its mixture of spatial and temporal effects—as in the deliberate blurring of the locational and causal meanings of the conjunction "whereupon"—produces some unease. The objects held up to sight will not hold still; they "slide each on the other," and what had appeared definitive begins to slip. The word "wade," which seemed so apt, is more appropriate to creatures with feet than fins. Crows do not consort with mussels. Other distinctive details merge what they had seemed to separate: the water, with its "black jade" and iron wedge, is as stony as the cliff that repels and borders it; it becomes increasingly unclear whether the sea contains the rock or the rock contains the sea. Perspectives shift. The conventions of realism presume that language is a transparent medium for bringing the world before our eyes. But much of the poem's descriptive language is opaque. In order to make the scene present, Moore relies on comparisons with objects that are very much not there: jade, ash heaps, a fan, spun glass, a spotlight, rice grains, toadstools, and lilies. Those terms have descriptive value, but they also distract from the scene, reminding us that artfice compromises the representations it alone is able to create.

By using the word "stars" for starfish, Moore exposes the way in which analogy obscures distinctions while helping us to know. This also recalls the arbitrary relationship of words to things: real stars lack the five points of the stylized depictions from which starfish take their name. Such effects culminate when the natural cliff is described as a ruined "edifice" lacking its "cornice" and bearing the scars of human assaults on natural or other structures: "dynamite grooves, burns, and / hatchet strokes." Earlier in the poem, Moore uses the phrase "ink- / bespattered jellyfish." The adjective may describe a pattern of markings or coloration; or it may be a comment on writing, implying that poets spatter and partially obscure things with ink in order to get them into poems. Perhaps "ink- / bespattered" simply conveys an effect of light and shadow. Yet the sense of an analogy with writing persists, for the poem, like the sea or the cliff, contains the ruins of life and death and, a ruin itself, is also contained by them.

Those disturbances of what had seemed a perceptual surface are amplified by the poem's eventual addition of explicitly abstract and thematic dimensions to its apparently pictorial scheme. In the final stanzas, the record of a pleasant outing to the sea becomes a revelation of threatened death and damaged but brave endurance. Those matters were present from the start, but the emphasis on description submerged them. Now it becomes clear that everything here is wounded or embattled: the fish are hindered as they swim; a single mussel, "opening and shutting itself like / / an / injured fan," moves in the ash heap of its fellows; the barnacles "cannot hide"; "The water drives a wedge / of iron through the iron edge / of the cliff." Description *is* evaluation, and the notion of a fully objective representation is a cheat. The invasion of observation by subjectivity is felt with special force when we recall that "The Fish" was composed during World War I, at a time when Moore's brother, a navy chaplain, had been assigned to duty at sea. (Slatin makes the case for reading "The Fish" as a war poem and shows its relationship to the repressed poem "Reinforcements," an anti-epic discussion of a troop ship, in which the soldiers going overseas are described as "advancing like a school of fish through / / still water.")[74]

Moore has almost completely removed herself as witness from the scene of "The Fish," and through much of the poem her wartime fears of destruction and death are controlled or suppressed, but personal feelings suddenly surface in the startling image of "the / turquoise sea / of bodies." From then on, descriptive and thematic images of violence enacted and endured inundate the poem. The power of poetry to resist danger and death is indicated by the fact that the image of a sea of corpses is so nearly submerged in the wash of other, more "natural" details; the presence of that image, and its controlling force over all the other facts the poem describes, indicates poetry's limits. Artistic control and comfort, like the ideal of perfectly transparent apprehension and description, is an illusion. It can sustain but not revive us; we grow old in it.

In part because Moore suppresses the presence of the poem's speaker and withholds narrative or other contextual details, it is difficult to tell whether "The Fish" is a representation of reality, an abstract or specific meditation on life and death or the current war, or an autonomous textual artifact. The latter possibility is suggested by the poem's impersonal surface, and especially by its technique. Its five-line stanzas, each arranged in a more or less exact 1, 3, 9, 6, 9 syllabic pattern; its syncopated movement and abrupt rhymes; the way it throws unusual emphasis on the articles "an" and "the" by isolating them in separate lines; and its overdetermined hyphenating of the word "accident" so that the syllable "ac-" is printed as a line and the sound "ax" is heard in a stanza containing a hatchet: all of these emphasize the poem's status as a self-contained and arbitrary system. Yet the poem's structural autonomy collapses at precisely the moment when the thematic emphasis on threat is greatest: the "live"–"revive" rhyme that the eye sees in the final stanza is undone by the mind and the ear; the "i" in "live" is short, not long. No final sorting out is possible. Art can represent the world, engage in abstract thought, and create autonomous structures. But it can do none of these with complete or final success. Each will compromise the others, and all are subject to the delusions of point of view. Poetry describes facts and pronounces general truths, but both its descriptions and discoveries are conditioned by subjective and accidental forces. A poem can create an artificial space, worthy craft in which danger and death are briefly resisted and endured, but that space is an illusion fated to sink.

"A Grave" is also a seascape, and Moore confirmed a personal source for this one. She recalled that its origin "was a man who placed himself between my mother and me, and surf we were watching from a middle ledge of rocks on Monhegan Island after a storm. ('Don't be annoyed,' my mother said. It is human nature to stand in the middle of a thing.')" Moore also affirmed that "A Grave" has "significance apart from [its] literal origin."[75] The syllabic draft of "A Grave"—it was later revised into free verse—is roughly contemporaneous with "The Fish" and with Warner Moore's service in the North Atlantic. The poem's wartime aspect appears in a few of its details: the word "phalanx" indicates both an ancient battle formation and the bones of the hands and feet; the sea has swallowed men so thoroughly that even "their bones have not lasted"; the word "breathlessly" conjures drownings. Nonetheless, the sharpest focus of "A Grave" is on perception, on the possibilities and limits of clear seeing. In its frontal attack on a single figure, the "Man looking into the sea," "A Grave" recalls earlier poems in which Moore uses direct address to challenge or correct the errors of assured subjectivists. Here, though, the stark contrasts that typify the characters, judgments, and structures of those poems are replaced by something a good deal more intricate.

Moore presents herself and the "Man" as different in degree but not in kind in their ways of bringing subjective preconceptions to the sea. In fact, to some extent the man's perspective and Moore's cannot be easily distinguished; issues of "rights" are deliberately confused, and he takes on as well as takes away her view. His seeing is secondhand, but hers must be as well—

the idea of the sea as a grave is older than the phalanx. Still, there is a critical difference between the man's view and Moore's. His perspective is possessive, wholly subjective, "rapacious." What he finds in the sea is what he brings to it: "the sea is a collector, quick to return a rapacious look." He assumes that the sea and his interpretation of it as a malevolent threat are identical. Moore shares the man's conception of the sea as a grave, a metaphor for death, but she continues to "investigate" both the actual sea and her conception of it, all the while remaining aware of the gap between the two.

From the start, Moore is suspicious of the process by which we presume to discover meaning in the world: "the sea has nothing to give but a well excavated grave." Any exchange with the sea is one-sided; there is no transcendent analogue. The sea does not respond or reveal; it merely reflects then buries what is brought to it (in something like the way the free verse rendition of "A Grave" swallows the rhymes of the syllabic version). Moore's mother's forgiving remark that "it is human nature to stand in the middle of a thing" provides a useful clue. Moore's ideas about human nature are rooted in the paradigm of the Fall; thus, the means that permit our approximations of knowledge obscure the knowledge we attain. When our rapaciousness is such that possession matters more to us than facts, we imagine that our knowledge of such immense matters as the sea or death comes from objective observation, from standing in the middle of a thing. But, as Moore says, "you cannot stand in the middle of this." Still, we have to try to comprehend. The man, like the fishermen who put to sea and "lower nets, unconscious of the fact that they are desecrating a grave," errs not so much in his conception as in confusing that conception with reality, in perceiving the sea as nothing more than an extension of his own desires and fears.

Moore, too, conceives of the sea as a metaphor for death. But in making the comparison she also emphasizes difference. If the sea is a grave, then the fir trees beside it "stand in procession." This is how a metaphor expands to shape the world in its own image and thereby create a pattern of meaning. But Moore disrupts the procedure. The trees do not move in procession; they stand stock-still. Their funeral dress—each wears "an emerald turkey-foot," like a hat—is symbolically and literally absurd, although the description is precise. Just so. Moore is not rapacious: metaphor does not possess the world; the world mocks metaphors. The trees are reserved, but not out of respect; they are simply "saying nothing." Nature neither signifies nor speaks; it is. Moore once said, "Any pastoral seems to pall,"[76] and one of the things she erases in "A Grave" is pastoral elegy, that classic mode in which fears of death find comfort in a healing nature that reflects our moods.

Still, to regard the world as wholly without meaning is to ignore other realities. The fishermen, who are "unconscious of the fact that they are desecrating a grave," "row quickly away . . . as if there were no such thing as death." But death is real, and although there is no way to evade it, human beings do need structures for controlling and containing it. Poems, with their rhythms and rhymes, are like "the pulsation of lighthouses and noise of bell-buoys": ways of lighting and mapping experience, means of guidance and protection. The danger is in claiming too little or too much for them. This poem describes "birds [that] swim through the air at top-speed, emitting cat-calls." Anyone who has heard gulls mew or seen them stroke the air will certify the accuracy of that. But the description confuses birds and mammals and fish. Nature's cat-calls mock the presumptions of language, which can, at best, approximate. Nonetheless, human structures do have value. "A Grave" is much concerned with decorum—politeness and rudeness, sanctification and desecration. A poem is a ceremony. Like a lighthouse or a well-buoyed channel, it can mark out an area of relative comfort and safety; it is useful, but ultimately an illusion, an "as if." "A Grave" mocks one kind of ceremony and makes another. Its sea is a metaphor with human value and consequence, but the metaphor cannot contain or alter the sea—or death. Each is what it is, neither malevolent nor benevolent, not comic or tragic, but unknowable, unutterable, indifferent:

> . . . the ocean, under the pulsation of lighthouses and noise of
> bell buoys,
> advances as usual, looking as if it were not that ocean in which
> dropped things are bound to sink—
> in which if they turn and twist, it is neither with volition nor
> consciousness.

Other poems of the 1918 to 1924 period take up related issues. "Sea Unicorns and Land Unicorns" and "The Monkey Puzzle" both explore the possibilities and limitations of perception, knowledge, and art in the context of nature. But the most important epistemological nature poem of these years is "An Octopus," which, despite its marine title, is a landscape. Moore's octopus is the tentacled glacier of Mount Rainier, not an animal at all, yet equipped with octopus-like "pseudo-podia" and capable of "killing prey with the concentric crushing rigor of the python." Such "confusions" are present from the start, as Moore sets against one another the clarifying and obscuring aspects of language as a perceptual and conceptual tool. Once more her pattern book is the story of the Fall. In the summer of 1922, Moore and her brother climbed Mount Rainier, the "Big Snow Mountain" or "Mount Tacoma" of the poem. Their ascent into this wilderness began from a meadow called Paradise, a fact that lends resonance to Moore's wry quotation of this rather biblical and Miltonic pronouncement by the Department of the Interior: "'disobedient persons'" will be "'summarily removed / and not allowed to return without permission in writing.'"[77]

Fallen human senses and sensibilities—perhaps they are fortunately fallen—are very much the subject of "An Octopus," as its remarkably "removed" speaker attempts to come to terms with the mountain's gloriously beautiful and bewildering array of vast and intimate facts. In addition to the immensities of the glacier and the mountain itself, there is an arkful of animals: bears, elk, deer, wolves, goats, ducks, a porcupine, a muskrat, beavers, a chipmunk, the water ouzel, the white-tailed ptarmigan, eagles, marmots, and spotted ponies (these last are domesticated but nonetheless a mystery "with glass eyes," "Instructed none knows how, to climb the mountain"). Vegetation is equally profuse; there are periwinkles, fir-trees, larches, spruce, berry-bushes, heather-bells, alpine buckwheat, birch-trees, ferns, lilies and lily-pads, chlorophylless fungi, moss, and rhododendron—as well as other plants whose names confuse flora with fauna, and recall human attempts at description as well: bear's ears, kittentails, and Indian paintbrushes. There are also minerals and rocks: onyx, manganese, iron, gold and silver ore, turquoise, calcium gems, alabaster pillars, topaz, tourmaline, amethyst quartz, marble, jasper, agate, stalagmites, lava, and pumice. And a polychrome of colors, too: cyclamen-red, maroon, a green metallic tinge, iron stains, manganese-blue, filtered sunlight, pea-green, indigo, blue-green, turquoise, blue, black, and white in shades from vaporous cloud to acetylene.

In addition to all these, there are animals, plants, minerals, and colors not actually present in the scene but imported into it by language in its struggle to name, describe, and contain (like happiness, those are powers "Adam had and we are still devoid of"). There are: octopus, python, spider, stag-at-bay, antelope, ermine, and snail; a fossil flower, cyclamen, anemone, cypress, and pea; moonstones, silver, and gold; gold and silver; and so on. There are people present, too—not so much in the scene as in the consciousness that perceives it. Human history is added to geological and natural ones as native Americans give way to trappers, then to mountain guides and businessmen-tourists. And there are hosts of other things as well: for instance, rice, prunes, dates, raisins, hardtack, and tomatoes—foods recommended to those who would "'conquer'" the peak. But Moore wants less to conquer than to come to terms with the scene, including its representation in the language of others. She incorporates into the poem a plethora of quotation, voices that amplify, mute, and qualify her own. Her sources range from *The National Parks Portfolio* and travel books to newspaper articles, religious and philosophical studies, statements by Cardinal Newman and John Muir, and remarks overheard at the circus. Many of the quotations have nothing apparent to do with Mount Rainier; they represent the emotional, intellectual, and cultural baggage any observer carries: like language itself, they impede our progress while they enable us to see and think, to write and speak.

These lists are wearying; the stuff of exact perception, they honor the world of fact and are essential to any objective knowledge, but they are also mired in subjectivity and are arbitrary or accidental in their application; they threaten to overwhelm abstraction in a Babel of sheer linguistic profusion. In this, they join the other dangers of the mountain: there are "'several hours of frost every midsummer night'"; the exploded volcanic landscape looks "'as if whole quarries had been dynamited'"; and even a summer climb guided by Park rules is perilous enough that it is necessary to "stipulate 'names and addresses of persons to notify / in case of disaster.'" There is the added danger that abstraction will stifle detail and smother the world it intends to comprehend. Seen from a distance, the mountain's "'graceful lines'" "'prove it a volcano.'" This deduction has value, but without the catalogues of detail it would present a reduced and impoverished thing and smugly misrepresent the mountain as it is.

For Moore, coming to terms with something involves perception, conception, and composition. "An Octopus" includes all three. Its perceptual language is a dizzying mix of certainty and imprecision. These words: "clearly defined," "recognized," "prove," "Distinguished," "a nice appearance," "supervise," "observatory," "conspicuously," and "self-evident," consort with these: "Deceptively," "misleadingly," "seems," "deceived," "prejudices," "concealed," "as if," "seeing nothing," and "hard to discern." They converge in the precarious word "perspective." Moore's early confidence that objectively exact perception could rectify error and conduce to truth is not condemned, but it is severely chastened. The human ability to move from facts to abstractions is as problematical as is our capacity to see clearly.

Although it has many concealed rhymes, "An Octopus" is a free verse poem. Its nearly two hundred lines (earlier versions are many lines longer) are printed with only one stanza break, but that break indicates a shift in emphasis from description to analysis and commentary. Like her accommodating descriptions, Moore's judgments prove flexible and intricate. For much of this poem, she has been unable and unwilling to organize her experience into systematic patterns, even narrative ones: description is the only plot. Perhaps Moore believed that systematic patterns would violate the nature of her encounter with the mountain (certainly their absence requires us, in reading and attempting to interpret the poem, to replicate certain aspects of that encounter). But Moore's interest in meaning remains as strong as her interest in facts. In the second section of "An Octopus" she considers ways of organizing and resolving complications. She discusses the

Greeks, who "liked smoothness" and who, applying philosophical rigor, resolved complexities "with benevolent conclusiveness."

That, Moore thinks, is admirable and damnable both: "distrusting what was back / of what could not be clearly seen," the Greeks too willingly ignored some kinds of surfaces in favor of clarity and supposedly certain depths. Their conclusive resolutions were clearer than experience permits. In "resolving with benevolent conclusiveness, / 'complexities which still will be complexities / as long as the world lasts,'" they show that if they were "'Emotionally sensitive, their hearts were hard'; / their wisdom was remote." Moore's evaluation of the power of philosophical intelligence to make sense of contradictory experience is remarkably involved. In the process of that evaluation, she challenges, criticizes, and vindicates her own rough method, too, including its refusal to ignore "what could not be clearly seen." Sight, she seems to say, needs room for the invisible; thought, for what cannot be conceived. Moore further chastises the admired Greeks by contrasting them with native Americans, whose adaptive intelligence kept them alive (and "'alive to the advantage of invigorating pleasures'") and with the authors of the Park's pragmatic instructions and rules. At the same time, those last are also attacked for their too-confident assumptions about authority, conquest, and control.

"An Octopus" is concerned with esthetic as well as epistemological issues. Having contrasted her methods of abstraction with those of the Greeks, Moore comments on the rugged surface of her own work by considering the example of Henry James. She defends his decorum, "not decorum, but restraint," against "a public out of sympathy with neatness." She seems to imply that James, too, was willing to "trust what was back / of what could not be clearly seen." Yet her own poem is anything but neat and not in any obvious way restrained. The repeated exclamation "Neatness of finish!"—especially notable in a poet who said "iteration is wasteful"[78]—is an outcry on several fronts. It notes a certain fussiness in James, yet Moore is shocked that there are readers blind to his corrugated complications, to the explosive "diversity of creatures" his shapely surfaces reveal. Perhaps Moore is astonished by the shagginess of her own poem, while also claiming for herself a neatness of finish beyond conventional kinds. Surely she implies that neatness of finish as an absolute esthetic value can only betray an experience like the one "An Octopus" describes.

Moore ends the poem by returning to the particulars of the mountain, to the world of her octopus of ice. Yet issues of seeing, knowing, and making continue to appear. The glacier is uncontrollable and uncontrolled, beyond perception, knowledge, or art: "it receives one under winds that 'tear the snow to bits / and hurl it like a sandblast / shearing off twigs and loose bark from the trees.'" But wild as it is, the glacier is artful, too: "symmetrically pointed," it creates its work, the "hard mountain," " 'planed by ice and polished by the wind.' " Those descriptions attack both an artless surrender to natural chaos and an art so symmetrically potent that it destroys particulars with an excessive neatness of finish. Perhaps the stunted alpine trees Moore next describes suggest a kind of art she could approve. Though "flattened" and "shrunk" by the cold and wind, they find "strength in union, forming little stunted groves." Yet the difficulties of language as the tool for mediating such survivals remain: "Is 'tree' the word for these things / 'flat on the ground like vines'?" "An Octopus" has no "conclusion," no "finish"; it is not resolved in judgments or ideas. Instead, Moore lets the curtain fall on her troubled, exuberant work. She recognizes that there are theatrical dimensions to even her ruggedly "natural" poem as it dissolves "in a curtain of powdered snow launched like a waterfall." The poem returns us to the beauty, mystery, and terror of a world beyond us. Inexhaustible in urging us to meaning but eluding our conceptions, it is wordless and blank—a surface like an empty page, where there is nothing certain to read, and room for writing that helps us to survive and is sure to be erased.

By the time of the later poems of *Observations*, all the aspects of Moore's work essential to consideration of her as a nature poet with epistemological and esthetic concerns were in place. It remains only to consider certain developments in her poems of the 1930s and to glance at the markedly altered emphases of her later work. The hush at the end of "An Octopus" presaged several years of poetic silence during Moore's busy tenure as editor of *The Dial*: after "The Monkey Puzzle" in 1925, she published no poems until "The Steeple-Jack" appeared as the first section of a three-poem sequence in 1932. "The Steeple-Jack" and several long poems on animals (Moore called them "animiles") are her major work of the 1930s. Those poems have much in common with "An Octopus." They remain aware that subjectivity invariably conditions perception; at the same time, they persist in using increasingly objective modes of presentation. The poems are typically long. They continue to suppress the subjective and organizing "I" of an experiencing, authoritative speaker. And they incorporate extensive prose quotations or otherwise employ information usually considered disruptively nonpoetic, often in expansive catalogues that detail facts of natural and cultural history.

There are differences as well. The amount of natural and other factual material in these poems continues to be uncommonly large, but now the amount of artistic or otherwise "non-factual" material is equally extensive. This matter of content is reflected in Moore's return from free verse to syllabic patterning, regular stanzas, and less covert uses of rhyme, all devices that heighten the poems' contrasts of nature and art. Of course, "The Fish,"

"A Grave," and "An Octopus" are also concerned with the opposition of art and nature: on the one hand, the human need to discover or create and impose patterns that can control the perils of an indifferent natural world; on the other, the danger that those patterns will go too far in seeming to tame or conquer nature, and will therefore destroy the profusion that occasions ecstasy and grants to creatures and things their rightful place beyond our conceptual grasp. But in the later poems of *Observations* (and for all their remarkable poise) Moore often seems nearly overwhelmed by intensities of ecstasy or fear. Although art in a way keeps pace with the dangers and attractions of the sea and the glacier, and does so without a fraudulent presumption of control, a mood of "much unease" dominates "An Octopus," "A Grave," and "The Fish." The source of that unease is the unbridgeable gulf between the human realm of feeling, thought, and art and the realm of nature, between the desire for absolute and objective truth and the subjective contingencies of experience.

In the poems of the 1930s Moore's unease is greatly decreased, for she reaches not a resolution or a reconciliation but an accommodation of her several and intricately opposed concerns. Moore's early poems exercise a confident empiricism to expose or correct perceptual, conceptual, and esthetic errors—poems are used as vehicles to convey experiment's results. The later poems of *Observations* enact intense awareness of the relative limitations of perceptual, conceptual, and poetic power, the dizzying and thrilling multiplicity of facts and perspectives. Those poems are embodiments. Moore's poems of the 1930s are both thematic vehicles *and* embodiments. In them, she contrives ways of including—without reconciling—the opposed values of observing and making observations, of nature and art. This is not a matter of balance or containment; it is, rather, as Moore puts it in "The Staff of Aesculapius," "A 'going on'; yes, *anastasis* is the word."

Denis Donoghue discloses Moore's characteristic stance in the poems of this period. For Moore, he writes, "Poetry is a way of looking, various because vision is irregular, reasonable because, irregular, it is not indiscriminate. . . . The distinction between appearance and reality is not to Miss Moore a cause of persistent distress. To think appearance significant is not a mark of folly; it is a mode of appreciation, or predilection. Things may be deceptive, but a relation between one thing and another is something achieved."[79] Moore had set out to realign appearance and reality, but she refused to force a unification where subjective and objective multiplicities prevented her. That bravely modest refusal is a source of the distress that is one aspect of "An Octopus," where art is an illusion. In the poems of the thirties, Moore comes to terms with illusion, continuing to expose it for what it is while realizing that we need its fictions in order to survive. She comes to terms with nature as well; although it can never be known or contained, nature offers well-adapted animals as models for our own more fallen ways of being in the world.

"The Steeple-Jack" is the clearest example of Moore's accommodation in the 1930s of such contrarieties as art and nature, appearance and reality, generalization and perception, and subjective and objective ways of knowing. Art and culture exercise order, but the dangers of nature and of excessive modes of control remain. "The Steeple-Jack" opens like a brochure. It describes a picture-perfect town that is quiet and orderly, well-situated and beautifully arranged. A tourist's paradise, the town affords attractive views of the sea and of graceful buildings and trig yards that are scrupulously maintained. Nature is shapely as well. On "a fine day," the town is awash with "sweet sea air." Seagulls fly regularly "back and forth" in neat trios and pairs. And the sea itself is "etched / with waves as formal as the scales / on a fish." Social signs of measurement and order are also in place: "the town clock," a lighthouse, boats that move "as if in / a groove," "a post-office in a / store," a school, and a church. The poem's carefully crafted stanzas and modest rhymes reflect the way in which human structures at their best can control and shape without dominating the world. This is civilization as idyl, as art. But Moore disrupts as she conveys.

The clock and whales betoken time and death; the lighthouse signals the perils of night and storm or fog. "The Steeple-Jack" uses representational conventions that treat language as a transparent medium for making an actual place present to consciousness through words. But the opening lines do not say that Dürer would have seen a reason for living in *this* town, rather, for living in a town "like this." Moore suggests from the beginning that what seems so specific, so very much *there*, is in fact imagined and abstract. The poem names names and places, catalogues particular things, and is numerically exact: there are eight whales and a twenty-five-pound lobster; the gulls fly "One by one in two's and three's." But those features sort oddly with deliberate imprecisions. The specificity of frequent "the's" and "a's" is contradicted by such vaguer words as "might," "would," "could," "as if," and "if." The notion that we are being presented with an achieved reality, a place where we might visit or live, an actual location in time and space, is disrupted by confusion about whether it is fair or stormy, night or day: a "fine day" is mentioned, but so is fog, and a storm that disturbs the stars. Nothing places these in any "natural" sequence.

Like other potential dangers in the poem, the "whirlwind fife-and-drum of the storm" seems tamed by its artful setting ("fife-and-drum" suggests music, not chaos, or perhaps a parade). Yet a storm that disturbs a steeple and the stars has cosmic dimensions; the music of fife and drum is for war; the whirlwind is apocalyptic. Similarly, the town's gardens present a domesticated version of the more threatening lushness of the tropics. The paradigm of the Fall is again at play. The gardens are works of art, Edenic in nurturing a delightful profusion that is also contained and "trained." But there are weeds among the flowers—and animals concealed in the seeming safety of names: snap-dragon, cat-tails, spiderwort, toad-plant, and crab-claw ragged sailors; among the lilies, "tigers" lurk. Of course, Moore admired dragons and cats, toads and tigers; all find favor in her poems. Tiger *lilies* are tame. Such accommodating turns and twists of judgment are everywhere in "The Steeple-Jack"; its disruptions delight and disturb at once: it is both perilous and "a privilege to see so / much confusion." These gardens harbor no "exotic serpent / life," but they are not so paradisal as to lack the native snakes; if "they've cats, not cobras, to / keep down the rats," they do have rats.

In "The Steeple-Jack," the "ideal" of nature controlled by civilization and art is significantly qualified. Culture is admired for its potent orderliness, but nature retains the power to threaten and destroy. At the same time, nature's ability to remain beyond the reach of our conceptions and contraptions grants pleasure and inspiration; the Fall seems not unfortunate. Moore's poem praises art and also exposes the threat that art will carry its proclivity for order too far: the sea's etched waves are overly simplified; "white and rigid" in their groove, the boats seem dead or fake. The rhyming of "the" and "sea" and "a" and "way" is strained. The artist Dürer presides over this poem, and rightly so: Moore shares his interest in both details and generalizations. As Moore would have done, he traveled far to see a stranded whale with his own eyes; he arrived too late, and much of his best work, again like hers, presents material already represented. In a process that Moore's rhyme approves, Dürer artistically "changed" what is to what is usefully "arranged." But Dürer, like Moore herself, could exceed what Moore could ratify. His "realistic" pictures are geometrical abstractions based on what he assumed are the objective absolutes of mathematical perspective. In consigning the town to him, Moore both praises and disclaims. He could see a reason for living in a town like this. She could, too, while seeing others for staying away.

"The Steeple-Jack" begins as an etching, then adds color to the scene, then people. The picture begins to move. As it does, it gathers social and political application. There are snakes and rats in lovely gardens; there is also human suffering and evil in this pristine place. A steeple-jack—perhaps he has been repairing storm damage (although, as if to further confuse our expectations, Moore says "he might be part of a novel")—lowers himself from the steeple of the church. He seems able; like an artist he "signs" his work, and he recognizes and warns his fellows of danger. But his scarlet garb and spidery movements have a devilish cast. Whatever the quality of the steeple-jack's work, "the pitch / of the church // spire [is] not true"—as the student named Ambrose insightfully knows. The church is white, but "pitch" defiles. Whether or not the steeple is "perpendicular," it is "not true" in some more metaphoric and essential sense, one it requires vision to perceive. Moore's response again accommodates. The church's white-washed columns suggest both modesty and a whited sepulchre. "True" or not, the church is "fit haven" for those who deserve it: "waifs, children, animals"; it is perhaps even an apt sanctuary for "prisoners." But the church can also be a "front" to conceal the real motives of those who use piety and politeness as artful cultural screens to evade their moral and ethical duties— like the "presidents" who conveniently and decorously ignore "sin-driven // senators."

"The Steeple-Jack" manipulates the signs of art and nature and of form and danger in order to accommodate the contradictory human need for significant shapes that resist the flux of experience but that do not dominate and destroy it. Moore praises and condemns, but finally accepts, and per-haps forgives. Her conclusion—after asserting both with and without irony that "[i]t could not be dangerous to be living / in a town like this"— compares the artist to the steeple-jack. Each places "danger-signs by the church" while "gilding" the star on the steeple. We use art to decreate false constructs, to repair "untrue" creations, and to make "untrue" creations of our own. The greatest danger of all is that we will confuse the sign for substance or give up any hope of contact between sign and substance at all. Like art or social institutions, the star on the steeple "stands for hope." To stand for does not prove, and there are stars that stand for nothing. Gilding may be a guilty imposition. Yet hope is not undone. Moore ends "The Steeple-Jack" and other poems of the thirties as she said Stravinsky ends his compositions, "with the recoil of a good ski-jumper accepting a spill."[80] It figures human helplessness and skill, as if illusion revealed keeps illusion sustained.

The enlarged social context of Moore's epistemological and esthetic vision in "The Steeple-Jack" is also a feature of "Virginia Britannia," an examina-tion of America's history of actual, conceptual, and esthetic plunderings of nature. But the most characteristic aspect of Moore's work in these years is her frequent treatment of rare or mysterious animals: the jerboa, the frigate pelican, the plumet basilisk, the pangolin. Unlike the swan and the ant, unlike the chameleon, or the vulture, goose, and loon of her early poems, these uncommon creatures exist without an attendant haze of emblematic or other prejudice. Free to generate and to resist perceptions and concep-tions, they suggest and shrug off esthetic and other implications of signifi-cance. As in "The Steeple-Jack," there is a return to judgment in these poems, accompanied by a movement from contrast and conflict to comple-ment and accommodation.

In her "animiles" Moore describes creatures with an exactitude that "honors" their separate and independent existences. In the process she employs without distress the subjective cultural "filters" that protect us from the threat of wholly wild nature and that are essential to representation. She does so in ways that never presume completely to control or possess nature and that expose repeatedly but without anxiety the illusions of art. At the same time, Moore uses analogies with animal activities to chide, correct, and model human behavior, insisting all the while that "as if" is different from "is." Moore is neither a taxidermist nor a field ecologist. Her poems are a menagerie with open habitats instead of cages, a place where the realms of art and nature meet, mingle, and separate, where conflicting claims cannot be reconciled but, at best, can coexist. She creates an artful, artificial space where "unease" is not dispelled but restrained. In the mid forties, Moore began her translation of La Fontaine. Of his fables she said, "To La Fontaine animals are vehicles for his philosophy, not studies in natural history."[81] Although Moore's own animal poems come by way of libraries and museums, they *are* studies in natural history; they permit to animals their own appearance and behavior, and are neither bestiary, allegory, nor fable. Still, as their cultural sources suggest, Moore's animal poems are studies in morality, art, and philosophy as well.

"The Jerboa" is exemplary. The poem is divided into two uneven sections that delineate its sharp contrast of plundering, dissonant art and adaptive, harmonious nature. But the sections overlap, and, without surrendering discrimination or judgment, Moore includes accommodation. The first section is called "Too Much," a comment on its subject matter, length, and bristling attack; the second, called "Abundance," is smaller, with more to admire. "Too Much" describes ancient artifacts that violate the natural world they use as a source. Obsessed with size and with absurd and incompetent mimesis, as in a gigantic bronze fir *or* pine cone, the Romans are mocked for imperial pretentiousness. Their appetite for power and possession imprisoned and enslaved others. Even their artists were owned, able to "contrive" only what—Moore says damningly—"passed / for art." The Egyptians are condemned as well. They also made "colossi" and claimed the ownership of people and creatures: they "use[d] slaves," "kept crocodiles," "had their men tie / hippopotami," and "looked on as theirs / impalas and onigers." But as Moore's description of Egyptian products progresses, damnation is modified.

Those who had "power over the poor" remain as monstrous as their pyramids or fruit-picking baboons on the necks of giraffes. They usurped the "fine linen" spun from flax to be used as "cordage for yachtsmen"; they treated their servants as things and themselves as gods. In an attempt to remake nature in his own image, the king, fearing snakes, tamed the mongoose and named it "Pharaoh's rat." But perhaps even Pharaoh shared the mongoose's excellent "restlessness." Surely some Egyptians made less brutal orders: beautiful, tree-lined gardens filled with animals and flowers. "These people liked small things" and pairings that are odd but apt. They constructed artful toys for their children and themselves, articles that show both splendid craftsmanship and respect for natural facts. Moore's admiration brims into catalogues of description. But here, too, her evaluation is intricate. Egyptian art is unnaturally abstract; the pools in the gardens are "square." Even skillfully made and attractive objects are betrayed by the desire to contain. Consumed by a fraudulent verisimilitude, a naive desire for a perfect match of function and form, the Egyptians made an art of entrapped entrapments, keeping "goose-grease" in a bone box "incised with a duck-wing," "ground horn" in a "buck / or rhinocerous horn," "locust oil in stone locusts."

Moore is restless. She can admire a culture's best efforts to protect itself from nature and death and to order and beautify its life, while still seeing those efforts as implicated in more vicious, possessive, and delusive kinds of transformation. Before the first section of "The Jerboa" ends, she turns away from the Romans and the Egyptians to the "small desert rat" that "lives without water," finding abundance in what seems to be nothingness. Unlike humans, who are everywhere beset by excess or by lack, the jerboa is perfectly at home in its seemingly hostile world, at ease in "boundless," "stupendous" emptiness. The poem's second section, "Abundance," uses the jerboa to criticize human failings and to offer a model for improvement. Unlike the Romans (in the person of Scipio Africanus), the jerboa does not conquer and plunder foreign lands; it is at home in its own. Energy, camouflage, and speed keep it safe from conquest by others. Insofar as the jerboa has to do with resemblances—it is said to be like the mongoose, the fawn-breasted bower-bird, a chipmunk, a kangaroo, and a fish—those resemblances result not from any invasion or appropriation of others but from its being part of the web of life. The jerboa makes no art; it leaves no sign but "fern-seed / foot-prints." This is Moore's prelapsarian ideal again. With its "pillar body erect," the jerboa is one with the lost perpendicular of "In the Days of Prismatic Color." Its own coloration is not spectral but the same as its world's.

While Moore offers the well-adapted, retreating jerboa as a corrective to the cruder, predatory adaptations of human culture, she knows that the animal represents an ideal that fallen human beings can never attain. Art is our sad and happy fate. If we will never have abundance but always too little or too much, we still can do our best to approximate perfection. Ascetic Jacob may have been deluded by the desert, but his "translucent mistake" suggests that the human desire to join the "terrestrial" and "celestial" can

take better—although still illusory—forms than offensive, luxurious impe-
rial ones. Moore's poem is her argument. Like the Romans and the Egyp-
tians, Moore imitates nature in representing the jerboa. Describing its "leaps
of two lengths," she reflects its "fifths and sevenths" in the syllabic structure
of her stanzas, each of which begins with two five-syllable lines and ends
with one of seven. But this device, although abstract, is neither gigantic nor
enslaving. It "honors" rather than captures or tames the jerboa. Still, it is
artificial; for human beings there is no other way. Moore accepts the condi-
tion. We can learn to be *like* but cannot *be* the jerboa. As Moore had tem-
pered her judgments of the Egyptians, so she tempers her contrast of nature
and art. Her poem's formal perfections—precisely regular stanzas, exact
syllabic patterning and rhyme scheme—complicate any simple evaluation
of art as malevolent and nature as good. Ours, like the jerboa's world, is
fraught with danger. Art is our camouflage and "burrow." "The Jerboa"
does not end by blending art and nature; they are immiscible. But it places
them together, the jerboa's speeding leaps and music's (and poetry's) mea-
sured intervals. Thomas Chippendale borrowed the clawed feet of his sofas
and chairs from nature. Moore gives them back and at the same time ex-
poses the artifice of representation. The jerboa "leaps to its burrow" and
escapes; it is also gently held within art's liberating space, where a wild
desert rat moves on the domesticated castor of a "three-cornered smooth-
working Chippendale / claw."

Many of the animals Moore writes about in the thirties are remarkable for
camouflage. Costello offers the best gloss on this fact when she says,
"Camouflage is the perfect emblem of a confusion between metonymy and
metaphor, for it creates the illusion of contiguity where there is actually
separation."[82] This goes to the center of Moore's best work. Metaphor
promises what metonymy denies, a perfect union of objective and subjective
realms, of fact and truth, of art, the world, and the Word, a place where "as
if" is one with "is." Moore believes neither and both. She contests each one
with the other and writes in the space between.

Moore encountered another period of poetic silence in the last years of the
thirties. When she began to publish again in the forties, there were more
animal poems, but the social dimension that had emerged in "The Steeple-
Jack" and "Virginia Britannia" became increasingly central; even in "The
Jerboa," ideas about wealth, poverty, and "abundance" reflect conditions of
the Great Depression. In her poems of the teens, Moore had trusted empiri-
cism to discover truth. In the twenties and thirties, she discovered and
learned to accommodate the notion that art and culture, and to some extent
knowledge itself, are necessarily illusions, fictive impositions on the world.
In the poems of her later career, Moore's interest in epistemological and

esthetic matters is secondary to the ethical requirement that artists—whether poets, carriage makers, engineers, or politicians—create and preserve those cultural illusions that lend order and significance to a life that otherwise may have none. A number of factors bear on this change in emphasis: World War II and attendant threats to civilization, the death of her mother in the late 1940s, Moore's own increasing age, and her intensifying fame. All contributed to an expanding need to have something useful to say on public matters.

The shift in emphasis is reflected in changes in technique. Quotations are used less often to disrupt delusions of certainty, more often to reflect consistent values. "Contractility" again becomes "a virtue." Regular syntax and verse forms are praised. The speaker's "I" is restored. Poems again are vehicles for themes. However, as Holley says, this return to earlier modes signals a new orientation, "a shared sense of social and historical urgency" and an "advocacy of value."[83] Even Moore's best critics disagree about the merits of her later work. Costello and Slatin see in it a drastic falling off and nearly dismiss the later poems. Holley and Stapleton think the late poems culminate "the poet's advance" toward social vision and expressive clarity. The later poems do have the pleasures of celebration and preservation, but they are too often preachy, nostalgic, cozy, or coy. Moore sometimes "contrives glory for ashes" in them, but they are more aptly described by a quotation she cites: "e'en in our ashes burn our wonted fires."[84] Moore remains interested in perceptual, conceptual, and esthetic delusions, but now she is more bemused than annoyed or distressed that what we call an arctic ox is more nearly a goat. When her brother said that her poem "The Arctic Ox" resembled an advertisement, Moore replied that it was one. Moore wants now to retail truths: preservation, humility, and restraint, a quiet joy, and modes of possession that neither hold nor hurt. There was nothing naive in this. Her exhortations to save the Camperdown Elm in Brooklyn's Prospect Park include necessity, hope, and hopelessness: "It is still leafing; / still there. *Mortal* though. We must save it." Her sharpest epistemological and esthetic outcry comes from the late poem "Elephants" (1943): "As if, as if, it is all ifs; we are at / much unease." That, she had come to know, is the case. There would be no cure, but medicines, palliatives, pragmatic remedies, those the artist might purvey. Moore seems at last to have felt that she could "perceive and champion determinate values" even though she remained a "vessel of indeterminacy" herself.[85]

CHAPTER FIVE

ELIZABETH BISHOP

A window across the river caught the sun
as if the miracle were working, on the wrong balcony.

ELIZABETH BISHOP had a predilection for balconies and other points of vantage. In daydreams she imagined herself as a lighthouse keeper. Her homes in Rio de Janeiro and Petrópolis, in Brazil, and at Lewis Wharf in Boston, perched high above the surrounding landscapes. A watercolor she drew in Mexico, reproduced on the cover of her collected poems, places the viewer on a roof, looking out and down across a balustrade to the scene beneath. Bishop's fascination with perspectives and points of view motivates a poetry of seeing, of aspects, prospects, and retrospects, a poetry of vision and visions—although, since "'visions' is / too serious a word," Bishop preferred to call her visions "looks." Her early reputation was as a meticulous observer. But Bishop was never content with description. As David Kalstone points out, Bishop was "eager" from the start "to move from observation to symbolic resonance." Kalstone quotes an early notebook entry in which Bishop writes that the poet uses her "proper material[s]" in order "to express something not of them—something I suppose, spiritual." This something spiritual "proceeds from the material," she says, and although "Sometimes it cannot be made to indicate its spiritual goal clearly . . . even then the spiritual must be felt."

Kalstone concludes from this that what most engages Bishop's attention as a poet is "the mysterious relation between the observed and what it spiritually' signifies." The engagement has as much to do with doubt as with faith. The notebook passage conveys both bold assertion ("must") and corrective hesitation ("I suppose"). Each is characteristic of Bishop's work; she stresses the gap between spirit and matter equally with their possible

187

connection. Bishop's demotion of "visions" to "looks" disturbs without utterly destroying belief in a relationship between matter and meaning. As Kalstone says elsewhere, "Bishop almost always took an ironic view of her allegorical yearnings."[1] She almost always had them, too. She admired Darwin for "the beautiful solid case being built up out of his endless, heroic observations," as well as for his "sliding giddily off into the unknown."[2] Contrasting attitudes about the "fit" of observed surfaces to significance are a mainspring of Bishop's verse. How is it that the "spiritual," although "not of" the material, yet "proceeds" from it? Do our observations build up a solid case or dismantle knowledge and send us tumbling into giddy ignorance? Bishop often turned to nature to consider such questions, as well as their epistemological and esthetic implications.

Bishop was not a believer; her use of the word "spiritual" is largely secular, as an equivalent for "significance." Nonetheless, much of Bishop's childhood was lived in an atmosphere of traditional Protestant faith. She spent formative years with her maternal grandparents in a Nova Scotia village. Her grandfather was a deacon; her aunts sang in the Baptist choir; and Bishop described herself as "full of hymns." Bishop's secular interest in the relationship of the seen to the significant does have a religious dimension: her tendency to "read" the world for signs of truth reflects the traditional Christian view of nature as God's second book. At the same time, her inability to find such signs, her insistence that "finding" them is not a matter of discovery but of subjective imposition, undermines all religious and metaphysical systems.

Several poet-critics testify to the religious tenor of Bishop's work, including her frequent use of such religious materials as miracles, revelations, Bibles, feast days, and hymns. Yet each observer also thinks that Bishop would have firmly repelled any description of herself as a "religious" poet. As Richard Wilbur says, "she had no orthodox convictions, and wondered at such certainties in others." In an interview, Ashley Brown asked Bishop if she thought it "necessary for a poet to have a 'myth'—Christian or otherwise—to sustain his work." The response was one Bishop gave elsewhere when faced with questions she found either too incisive or too abstract: "It all depends—some poets do, some don't." When pressed, she replied, "Some people crave organization more than others—the desire to get everything in its place."[3]

Perhaps Bishop did "crave organization" less than others. Surely she subscribed to no religious or other comprehensive "myth." But it may be more accurate to say that although she craved organization a good deal—not least because of the disruptions and dislocations of her early family life—Bishop was less willing than most to force the particulars of experience to fit a satisfying or comforting pattern. She refused to impose a myth where none could be discovered. Still, Bishop's concern with how the spiritual proceeds from the material has religious roots. In the notebook entry quoted above, Bishop concludes her esthetic speculation about matter and meaning with this remark: "Genuine religious poetry seems to be about as far as poetry can go—and as good as it can be." The poetry she had in mind often proceeds from description to assertions of spiritual significance. Religious poetry—especially the devotional verse of George Herbert and Gerard Manley Hopkins—was an important model for Bishop's work. But Bishop lacked Herbert's and Hopkins's belief that the relationship of the seen to the significant is guaranteed by God no matter how dimly visible to human perceptions the relationship may be. She doubted the formulas of preconception. Nonetheless, like Moore, Bishop worked at the boundary of the visible and the invisible, interrogating human claims to knowledge and questioning whether we discover or impose the meanings we—and works of art—assert. Like Frost and Stevens, she might be called a religious poet without religious faith.

Bishop's version of natural supernaturalism—her secular concern with the relation of seeing to significance—has an additional source in the work of the New England transcendentalists. Bishop claims the connection herself. In a letter to Anne Stevenson, she says (with her usual quantum of restraint), "I . . . feel that [Robert Lowell] and I in very different ways are both descendants from the Transcendentalists—but you may not agree."[4] Lawrence Buell's taxonomy of New England poetics can assist speculation about what Bishop might have meant. According to Buell, poem after poem in the transcendentalist tradition begins by describing a scene or event in nature and then moves to assert a discovered truth, a religious or other revelation. Buell's examples are chestnuts: in "The Rhodora," for instance, Emerson describes a shrub "Spreading its leafless blooms in a damp nook," wonders why its "charm is wasted on the earth and sky," decides that "Beauty is its own excuse for being," then makes an epistemological claim, an intuitive supposition of providential truth: "The self-same Power that brought me there brought you."[5]

Descriptions are the most evident feature of Bishop's work, but it is obvious that her portrayals reach quite different ends from those of the transcendentalists. Bishop's favorite word is "or," not "thus"; she suspects with Wittgenstein that all we can see or describe "could also be otherwise." One critic writes that Bishop's poems have the "lowest density of generalization that it is possible for poems to contain."[6] Nonetheless, Bishop's poems frequently recall "the correspondence game," the process of moving from image to idea, from something seen to something known and believed. They do so in ways that question, thwart, and deny the analogies earlier poets claim. They reject the theocentric, logocentric, and idealist or symbolist epistemologies and esthetics upon which Puritan and transcendentalist doctrines of correspondences are based. In this Bishop can be harshly satirical and either warmly or achingly nostalgic. Eventually, though, she develops a "diminished" mode of correspondence central to her work. In it, her hunger to have significance proceed from what is seen is famished and fed. Chastened by an awareness of subjectivity and its projections, and by a recognition that our appropriations of nature, art, and others for systematic truth abuses use, Bishop's reenactments of the search for correspondence offer a bearable but neither certain nor redemptive way of being in the world. Those matters are the subject of much that follows. For now, the poem "Filling Station" can preface Bishop's transcripts from the correspondence school of verse.

Just after her graduation from Vassar, Bishop worked for a while on the staff of the U.S.A. School of Writing, a shady operation that offered a correspondence course for would-be authors. In a memoir, she remarks upon an aspect of her students' work that might comment as well on certain poems by transcendentalists, the tendency in ending a story "to make it all right, or of real value to the world, by tacking on a grand, if ill-fitting, 'moral.'"[7] "Filling Station" parodies that tendency—the expression of our desire for a well-oiled consistency to give coherent resolution to the world. It cradles and rehearses it as well. In part, Bishop's poem is a still more deflated and secular version of Frost's "Design." Frost disrupts the conventional analogy between orderly nature and an orderly cosmos or God by introducing doubts about his natural facts as well as about the logic of correspondence—which proves to be both more provisional and more appallingly sure than we had thought. Bishop goes Frost one, or several, better.

Bishop's description begins with an unnatural landscape that is as fully, if foully, patterned as a transcendentalist nature scene: "thoroughly dirty," the filling station is "oil-soaked, oil-permeated / to a disturbing, over-all / black translucency." Everything is pregnant with grease. A "big hirsute begonia" seems oiled, not watered. In a parody of the transcendentalist goal of reattaching words to things, even the language is stained, so that "oily" soaks the "big dim doily." Such consistency eventually produces the corresponding "moral" that a transcendentalist expects. It comes as a kind of jest, or so it seems. Someone has aligned the rows of oil cans "so that they softly say: / ESSO—SO—SO—SO / to high-strung automobiles." This demonstration of "coherence" (a parodic version of poetic and analogical repetitions) prompts an apparently ironic summary remark: "Somebody loves us all." As a glib version of comforting resolution, a slightly mocking echo of myriad poems secure in the confidence that God inscribes the world and poets can read the text, this banality satirizes closure. The precipitating detail, the design of oil cans, transmutes the conclusive "therefores" of analogical logic to a dully reverberating "so"; "so what," the soft repercussions demand. (In the Brazilian memoir "A Trip to Vigia," Bishop describes a store where bottles of *cachaça*, the local alcohol, are lined up on a shelf so that the labels speak their name, "Esperança, Hope, Hope, Hope."[8] The similarity indicates what "Filling Station" has at stake.)

Bishop mocks the unifying vision. Her words deny what they invoke: "black translucency" blinds Emerson's transparent eye; "over-all" deflates the "Over-Soul." In Hopkins's "God's Grandeur," an "ooze of oil" gathers to greatness as the earth manifests the glory of its creator. "Filling Station" smears that "ooze" with "toil" and "trade," "man's smudge." Here, coherence neither proves, elates, nor elicits praise. It offers no spiritual comfort or truth. Instead, it agitates. But agitation does more than cancel the contentments of transcendentalist or religious certitude; it also disrupts the security of sarcasm. Bishop's poem has another voice to challenge its parodic one, a voice with a reverential tone, a nearly religious hush.

"Filling Station" begins with a ladylike recoiling ("Oh, but it is dirty!") from a scene superintended by "Father," who is named to suggest both God and other patriarchs. His "oil-soaked monkey suit . . . cuts him under the arms" and is as ill-fitting as a tacked-on moral. His "greasy sons assist him / (it's a family filling station)." The word "family" is always resonant for Bishop; it prompts a second look. Perhaps the family lives here at the station. Soon, the repellent place (so thoroughly male and soaked with impregnating fluids) begins to seem almost homey. On the porch behind the pumps is a set of wickerwork; on the wicker sofa lies "a dirty dog, quite comfy." There is a begonia and, "draping a taboret / (part of the set)," a doily, "Embroidered in daisy stitch / with marguerites, I think." Although they are hard to see ("marguerites, I think") and dimmed by penetrating oil ("gray crochet"), those womanly touches suggest a counterorder to the hegemony of grease. This is tenuous, of course: does "taboret" rhyme with "set" or "crochet"? The descriptions are partly comic, and if the porch is a sort of living room, it, too, is "oil-soaked." The porch is fragile and exposed, and, if there is a house (no house is mentioned), we are never allowed inside for the privileged "interior" view a transcendentalist's eye would disclose. Uneasy suggestions of male dominance and female absence threaten the domestic scene throughout.

Still, the wickerwork *set*, the carefully arranged furniture, the "comfy" dog, the nurtured houseplant, the embroidered doily, and the patterned oil cans all suggest a guiding, caring, but not insistent or dominating hand. The Esso cans speak "softly." They represent the sort of unassuming art that Bishop most respects, art that offers some minimal pattern to moderate soiled life without making false claims or grandiose assertions. With the other domestic details, the arrangement of oil cans provides some color against the black translucency of overdetermined design. Perhaps there *is* someone—mother as God?—who really loves us all: "Somebody embroidered the doily"; "Somebody waters the plant"; "Somebody / arranges the rows of cans"; "Somebody loves us all." This is litany: like the repeated "SO," a quiet prayer. Perhaps it is Bishop's version of Hopkins's Holy Ghost brooding maternally over the bent world "with warm breast and with ah! bright wings." But when Bishop follows Hopkins and interrupts herself, it is not to include elation ("ah!") but a sardonic, poisoning doubt: "Somebody waters the plant, / or oils it, maybe." This checks sentimentality without defeating feeling, and it joins such words as "comfy" and "hirsute" in keeping the poem and the reader off-balance, like the jittery speaker, who projects her case of "nerves" on the "high-strung automobiles."

Those disorienting details permit the poem to replace a "disturbing" consistency without becoming overly coherent itself, without succumbing to another "over-all" order that might impose an opaque "translucency" and be anxious to dominate and conceal, not nurture and reveal. The refusal of generalization allows signs of comfort *and* distress to appear. But the poem's quieter, less grand and all-inclusive patterns have a cost beyond even their vulnerability, one expressed in yet another tone of voice. Alarmed by an "oil-soaked" world, then calmed by more gently woven shapes (the work of a woman's hand that arranges "so's," that sews and sows), the speaker is also profoundly disturbed by the signs of an absent mother, for if "Father" and sons are there, mother is out of sight. As comforting details accumulate, so does the speaker's distress about their source: "Why the extraneous plant? / Why the taboret? / Why, oh why, the doily?" The origin of this distress is partly autobiographical, since Bishop's mother was lost to her when Bishop was very young. The disturbance has an esthetic source as well. Those patterned "so's" almost spell S.O.S.; Bishop thought "an element of mortal panic and fear" underlies "all works of art."[9] Psychological, epistemological, and theological issues are also involved: the speaker's distress reflects the loss of the nurturing mother, and the difficulties of "reading" the work of any absent designer, human or divine. Presence is known only through signs; the signs are nearly obscured and all but impossible to read; they may be accidents, or projections of the self.

"Filling Station" does not resolve its several voices. It mixes mockery and fear into a moment of enlarging sympathy and hope. Neither comfort nor terror is complete. Like Dickinson and Frost and Stevens and Moore before her, Bishop challenges and extends the transcendentalist tradition she evokes. Bishop writes a poetry of correspondences, but she complicates both the descriptive and analogical levels of the image-to-idea poem in order to question the meaning of meaning. Her poems disrupt the traditional redirection of description to "creedal formula" and resist, reject, and unravel "premature closure"; they do so while still engaging in the effort to reach conclusions, to proceed from experience to knowledge.[10]

Bishop descends from transcendentalist and other idealist sources in several senses of the word "descend," but her work is not a falling off, no comedown. In J. D. McClatchy's frugal economics, "A poet's debt is her starting-point; her interest cancels it."[11] One mark of Bishop's debt-canceling interest in the transcendentalists is her veering away from her own attraction to their ideal: a transparent world through which the signs of God or other absolutes show clear. In "Filling Station," transparency is replaced by a pseudotranslucency that reflects rather than reveals; it is nearly opaque. The signs of love that still appear are human, relative, and dubious; if they are there at all, they are vulnerable to total concealment or to obliteration. In the autobiographical story "In the Village," a child stops and stares down into a river from the vantage of a bridge: "From above, the trout look as transparent as the water, but if one did catch one, it would be opaque enough, with a little slick moon-white belly with a pair of tiny, pleated, rose-pink fins on it."[12]

Similar versions of vision abound in Bishop's work, descriptions in which the relationship of seeing to the transparent and opaque is nervously construed. Her interest in that relationship appears even in minor matters, although "minor" is the wrong word, since Bishop rejects the hierarchical and grand. Looking at a still life of fruit on a table by the primitive artist Gregorio Valdes, Bishop discovers that "[t]he blue background extended all the way to the tabletop and where the paint had cracked the blue showed through the fruit. Apparently [Valdes] had felt that since the wall was back of the fruit he should paint it there, before he could go on and paint the fruit in front of it."[13] This is partly a joke: Emerson's transparent vision made literal as a cracked verisimilitude. But "primitive" art often set Bishop's "vision" to work, and, as Marianne Moore declared, "One's humor is based upon the most serious part of one's nature."[14] Images of transparency and opacity figure again and again in Bishop's descriptions and esthetics. In the poem "The Fish," the subject is brilliantly observed, yet the fish's eyes, "backed . . . with tarnished tinfoil," are more like mirrors than transparent glass, and more opaque than mirrors: "more like the tipping / of an object toward the light."

Efforts to see through or into, discoveries of the self reflected back, glances into interiors where we can and cannot see or understand, these are characteristic dramas of Bishop's verse, as in the opening lines of "Twelfth Morning; or What You Will": "Like a first coat of whitewash when it's wet, / the thin gray mist lets everything show through." Twelfth Day is Epiphany, a time of revelation and heightened seeing, of spirit made manifest. In the poem, a miracle of sorts occurs: a boy appears through the mist. He carries a gleaming tin of water on his head and bears himself as if to say, I come to you in glory, the highlight on the world's bright pearl. This is at once wholly secular and holy in its resonance, recalling the pearl of great price and the coming of Christ with the waters of resurrection and rebirth. But if "everything show[s] through," is the morning world miraculous, transformed, redemptively transparent? Or is it all a trick, a pretty artifice we ought to be able to "see through"? "What You Will" incriminates as it answers. As with most descriptions of transparency in Bishop's work, this "vision" is obscure. Whitewash is used for cover-ups. Even the sheer first coat will dry opaque; there are other coats to come. Gray mist, however thin, is apt to blur what it reveals, and "lets" locates authority beyond the reach of sight. A local boy as Christ? There are "visions" or "looks" in Bishop's work, but they are tentative and earthly, a little comic, easily assailed, and apt to be reflective shams of eye or air. Nevertheless, they appear, and shine with a lovely light; or is it merely pretty.

A concomitant of the transcendentalist ideal of a reality transparent to the inspired eye is a view of the world as a book or text—a conception in which nature is seen as an inscribed surface that reveals an ultimate authoritative Word. Here, too, Bishop follows to diverge. In the short story "The Sea & Its Shore," Edwin Boomer ("Boomer" is a common pronunciation of Bulmer, Bishop's mother's family name) has been appointed to keep a large public beach free from papers. The story's tone is comic Kafkaesque, in which symbolism, parody, and reportage drily merge. Boomer collects scraps of paper, which he sometimes reads, arranges, and conserves, and which he eventually burns. He sees those fragmentary texts as possible sources of truth *and* as distracting trash that disfigures the actual world. For those reasons he is said to have "lived the most literary life possible." Eventually, "Either because of the insect armies of type so constantly besieging his eyes, or because it was really so, the world, the whole world he saw, came . . . to seem printed, too." When he watched a sandpiper, "It looked, to his strained eyesight, like a point of punctuation against the 'rounded, rolling waves.' It left fine prints with its feet. Its feathers were speckled; and especially on the narrow hems of the wings appeared marks that looked as if they might be letters, if only he could get close enough to read them."

For a while, Boomer kept some of the papers he collected, attempting to puzzle them out and to discover in them some orderly system, an application to his life. He tried to get "close enough" to interpret nature's text. "But the point was that everything had to be burned at last."[15] It's left at that. There is a multitude of texts. And the world itself seems to have a textual dimension—although whether it is really so or only looks that way to eyes attacked or strained by too much print is left unsettled or unsaid. In any case, we try to sort it out, to read it, but we cannot. We burn and otherwise erase what texts we are able; others are constantly being prepared, inscribed by writers—or by eyes that engender print. There are many texts, and the world itself may be a book, but the pages we have are fragments—subjective projections, palimpsests. Meaning is elusive and plural, never to be restored to the accessible and unitary text so comforting to transcendentalists (unless by some final and inhuman conflagration). In Bishop's story, this is a matter for tragic, comic, and parodic distress. No matter how much we want or will it otherwise, without a single author and a single text there is no authority—and no authoritative voice or stance, no writer or reader with an absolute or sovereign interpretation to present. We are free, belated, and bereft.

In part, this fable of reading and writing is as far as it is possible to get from the transcendentalist valorizing of the poem—and the earth—as sacred text. And yet the story itself is runic; Bishop is never quite free of the thought that life is a code we almost apprehend. Raised to believe that the world is comprehended in—and as—a book, Bishop reflects the Puritan and transcendentalist habit of describing nature as a kind of Bible or supplemental text, but she does so without subscribing to—and often while subverting—the theological, epistemological, and esthetic implications that Puritans and transcendentalists upheld. Bishop's work often describes nature as thick with signs of print. In one poem, a flock of "fine black birds" hangs "in n's in banks." Other birds are "S-shaped." There are "big symbolic birds" as well, and "the weak calligraphy of songbirds' cages." A sandpiper scours a shoreline like some student of Blake, anxious to read the cosmos in a grain of sand. In one landscape piece, boats are stacked like "letters" on a shore "littered with old correspondences." In another, there are stones inscribed with "scriptures," recalling Shakespeare's "sermons in stones."

But the textual elements of Bishop's descriptions are always broken or blurred. Like the "assorted characters" of Frost's "Design," they are apt to be eccentric and to spell out either nothing or something a good deal less than palliative or grand. The textual fragments embedded in or imposed on Bishop's natural scenes never cohere, are never complete: as one of her characters says of books and landscapes he has read, they all are "full of blanks." Textual details emerge in Bishop's poems, but they are not the work of an authoritative hand. Often they prove no more than clichés of representation (a painter depicts a flock of birds as amateurish n's) or the result of some natural accident ("scriptures" are "made on stones by stones" themselves, not God's inscribing hand). Such texts have authorship, perhaps, but no authority. Nature can be a teacher for Bishop, but its teaching is "never a priori."[16] Nature's text is not the holograph or hieroglyph of God, a book of truths just waiting to be read. Texts are imposed by us or others of our kind. In reading them we do not discover "truth," although we might learn something of ourselves.

Writing about one of Bishop's most "bookish" works, a poem in part about a Bible ("Over 2,000 Illustrations and a Complete Concordance"), David Bromwich summarizes her view of the textuality of nature: "The thought that troubles [her] . . . is that the book of nature . . . may not be either a clean text or an already canonical one."[17] The loss of a canonical text can leave us unanchored, with no absolutes that hold and none to discover. It might also free us from narrowly preconceived and oppressive beliefs, providing us with an empty space in which to invent and inscribe new meanings of our own, permitting a provisional making-do that delights—and is authorized by ourselves if by no one else. For Bishop, however, the loss of a canonical text does not leave a clean one in its place. The world is covered instead with fragmentary textual traces from which we cannot escape (perhaps, since the traces are human, we should not want to escape from them). Everywhere, inscriptions crowd in and compete. All seeing is seeing as, the subjective projection of some conscious or other interpretation—and without a master interpretation by which to adjudicate or select. This, as a source of trouble and of joy, vibrates in Bishop's work.

Bishop is a provisional poet. She courts no absolutes, whether of beginnings or of ends: she finds no originating Word, no transfiguring epiphany or apocalypse. Instead, Bishop's descriptions are moments of interchange between perception and significance. They enact and explore the relationship of what is seen to what is known and meant. Sure that no perception or conception is final or unindebted, Bishop sets her poems in medias res. Her details are already represented, whether by others or by the reference frames she inevitably brings to bear on them. Just as inevitably, other representations will succeed and supplant her own. This is what John Unterecker means when he calls Bishop "a poet of options and echoes"; what Robert Dale Parker has in mind when he says "First she sees . . . then wonders if she is wrong."[18] Bishop works at boundaries and edges, in the spaces between priority and culmination, seeing and signification, description and assertion, correspondences sought and disclaimed, nature as canonical text and vacant page. Her poems are set in border regions, on journeys and on shores, at the brink of sleep or initiation, in waiting rooms and filling stations, points of vantage and of transition or transit. Her style hovers between formal modes and conversation. In Bishop's poems, description subsumes or replaces argument and narration, exposition and persuasion.

Bishop is also a metonymic poet, always aware of what Octavio Paz called the "dissonance within analogy."[19] In choosing descriptive modes, she consistently prefers simile to metaphor. When thought of as a mode of representation, metaphor may be said to imply a theory of knowledge. So conceived, metaphor achieves understanding or truth by dissolving or overwhelming boundaries, converting apparent unlikeness to actual identity either by an act of inspired discovery or by the force of creative will. Seen in this way, metaphor asserts that the "vertical" analogy of the physical and metaphysical is guaranteed either by God or by human visionary power, as in the religious or natural supernaturalism of mystics, romantics, and transcendentalists. Meaning has authority and permanence. For Bishop, this claims more than eye, mind, and language can convincingly perform, more than anyone can know. Simile is a metonymic mode of representation and much more modest than metaphor. It is a "horizontal" figure, a figure of borders in which unlikely pairs can meet and overlap but not dissolve and merge. Simile suggests sameness while implying difference; its likenesses are likely and unlikely both. Rather than claiming identity, simile leaves room for deviation, for alternative verdicts, for "or" and for "and." Simile affirms that likeness is contingent, sponsored only by its human maker, and subject to revision. It is the home-made figure ("Home-made, home-made! But aren't we all?"), imaginative but not too ostentatious.[20] Bishop not only prefers simile, as a figure of speech and a mode of representation, she also uses similes additively, correcting, qualifying, and adjusting them as she goes: no single figure nor any accumulation can render reality or experience with absolute precision. Bishop's comparisons are always "askew, but braced," "perfect!—But impossible."

Bishop's similes give her materials their due while both controlling and exposing the willfulness involved in even the most restrained acts of epistemological or esthetic appropriation. "Wading at Wellfleet" is an exception (or seems to be at first); it proves the rule. Here, Bishop's figure is a metaphor; her treatment, metonymic. The sea, she says, "is 'all a case of knives.' " That description is the culmination of an extended comparison in which the waves, glittering in the sun as they roll to the beach, are identified with an Assyrian war chariot equipped with murderous sets of blades that revolve on the hubs of its axles. The effect is strangely disproportionate. In certain circumstances the indifferent machinery of the sea might seem as malevolent as a knived chariot bearing down on retreating infantry—but to a wader?, with waves, not knives, "directed at the shin"? The metaphor proves inappropriate; it collapses under the strain.

> The chariot front is blue and great.
>
> The war rests wholly with the waves:
> they try revolving, but the wheels
> give way; they will not bear the weight.[21]

The waves, forced by "gravity" and metaphoric logic to bear too "great" a burden, break—undone by their own weight (a crumpling felt as well as stated in the slumping enjambment of "wheels / give way"). The metaphor and its self-regarding dramatization break down, too, wrecked in a comically deadpan deflation. In the other drama of the poem, the poet recovers herself in time, dropping the overblown metaphor in favor of observation. The effect is a return from metaphor to more modest means of description and representation.

Bishop is one of the least "theoretical" of poets. The modernist revolution preceded hers, and, although her own breakthroughs anticipate postmodern ones, the arguments for those came after. Bishop published no manifestoes and few explanations or justifications of her work. In recorded conversations she often employed a maneuver she admired in Fred Astaire: in an interview she had seen, Astaire "refused to discuss 'the dance,' his partners, or his 'career' and stuck determinedly to golf." Asked by Elizabeth Spires about her attitude toward nature, Bishop danced away from the subject until she settled on automobiles.[22] Still, she gave directional signals here and there. In a piece called "As We Like It, Miss Moore and Edgar Allan Poe," Bishop uses lines from Moore ("As if, as if, it is all ifs; we are at / much unease") as an occasion for comment on representational figures. "It is annoying," she says, "to have to keep saying that things are like other things, even though there seems to be no help for it. But it may be noticed that although full of similes, and such brilliant ones that she should never feel the necessity of complaining, she uses metaphors rather sparingly and obliquely."[23] Bishop's remarks apply to her own work as well as to Moore's. It may be irritating to be restricted to comparisons that invariably fall short of "identity" and insist on their own limitations, but to resist the desire to soar in metaphor is to accept the nature of things and to avoid the fraudulent impositions of religious or romantic self-indulgence, claiming more meaning than the facts can bear.

Alan Williamson points out that Bishop's posthumous reputation soared in part because such works as "In the Waiting Room" and "In the Village" clarify the private sources of her calmly desperate poems: her desire for and distrust of "home," of all the "comfy" arrangements we make in life and art. Bishop's poetry is much more personal and emotionally intense than the preceding discussion reveals. However, until her later works, it is not obviously intimate or self-revealing—and it is never "confessional" (even though Bishop's homosexuality and troubles with alcohol might have provided her with standard confessional subjects). Confessional poetry is "strained" almost by definition, and what Bishop wanted was something she felt that Herbert had achieved, "to express a very deep emotion without straining."[24] In any case, the "deep emotion" in Bishop's poems does come from her personal life, most manifestly from the disruptions of her early years and their echoing effects. Knowledge of those events helps explain how the seemingly unstressed details of her poems convey their emotional charge, for in Bishop's work the personal defines epistemological and es-thetic concerns in a way that is finally inseparable from them.

Bishop was born February 8, 1911, in Worcester, Massachusetts, to Canadian-American parents. Her father, an executive in the family con-struction firm, died of Bright's disease when she was eight months old. In the next few years, Bishop's mother suffered a series of mental breakdowns and was hospitalized in Massachusetts. The child was sent to live at her mother's parents' home in Great Village, Nova Scotia. Mrs. Bishop's health did not improve, and in 1916 she, too, was sent to Great Village, in the vain hope that familiar surroundings might effect a cure.

With her mother ill, Bishop was raised by her maternal grandparents in a place both backward and idyllic. Situated where a river meets the sea, Great Village had few cars and no electricity or plumbing.[25] Bishop attended primer class in a one-room school, an experience she recalls in a memoir. Her description of the classroom's maps suggests that she had already devel-oped the sense of "everyday" surrealism that pervades her work:

> Only the third and fourth grades studied geography. On their side of the room, over the blackboard, were two rolled-up maps, one of Canada and one of the whole world. When they had a geography lesson, Miss Morash pulled down one or both of these maps, like window shades. . . . The light coming in from their windows, falling on the glazed, crackly surface, made it hard for me to see them properly from where I sat. . . . But I got the general impression that Canada was the same size as the world, which somehow or other fitted into it, or the other way around, and that in the world and Canada the sun was always shining and everything was dry and glittering. At the same time, I knew perfectly well that this was not true.[26]

The child's view of a perfection envisioned and denied is one source of Bishop's interest in representation and in seeing and significance, of her frequent shifts of scale, of her preference for the simile, of her hopes and doubts about knowledge and art, and of such characteristic conclusions as this one, from the story "The Sea & Its Shore": "It is an extremely pictur-esque scene, in some ways like a Rembrandt, but in many ways not."[27]

In the summer of 1916, when Bishop was five, her mother suffered the final breakdown described in the story "In the Village." She was deemed to be incurably insane and placed permanently in an institution. Bishop never saw her again. Now an "awful but cheerful" sound hung over the village: the nearly merged but divided reverberations of the terrifying scream that signaled her mother's mental collapse, and the artful, familiar, and healing "clang" of Nate the blacksmith's hammer. There, perhaps, is the source of Bishop's lifelong sense that all human systems—whether domestic arrangements or the structures of religion, knowledge, and art—are comforting but merely invented: contingent, vulnerable, and transient. In "In the Village," the scream that signals the mother's disappearance occurs while she is being fitted for a purple dress to wear for coming out of mourning. That failed "fitting" is set alongside the successful artistry of the blacksmith, who makes horseshoes and fits them with efficient skill, controlling a potentially dangerous situation: "Nate does wonders with both hands; with one hand. The attendant horse stamps his foot and nods his head as if agreeing to a peace treaty." Several other attempts at protection, control, or permanence appear in the story. They lack the purity of either the mother's chaotic scream or Nate's beautiful, orderly "clang," of either a house fire out of control (also described in the story) or the contained and useful flame of the blacksmith's forge. These other "fittings" succeed and fail at once; they set a pattern for Bishop's versions of the possibilities and limits of domestic life, and of poetry and knowledge.

While the grandmother and aunts arrange the mother's belongings, the daughter "abscond[s] with a little ivory stick with a sharp point. To keep it forever I bury it under the bleeding heart by the crab-apple tree, but it is never found again." When the dressmaker, Miss Gurley, gives her a nickel, "I put my five-cent piece in my mouth for greater safety on the way home, and swallowed it. Months later, as far as I know, it is still in me, transmuting all its precious metal into my growing teeth and hair." When packages are sent to her mother, "The address of the sanatorium is in my grandmother's handwriting, in purple indelible pencil, on smoothed-out writing paper. It will never come off."[28] And her mother will never come back. Those passages all reward attention. They combine the sentimental and the acerbic (as in the "casual" conjunction of bleeding heart and crab-apple). In their level presentation of the attractions, dangers, successes, and failures of an instinctive urge for permanence and safety, for the "smoothed-out" and "indelible," they are vintage Bishop. Home and art, ownership and knowledge, and, of course, writing ("smoothed-out writing paper"; "indelible pencil")—all can master and be mastered by disaster, and all at once. From such awareness comes a major aspect of Bishop's work: "a language unblinking as childhood, open to and unembarrassed by anomaly."[29]

When Bishop was six, she was taken to live with her paternal grandparents in Worcester. Perhaps both families thought that the Massachusetts relations' more ample means would serve the child better. But, as Stevenson says, "the peaceful home, the family affection, and the simple life she had known in Nova Scotia vanished. The change was like a fall from innocence and she never forgot it."[30] Compared to her mother's family, to the devout and affectionate grandfather who smuggled her Canada mints in church and taught her country manners, Bishop's Worcester relatives were kind but cold. In the memoir "The Country Mouse," Bishop describes her journey with them from Great Village to Massachusetts: "I felt as if I were being kidnapped, even if I wasn't." The family tried: there was a delightful gift of three Golden Bantams, and attempts to provide her with appropriate friends. One night her grandfather, relaxed in his nightshirt and dressing gown, joined her game of squinting to exaggerate the effects of light on trees sheathed in ice. But this, she says, was "one of the few unselfconscious moments of that whole dismal time."

The atmosphere of the house as it felt to the child is conveyed by two other anecdotes from "The Country Mouse." In one, the family dog, a Boston terrier named Beppo, disappears. He is found in a closet, punishing himself for having vomited; Bishop attributes this self-punishment to "his peculiar Bostonian sense of guilt." The dog's illnesses and sensitivity reflect her own. She says they became "very attached" and that Beppo "adopted" her, "perhaps as being on the same terms in the house as himself." In the other anecdote, Bishop is taken out to what was once a barn by her Aunt Jenny. The child is fascinated by the cars, "but what had caught my eye was a carriage sitting at the back of the garage." The carriage was her grandmother's and had not been used for years. "It was dark green. I climbed inside. . . . It made the most beautiful little house imaginable. I wanted to stay in it forever, but Aunt Jenny . . . invited me to ride down as far as the house with her, so I had to go." The intense desire for a permanent, imaginary home to replace a lost one, the sense that any realization of that desire is fragile and quick to dissolve, the feeling of powerlessness in a world ruled by large and careless forces, these resonate in Bishop's childhood and in her poems.

At the end of "The Country Mouse," Bishop describes the following incident as the source of a "great truth" that "came home" to her during her brief stay in Worcester. A playmate asked about her parents:

> I said my father was dead; I didn't ever remember seeing him. What about my mother? I thought for a moment and then I said in a *sentimental* voice: "She went away and left me . . . She died, too." Emma was impressed and sympathetic, and I loathed myself. It was the first time I had lied deliberately and consciously, and the first time I was aware of the falsity and the great power of sentimentality—although I didn't know the word. My mother was not dead. She was in a sanatorium, in another prolonged "nervous breakdown." I didn't know then, and still don't, whether it was from shame I lied, or from a hideous craving for sympathy, playing up my sad romantic plight. But the feeling of self-distaste, whatever it came from, was only too real. I jumped up, to get away from my monstrous self that I could not keep from lying.[31]

The refusal to falsify facts in order to attain effects of heightened significance is a principle in Bishop's writing. It affects not only her willingness to include anomaly, and her relentless self-correction, but also such expressive characteristics as her reluctance "to allow technical intensity and thematic passion to correspond in her work," a reluctance reflected in slant rhymes, irregular rhythms, and disproportionate stanzas, as well as in oblique allusions, violations of genre, and deliberately flattened tones.[32]

Bishop's loneliness in Worcester was a little moderated by the affection of a Swedish maid named Agnes. "Then," in a pattern that seemed to define the nature of things, "Agnes left. She was going back to Sweden to get married. I wept and clung to her skirts and large suitcase when she kissed me goodbye. After that, things went from bad to worse." Abandoned again, Bishop began to suffer from illnesses that seem to reflect her history of displacement, her psychic distress. "First came constipation, then eczema again, and finally asthma. I felt myself aging, even dying. I was *bored* and lonely with Grandma, my silent grandpa, the dinners alone, bored with Emma and Beppo, all of them. At night I lay blinking my flashlight off and on, and crying."[33]

Perhaps frightened by her illnesses, Bishop's grandparents decided she would be better off with her mother's sister, Maud, who lived in a suburb of Boston. Another displacement. But although illness kept her from regular attendance at school for several years, Bishop began to recover. Books, writing, and music stood in more or less for parents and childhood friends, and by the time she was thirteen Bishop was able to begin a series of summers at a camp in Wellfleet on Cape Cod. In 1927 she entered boarding school at Walnut Hill in Natick, Massachusetts, and in 1930 enrolled at Vassar. She remained shy, asthmatic, and bookishly aloof, but made friends, was editor of the yearbook, and contributed to the *Vassar Review*. She graduated in 1934. In that same year, her mother died, and Bishop met Marianne Moore. The two began a long relationship, chronicled by Bishop herself and by several others.[34] In the years immediately after college, using a small inheritance, Bishop lived in New York City and traveled to France, England, North Africa, Italy, and Spain. In 1938, she moved to Key West, where she lived for several years, while also spending time in Mexico and Washington, D.C.

Bishop "emerged into young adulthood feeling she had always been a guest in other people's houses."[35] From the late thirties on, she began to make homes for herself, and to lose them, too. By the mid 1940s, she found Key West had altered for the worse, and in 1951, after suffering an allergy attack during a trip around South America, Bishop settled in Brazil, where she lived in Rio de Janeiro, Petrópolis, and Ouro Prêto until the early seventies, most of that time with Lota de Macedo Soares, who committed suicide in 1967. From 1970 to 1973, Bishop alternated teaching fall semesters at Harvard with seasons at Ouro Prêto. In 1974, she moved permanently to Boston and continued to teach, now in the spring term as well. She died, at home, of a stroke in 1979.

Bishop's first book, *North & South*, was published in 1946. The title specifies a geographical division that has chronological and stylistic dimensions as well. Several of the first twenty poems in the book have explicitly northern settings, whether in icy seas or in Paris and New York; most of them were published in magazines between 1934 and 1938. The last ten poems are set in Florida and were written in 1939 and after, when an important alteration in Bishop's work had taken place. Exceptions to this arrangement are two northern poems, "Chemin de Fer" and "Large Bad Picture." Although placed with the earlier group because of their settings, they were written later and belong with the southern poems in several ways.[36]

As might be expected, the earlier poems in *North & South* reflect conventions of the period style of the 1930s, aspects of the neometaphysical, neosymbolist, and New Critical esthetics then in vogue. Witty, ironic, and allusive, impersonal and hermetic, these poems provide verbal and intellectual enigmas that demand explication. Some exhibit deft mastery of difficult verse forms, and many are self-consciously concerned with art. But from the beginning Bishop interrogates the esthetic and epistemological assumptions of the work she imitates. She mistrusts the power of poetry and the rational mind to comprehend the world or to give it shape. Bishop seeks out works of art and other imaginative domains as places of secure and safe enclosure; she suspects them of being traps.

One sign of Bishop's distrust of art as a rational tool for discovering and expressing truth is her interest in surrealism, a style defined by its disruptions of conventional "reality" and its allegiance to alternative ways of knowing. At Vassar, Bishop kept a pot of Roquefort in her room, having heard that eating cheese at bedtime inspires exotic dreams. She lived in Paris in the mid thirties, when surrealism was a dominant force in literature and art. Her attraction to such surrealist constructions as Joseph Cornell's "Medici Slot Machine" encouraged her to make at least one "Cornell box" herself. And she translated poems by Max Jacob and by Mexican and South American practitioners of the surrealist-influenced style called magic realism. But as in almost everything else, in following surrealism Bishop swerved from the path. In place of more esoteric effects, she preferred "the always-more-successful surrealism of everyday life," what Robert Pinsky calls her "formula of the normal as the 'strangest thing there is.'" And Bishop never subscribed to the surrealist claim that the unconscious provides the way to transcendent knowledge of absolutes, to perfection and truth, a permanent paradise.[37] Bishop's surrealist details and techniques subvert rational confidence in works of art and other human arrangements, but they offer no alternative faith to guide her navigation of the spaces separating seeing, significance, and signification.

Works of art and other imaginative structures play a major role in Bishop's early writings. In "The Map," "The Imaginary Iceberg," and "The Monument," she explores the relationship of observation and meaning and examines the powers and limitations of human arrangements to know and domesticate the world. By definition, maps, like paintings or poems, are overdetermined objects.[38] They interpret what they represent, as Bishop thinks all human constructions must. But because maps are effective tools that enable navigation, we usually accept their consensual conventions without demur and ignore their status as willful artifacts. In "The Map," Bishop reactivates cartography's artificial dimension, exposing the gap between the actual and its abstract representation, or, rather, the gap between the actual and its interpretation masked as representational equivalence (no wonder maps have "legends"). Bishop lifts the mask. By conflating land and sea and art and nature, by exceeding the boundaries convention commands, and by stressing the arbitrary strain in any "conformation" (drawing borders, conclusions, or lines; assigning names or colors), Bishop reveals the distance between the world and the map. But her purpose is neither correction nor complaint. The "opening" between the map and what it re-presents permits the questions that produce the poem, and the poem stands in the same relationship to the map as the map to the sea and the land, a relationship that is both artificial and accurate, uneasy and elating.

Bishop's attitudes about such matters are expressed in several ways. Because she sees reality as neither a canonical text nor a blank slate, representation is neither determined nor utterly free. Every depiction of the world is a negotiation between description and interpretative invention. This permits creativity; it also demands critique. "The Map" begins with descriptive statements, as if secure in its own representational conventions: "Land lies in water; it is shadowed green." But "lies" and "shadowed" are dubious words, and by the second line of the poem more substantive doubts begin to appear. Self-interruption shifts assertion toward inquiry: "Shadows, or are they shallows. . . ." The word "or" invokes investigation, which confuses the relationship of the map to the world—and of the viewer to the map. Perhaps "Shadows," as effects of chiaroscuro, belong to the world of art, while "shallows" are topographic. But there are shadows in the world, and foreshortened (shallow) perspectives in the realm of art. Topography is not the world but writing on it. Maps lack shadows and shallows both, yet they use shadings to indicate relative depths. The words "Shadows" and "shallows" themselves are unlikely in being alike. In the wake of disruption, the speaker "sees" what a map can barely suggest: "sea-weeded ledges." Inquiry generates both freedom and distress.

Other aspects of "The Map" produce similar effects. The opening stanza rhymes in a regular pattern. Its form artfully and artificially imitates the structures of the map. Some rhymes indicate convincing resemblances ("edges" and "ledges"); others are overdetermined. Not rhymes at all in the usual sense, they subvert the identities their sonic echoes stress, matching "green" with "green" and "under" with "under." The poem shares with the map both effective and excessive strategies of representation. As certainty is unsettled, the observer is free to speculate. At the same time, a lack of certainty limits freedom's range.

The middle stanza of "The Map" (the third stanza matches the first) is unrhymed and has eleven lines where the others have eight. Conventions slip, and the speaker is freed for invention. The map comes alive in a nearly surreal plurality of possible conceptions: "We can stroke these lovely bays, / under a glass as if they were expected to blossom, / or as if to provide a clean cage for invisible fish." In a related passage, personification domesticates what is usually beyond our grasp: "These peninsulas take the water between thumb and finger / like women feeling for the smoothness of yard-goods." This is exciting ("excitement"), as though if we were freed from a false ideal of representational perfection the world could blossom in our hands, as though our naming and writing could expand beyond constraints, the way on a map "The names of seashore towns run out to sea, / the names of cities cross the neighboring mountains." But this imaginative exuberance is also dangerous, even mad, related to what occurs "when emotion too far exceeds its cause." Chastened, the third stanza reestablishes orderly conventions—and their overdetermined, self-rhyming excesses. Now when the imaginative eye sees the shape of Norway as a sprinting hare, "Norway's hare runs south in agitation." If we can project onto the map our human exuberance in imaginative adventure (crossing mountains; heading out to sea), or the "tamer" excitements of considering existing material as the stuff of further creations (handling cloth to prepare for making clothes), then we can also project our fears and desperations. As in "Filling Station," art has to do with all of those.

Questions return: "Are they assigned, or can the countries pick their colors?" This sets out the poem's terms. If the colors are "assigned," then the forms are preserved and boundaries are sure: agitation can be contained, but both imaginative freedom and domestic comforts will be curtailed. If choice is free, then constraints are removed and imagination and language have infinite range, although that can leave us disturbed and afraid as well as enraptured. Assigned or free, canonical text or empty page? There is this for answer: "Topography displays no favorites; North's as near as West." As orientation, this disorients. The poem's concluding line—"More delicate than the historians' are the map-makers' colors"—is often taken as Bishop's statement of preference. Supposedly she chooses a life and art of travel, a poetry that explores space instead of time, geography rather than people, sequence in lieu of cause and effect, and surface in place of significance; supposedly she yields interpretation in order to describe. Those apparent choices have been variously judged as weak retreats or models of modest restraint. But Bishop's conclusion is neither weak nor modest, and no more clear than the blurred border between description and interpretation.

The specificity and singularity of the poem's title, "The Map," is challenged by multiple constructions and responses as the poem proceeds; it gives way to plurals in the final line ("historians'"; "map-makers'"). There are as many chronicles as chroniclers, as many charts as there are cartographers to make them. The comparative mention of historians includes rather than excludes political and social considerations. Historians and map-makers are often interdependent. This map is political as well as topographical, and national boundaries and colors are another area where representation is both actual and overdetermined, where description and interpretation overlap but fail to "fit." The words "More delicate" mean more vulnerable, threatened, and precious, as well as more artful, precise, and fine; they suggest fragility as well as strength. Bishop's closing line has the ring of resolution, the syntax of assertion, but it is less an epigram than an enigma. The statement about the relative delicacy of historians' and map-makers' colors does not answer or even address the question of whether the "colors" (read "interpretations") are freely chosen or predetermined. Nor is it clear which alternative should be preferred, any more than it is apparent what the grounds of choice would be if choice were to be involved: "[C]an the countries pick their colors? / —What suits the character or the native waters best." Each stanza of "The Map" pivots on the word "or." Three more are embedded in its final line: in "More," "historians,'" and "colors." Mapped out, at the beginning, middle, and end, the sounds are there. By accident? Or were they picked, or perhaps assigned? Arbitrarily? Or by design?

"The Map" is Bishop's introduction to her work. It questions and values human arrangements, including works of art, as it explores their relations with the world, the relation of seeing to meaning and knowledge. Bishop typically negotiates the open space between the total certainty of absolutes, a deadly perfection, and the total freedom of utter relativity, a hopeless chaos. In some of her early poems, perfection's temptation is great. "The Imaginary Iceberg" describes the attractions of a massive, ideal, and self-contained system. This work of art (the iceberg is imaginary) claims to be "natural" (an iceberg). Supposedly, it can freeze time into stable perfection ("stock-still like cloudy rock"), align misshapen planetary paths ("correct elliptics in the sky"), and unify nature and art in oxymoronic paradox (the "artlessly rhetorical"). This seems the pinnacle of art, the goal of humanity's preference for powerful, ordering forms: "We'd rather have the iceberg than the ship." Bishop also counts the cost of such a choice.

"We'd rather have the iceberg than the ship, / although it meant the end of travel." And it does: the end of life. The iceberg's perfection kills. Yet our desire for possession is strong: "We'd rather have"; "we'd rather own." "This is a scene a sailor'd give his eyes for." He would, and then be blind to the scene he bought. Moreover, the iceberg's power is "imaginary" in an illusory sense, a kind of trick. A frieze of "cloudy rock" is likely to dissolve. Elliptics are accurate orbits. And "artlessly rhetorical" or not, the scene is stagy, as such theatrical terms as "treads the boards" and "curtain . . . ropes" reveal. The iceberg has crystalline beauty; like poems that are wholly self-contained, it "cuts its facets from within." But in this, it is divorced from life, "Like jewelry from a grave." As the iceberg's dangers and limits are exposed, "the ship steers off," heading south, "where waves give in to one another's waves," a place of intimate contact, of conflict and compromise, a more human and natural place where dissolving and forming clouds (and works of art as well) "run in a warmer sky."

Finally, if very reluctantly ("Icebergs behoove the soul"), Bishop rejects the model of art offered in "The Imaginary Iceberg." Its achievements come at the cost of life; its power to control change and to unify variety in a single, sacramental structure is destructive; its grandiose claims are pretentious and probably fraudulent as well. But Bishop does not reject art itself. "The Monument" describes a work conceived, executed, and responded to in radically different terms. Although based on wood rubbings by Max Ernst, the "monument" Bishop describes is anonymous. It refutes claims of authority in authorship and rejects romantic notions of the artist as redemptive culture hero. The object itself consists of boxlike structures stacked in a regular but uneven pattern, so that the corners of each "box" point to the sides of the slightly larger one beneath it: an awkward balance, a shape uneasily or not too assertively framed.

The monument is modest. It hints at significance but does not insist upon grand or singular meanings. Its materials are exposed for what they are: ordinary wood, not crystal. One decoration is "a sort of fleur-de-lys of weathered wood." This is appropriately flowerlike (with "petals") but also wooden ("petals of board"). It is "pierced with odd holes." There is no attempt to make the materials a transparent medium of representation (the same may be said of the poem, where the word "board" may lead to "bored," that is, "pierced"). Part of the monument depicts a seascape, but the sea is made "of narrow, horizontal boards." There is a "likeness," a version of the sea and sky with clouds and sun. But difference is insistently revealed. The wood that imitates the sea also looks "like floor-boards." The sky is coarse "palings." The sunlight is "splintery"; the clouds, "long-fibred." There is always a gap between the world and the wooden work.

To return to the fleur-de-lys, it is clumsy ("stiff"), and somehow impressive ("ecclesiastical"). The monument is evocative and suggests significant patterns of meaning: the systems of church ("ecclesiastical") and state ("flag-poles"). But those suggestions are in no way singular or insistent. The flag-poles might equally well be "fishing-poles," and the presence of "jig-saw work" and "vaguely whittled ornament" undercuts high seriousness. The work was done with ordinary tools in a way that reveals the processes by which it was made. This is far removed from the lofty, autonomous grandeur of the imaginary iceberg.

"The Monument" is a dialogue poem. One speaker is showing the construction to another, who complains of the lack of realism, "finish," and clear significance in the work ("'Why does that strange sea make no sound?'"; "'Where are we?'"; "'the sky looks wooden'"; "'It's like a stage-set; it is all so flat!'"; "'It's . . . outlined with shoddy fret-work, half-fallen off, / cracked and unpainted. It looks old.'"; "'What is that?'"; "'A temple of crates . . . , what can it prove?'"). The first speaker rarely responds directly, unless to say, "It is the monument." Instead, she continues to describe the work as it is, without judging it against some abstract standard of realism or elegant finish, or against the requirement that a work of art express impressive or eternal truths. Gradually, her calm attention reveals a counteresthetic. She admires the work for revealing the process of its creation, for being frankly an "artifact," as well as for accepting "the conditions of its existence," including the circumstance that time will wear it out. The homeliness of the monument gives it an intimacy grander works lack.

The speaker's attention to surfaces in describing the monument (its materials and shapes, its physical condition, its "perspective") implies a rejection of pretentious claims of esthetic significance. She refuses to give an authoritative interpretation. But the work does signify. Unlike the autonomous iceberg, however, it has multiple meanings that in part depend upon the viewer's participation in "creating" the work (it "might" "mark a tomb or boundary, or make / a melancholy or romantic scene"; "It may be solid, may be hollow"). Nonetheless, the monument is not without ambition; it reflects the desire to create an artifact that resists time: "Wood holds together better / than sea or cloud or sand could by itself." But it also reflects awareness that art's claims for permanence are a relative matter. Embedded in time, the monument accepts "all the conditions of its existence"; it, too, will suffer change: "the rain falls on it, . . . the wind blows into it." When the monument's meaning does emerge, it is no grand truth, no redemptive or all-explaining system. It expresses a human urge: "to cherish something," to "'commemorate.'" Its achievement is clumsy and small, but sufficient: "But roughly but adequately it can shelter." For that, it merits attention.

At the end of "The Monument" the esthetic implications of the object are expanded: "It is the beginning of a painting, / a piece of sculpture, or poem, or monument." "The Monument" is an ars poetica, a description of the sort of work Bishop admires and wants to create: writing that will cherish, commemorate, and shelter, but without making grandiose claims for eternal and redemptive truths that no one can know or express for certain. In the calmly uninsistent poems of the southern section of *North & South*, it is the poetry she writes. Bishop describes the world but confesses that her representation is artifice and interpretation. Her poems are at once transparent and opaque. They attempt to discover truth but acknowledge that what they "find" may be invented. Bishop's is a poetry of process; it exposes its materials and procedures and is always incomplete. It postulates possible meanings while revealing the limits of consciousness and art to know and to give shape.

In the second part of *North & South*, beginning with the poem "Florida," Bishop approaches her mature style (although the relatively direct use of personal materials from her childhood does not emerge until later). She writes quiet, metonymic poems of great descriptive precision, pressing her details for meaning with a tentative gentleness that is almost wholly uninsistent. This delicate probing for meaning is characteristic of a number of nature poems in which description is the occasion for epistemological and esthetic exploration, for considerations of how and how much we know and of the power of art to discover or create significance. Although Bishop has other subjects and interests (love, the lives of the poor, differences of gender, class, and culture), from this point on nature poems with epistemological and esthetic implications are central to her work. "Chemin de Fer" and "Large Bad Picture," the two northern poems written later than the others, can serve as transition. "Chemin de Fer" exposes the limitations of art and nature as sources of meaning. It inverts the pattern of such romantic poems as Wordsworth's "Resolution and Independence," in which apparent failures of society and nature to cure distress or despair can be corrected by the wisdom of one who lives in closer contact with the natural world.

An anguished speaker walks down railroad tracks. The iron consistency of the railroad's artful pattern is out of step with human needs and dimensions: "I walked with pounding heart. / The ties were too close together / or maybe too far apart." The natural world is an equally bad fit: "The scenery was impoverished: / scrub-pine . . . [a] little pond." Failed by culture and nature both, failed as well by love ("pounding heart"; too intimate or distant "ties"), the speaker seems near despair. A "dirty hermit" appears. Convention predicts a version of Wordsworth's leech-gatherer, a source of wisdom and consolation, able by his simple words to restore confidence in the self, in art, society, and nature. But the hermit "shot off his shot-gun," an unwelcoming gesture. Still, his salute might augur annunciation. Nature vibrates in response to the shot; the hermit exclaims. Perhaps he offers wisdom; the words sound right, although the instructions are vague and, for a recluse who may have been injured by love, rather strange: "'Love should be put into action,'" the hermit proclaims. Any hope that those are restorative words is undercut by several facts. Nature accompanies or "responds" to the hermit's pronouncement, but in ways more mechanical and indifferent than transcendental: "the tree by his cabin shook. / Over the pond went a ripple. / The pet hen went chook-chook." The hermit did not speak in fellowship; he "screamed" in resentment or grief. Nature attempts to support his words as affirmation, but it fails: "Across the pond an echo / tried and tried to confirm it." This is even worse than it sounds, since, as James Merrill points out, nature would echo "action" by saying "-tion," "shun," "shun."[39] "Shun" is a hermit's word, not a lover's; nature's response reverses the hermit's advice, and defines his life.

As a nearly impersonal depiction of intense distress in carefully managed quatrains, a semisurreal fable with a darkly comic "moral," "Chemin de Fer" reflects Bishop's earlier manner. Its focus on nature foreshadows things to come. "Large Bad Picture" is also in quatrains but moves closer to Bishop's characteristically uninsistent descriptive style. Now, conclusions are all implied; impersonal methods of presentation give way to modes of disclosure in which the poet is intimately involved—yet they remain remarkably objective sounding and precise. In "Large Bad Picture," nature is not observed directly, but, as so often in Bishop, is mediated by someone else's vision. Here, the mediating filter or frame is an amateurish landscape painting by Bishop's great-uncle (in this poem, Bishop's voice is still impersonal enough that she calls him "a" not "my" great-uncle; where we might expect "I," we get "One"). A pictorial cliché, the painting employs conventional perspective—cliffs recede /"for miles on either side"—in order to create a customary scene of pastoral stillness, simplicity, and peace. It's a clumsy job. For all its "realistic" conventions, the picture is vaguely generalized and stiffly artificial. The attempt to render water visible conceals what it wants to reveal, producing a bay "masked by perfect waves"—they look more like a "quiet floor" than the sea. On that floor "sits a fleet of small black ships." The picture is large and bad. Illusions of scale collapse; representational artifice fails: the spars of the supposedly safely harbored ships look "like burnt match-sticks," not rigging seen from afar. Similitude betrays, as in the too literal "fine black birds / hanging in *n*'s in banks."

Those observations expose the dangers of artistic incompetence, of course; they also give the lie to conventional notions of art as a consoling system of order. The painting's pastoral depiction is invaded by just the threats that pastoral wishes away: change, destruction, and death. The fretwork of arches under the cliffs suggests erosion as well as decoration or support. The ships seem disastrously burned; they "sit" on the "floor" of the sea as though they had been sunk. The birds are hung. The criticism of the painting and its conventions is harsh. However, as elsewhere in Bishop's work, the gap in representational art between opaque techniques and supposed transparency (the cliffs are "semi-translucent") is more than a matter for complaint. It permits examination of the sources and meanings of artistic versions of nature, of the ways in which what we see can seem to signify. The picture attempts to memorialize a moment out of time: the waves are still; with their "sails furled," the ships sit "motionless"; the birds are suspended in the air. However unconvincing the result may be, the painter's effort to render nature as a permanent and therefore comforting pattern eventually proves intense enough to involve the viewer in the work. Suddenly, even though (or because) the depicted birds are so weakly portrayed,

> One can hear their crying, crying,
> the only sound there is
> except for occasional sighing
> as a large aquatic animal breathes.

A picture that can make us *hear* the world it depicts has had some representational success—perhaps Bishop is recalling the northern seas of her childhood. The stanza suggests complicity between the poet and the kindred painter in "making up" a world. It is rich with other suggestions as well. The repetition of the word "crying," and the "bad" rhyme with "sighing," implies complicity of a different kind, a sharing of amateur technique (Bishop once told Lowell that she felt she had "written poetry more by *not* writing it than writing it"[40]—of course, Bishop is being deliberate, where perhaps her great-uncle was not). The words "crying" and "sighing" also indicate that the viewer suffers from (and projects) the very difficulties that the painter hopes to resolve. And they recall the limitations of his work again, since in the sequential repetition of "crying" and in the timeful word "occasional" sorrow and time (saying *et in Arcadia ego*) invade the painting's motionless pastoral perfection.

The next stanza returns to description; eventually, the poet ackowledges that the painter has achieved an uneasy balance between time and stasis. However clumsily, he has contrived to provide some solace. The sun in the painting rolls "round at the same height / in perpetual sunset, comprehensive, consoling." The last stanza confirms the artist's achievement. "Apparently," it says, the ships "have reached their destination." Of course, "Apparently" casts doubt. A "perpetual sunset" may have apocalyptic connotations. And the "destination" may be a harbor more fiery and final than security can stand. The painting may seem "consoling" only because it pretends to be "comprehensive." The closing lines reopen every question: "It would be hard to say what brought them there, / commerce or contemplation." "[H]ard to say" considers the limits of knowledge and speech. With its disruptive "or," the phrase "commerce or contemplation" contests the superficially similar phrase "comprehensive, consoling." It wonders about the goals of both shipping and art, the commodification of explorations and visions alike.

"Large Bad Picture" turns an apparently casual surface to contemplative and consoling ends. Bishop exposes the incompetence of her great-uncle's painting, and in the process she reveals the flaws in all human claims to know or to order nature, to discover or to create meaningful and redemptive visions of life. At the same time, by giving her full attention to the clumsily amateurish picture, Bishop comes to see that the technical limitations that undermine the painting also "save" it from the "professional" excesses of "The Imaginary Iceberg" and other grand inventions. She discovers in her relative's modest, conventional painting a heavily qualified yet affecting communal consolation—a consolation she replicates in her own tempered words. The pattern is typical of Bishop's finest work and appears in several of the southern poems of *North & South*.

"Jerónimo's House" is a dramatic monologue of sorts. A Cuban resident of Key West "naively" describes his "shelter from / the hurricane." He is sentimental and practical at once, and his portrayal of his house reveals the tenacity and tenuousness of human efforts to build domestic enclosures, structures to withstand life's storms. His house is a "fairy / palace," a "love-nest," as delicate and vulnerable as those terms suggest. Made "of perishable / clapboards," it is a "wasps' nest / of chewed-up paper / glued with spit." A hurricane would make quick work of it. Still, it is a nest; though fragile, it nurtures and protects.

Jerónimo's catalogue of his possessions is partly comic. He is house proud and describes his cabin as *endowed* with a "veranda" and *adorned* with ferns. The ornaments he contentedly lists are these: "left-over Christmas / decorations," "two palm-leaf fans/and a calendar," "four pink tissue- / paper roses," and "an old French horn / repainted with / aluminum paint." For furniture, there is a wicker table, "four blue chairs," a high chair for the baby, and a radio. For food, "one fried fish" with hot sauce and grits. For pleasure, flamenco music. And for hope, the lottery numbers. Not much by conventional standards of wealth, interior decorating, or personal ambition, not much to set against the storm. But this is beyond condescension. Jerónimo survives. He plays his horn "each year" in the parade for José

Martí and is a kind of artist. His speech is calmly self-possessed; he is pleased with his house but never boastful, secure but not smug. He is ready to move at a moment's notice; he travels light; he knows the hurricane is beyond control or resistance. In all of this, there is something of Bishop's own desire for an unpretentious "home," a place that would be a little safe—a rough but adequate shelter, not so imposing or secure as to be a burden, fraud, or threat.

In part, Jerónimo's house is a parable for what Bishop sees as the artist's proper work. Unlike some painters or writers, he makes no excessive claims, "tacking on a grand, if ill-fitting, 'moral.'" His house is no more able to withstand "the hurricane" than Bishop's great-uncle's painting is to suspend time or to provide safe harbor for ships. And Jerónimo knows it. He is ready to move when the hurricane comes, not if, and to make a new house of what he has left. Still, for now his house resists the outer dark: "At night you'd think / my house abandoned. / Come closer" and you'll see it is inhabited. The house is like a certain sort of writing; a surface so calm as to make anything more than description almost invisible, on closer inspection it reveals much human art. The comparison with writing is delicate but exact: at night there are "writing-paper / lines of light." What Bishop admires in Jerónimo is his insistent uninsistence, his humbly accurate pride, his sense of limited but valuable achievement in ordering his life, his acceptance that such achievements are provisional and have to be revised. Stuck together with spit, the nests of paper wasps are strong for a while.

Bishop is not always so tender in exploring the relation of surface to significance. "Florida" subverts the picture postcard image of the Sunshine State: "The state with the prettiest name, / the state that floats in brackish water." Those rapid shifts in tone, judgment, and scale are typical. The recuperative Florida of lush vegetation and exotic beauty is real enough, but Florida is equally a landscape of death, destruction, and decay. Mangrove roots bear "oysters in clusters" while living, but they "strew white swamps with skeletons" when dead. Beautifully colored shells (they are also homes of a kind) are abandoned and "fade." Buzzards circle and wait.

> Enormous turtles, helpless and mild,
> die and leave their barnacled shells on the beaches,
> and their large white skulls with round eye-sockets
> twice the size of a man's.

In one sense, this is the order of nature, cycles of life and death. But as those measured eye-sockets imply, it has human dimensions as well. And not all the deaths are natural. Hummocks are like cannon-balls, and the description of the wrack-line woven with shells as a "buried Indian Princess's skirt" recalls the murdered Seminoles. There are other racial and political implications in lines depicting Florida in moonlight: "the careless, corrupt state is all black specks / too far apart, and ugly whites." To some extent, this is ecological description, a neutral presentation of the way things are, with human predation and change (including the destruction of the Florida wilderness, and even genocide) as just one more thread in the fabric of life. Yet in the last lines that distant perspective dissolves. The entire state is depicted as the buried Indian Princess. The whimper in her throat gives agony a voice, whether the agony of native Americans, women, or the violated land, or of Bishop's anguished life. Here, description, however uninsistent, reaches significance in moral evaluation.

"Seascape" takes a nearly opposite tack; it exposes moral certitudes as epistemological frauds. As so often in Bishop, and as the title implies (since seascapes are inventions of the eye, of paint and pen), the poem works as a critique of representation and figuration. Bishop describes a Key West or other Florida scene as paradise; she rejects puritanical (northern) fears that beauty and pleasure are snares, a view asserted in the poem by a "clerical" lighthouse. The lighthouse minister is skeletal, and dresses as he thinks, in "black and white." His authority is mocked by the uncertain style in which his certitude is expressed. He "thinks he knows better" than to see this scene as paradise. He thinks the shallow water is warm because hell is beneath his feet. He "knows that heaven is not like this." It is all a matter of getting the similes right, but his comparisons are hopelessly imprecise.

> Heaven is not like flying or swimming,
> but has something to do with blackness and a strong glare
> and when it gets dark he will remember something
> strongly worded to say on the subject.

This ministerial "knowledge" is vague ("something") and abstractly removed from fact (the sun, not hell, warms shallow waters). A useless sequence of failed comparisons, it is fervently believed in nonetheless. The poem's countervoice makes heavenly metaphors. The seascape is "celestial," with "white herons got up as angels." Terms from religion congregate: "immaculate," "illumination," "Gothic arches." Eventually, the whole scene seems a "cartoon by Raphael for a tapestry for a Pope." This is more than metaphor can bear. But unlike the lighthouse Puritan, who is wholly unself-conscious about his similes and fails to see that his heaven is a projection of himself, Bishop also undoes the metaphors she makes. The herons are "got up" as angels; the "illumination in silver" is from "bird-droppings"; the "Gothic arches" are mangrove roots. The entire heavenly scene (like religion itself?) is spume, "an ornamental spray of spray." With its talking lighthouse, misplaced art, and "heavenly" clichés, the entire poem is a kind of elaborate joke. Still, there is something exalting in its inventions. The description ends in affirmation: "it does look like heaven." "Reduced" to simile, this claims unlikely likeness and is firm in a way the dour lighthouse can not dispel, even though it, or he, has the final word. The minister's comparisons collapse because they claim too much on insufficient grounds: he relies on tradition and authority; he is confused and wrong. The speaker's extreme comparisons collapse as well, but her metaphors are refreshingly playful and come to rest in a simile that holds. As in "Anaphora," ascent is replaced by "assent"; the result is lofty enough.

These nature poems are Bishop's poetry of earth. They reject the extremes of heaven and hell in favor of a present but historical world that permits the free play of creativity and pleasure but also requires the exercise of judgment and art. To say it again, Bishop's world is neither a canonical text nor a blank page, but a palimpsest. It is neither definitively and finally written nor totally open to any inscription; it bears the traces of its past. This frees the poet to write, but it also leaves her responsible to attend to and judge the inscriptions of others—to read, and then to repeat, erase, or revise. Over and over, Bishop's poems negotiate the space between prior authority and unbounded relativistic freedom, often in encounters with nature that also explore ways of knowing and ways of making art. "Roosters" is a meditation on such matters. The poem begins at four o'clock, when the immediately echoed and repeated "first crow of the first cock" awakens a sleeper.

Irritation mixes with knowledge of barnyards and cockfights to produce the poem's initial description. With their "cruel feet" and "stupid eyes," roosters are seen as militaristic, vainglorious, and sexist. Representing the human male, they are the sign of "traditional" masculine authority run wild. Their cries are "uncontrolled"; they use their "protruding chests" (feathered with medals) to "command and terrorize" the "many wives" that they have "courted and despised." As to themselves, they demonstrate their swollen virility by killing one another, their "raging heroism defying / even the sensation of dying." This is accurate in its awakened (feminist) anger, but it is also a diatribe. It is modified by other matters. Bishop recalls Greek views of roosters and, while despising warriors, provides one of them with a "funeral" of Homeric directness, expressing pity as well as scorn. Meanwhile, the mention of funeral rites evokes the ancient practice in which a dead king's or hero's wives are killed to be buried with him. This further revelation of phallocentric patterns recalls a rooster in another cultural context (also patriarchal), the Judeo-Christian one—by way of a contrast between Peter's spiritual sin in denying Christ and that of the Magdalen, "whose sin was of the flesh alone." The connection, of course (modulated by another antithesis based on gender), is that Peter's denial was verified by the crowing of a cock.

All the transitions in this remarkable poem are similarly subtle and firm.

"Roosters" develops from private and local beginnings through seemingly casual meanderings to become a comparative history of how different cultures—pagan, Christian, and post-Christian ones—transform natural facts into emblems of art. In Christian iconography, the rooster was eventually converted from a symbol of denial to one of forgiveness, a process the poem records. This conversion pivots on "inescapable hope." And one source of hope, although not perhaps for pagans or Christians, is that the meanings assigned to things can change. Roosters can bear many and inconsistent signs. Men might be other than bullies and brutes; women not merely despised as sinners or wives. The revelation that meaning is historical—arbitrary, relative, and alive (and therefore subject to revision)— frees us from fate, from life as predetermined plot or text. But Bishop's reluctance to generalize extends still further. The poem returns to the backyard where it began, to the day announced by the roosters' cries. In part, this cyclical maneuver suggests that nature is simply "there" and indifferent, that any system of meaning, whether damning or saving, is a human imposition, a matter of perspective. Asking "how could the night have come to grief," the poem undoes the conventional significance of dawn as rebirth. Meanings change as easily for the worse as they do for the better.

The last line of "Roosters" describes the rising sun. Like Peter following Christ "to see the end," it is "faithful as enemy, or friend." This insists that while the absence of definitive or canonical meanings frees us from oppressive systems of significance, it also implies that any alternative meaning we create is itself provisional and without authority. A world in which there are no sure signs by which to distinguish enemies from friends is free but dangerous. Especially in time of war. Among other things, "Roosters" is a war poem, written in Key West as the nation prepared for World War II. In 1943, Bishop wrote to Marianne Moore about wartime's "terrible *generalizing* of every emotion."[41] "Roosters" suggests ways of avoiding the murderous consequences of excessive generalization, including Bishop's own, though perhaps at the cost of any certitude.

The best-known poem from *North & South* is "The Fish." Like "Roosters," it attempts to imagine ways of describing nature that provide alternatives to traditional, masculine strategies of authoritative possession and domination, while still providing human satisfactions. Bishop catches a fish that does not fight, examines it, then lets it go. She knows it by analogies that domesticate without complete control, comparisons to wallpaper, flowers, feathers, isinglass. She sees the fish so clearly that it becomes transparent to her eye and she can conceive of its interior reality without recourse to the knife. But this seeing has its limits. When she looks into the fish's eyes its otherness prohibits comprehension. Neither glass nor mirror, its eyes prove nearly opaque. With that, Bishop returns to surface observations and descriptions, in similes that depict the fish as a wise survivor, with attributes that are *like* but not identical with human ones.

This informed shifting back and forth between the transparent and the opaque gives rise to a vision—the rainbow sign of covenant with all its religious and transcendental implications. But the source of this vision is no divine authority or benevolently encoded natural world. The "vision" is a "look," an oil spill in the bilge of a "rented boat." This subverts the blessing it depicts. It prevents the generalization that exaggerates or kills. Bishop's poetry exhibits the esthetic and epistemological "pleasure of deep gaze," the look that shapes and understands, but she avoids the "corresponding desire" to give the shape authority and to objectify or possess the things on which her gaze is turned.[42]

Bishop published three collections of poems after *North & South*: *A Cold Spring* (1955), *Questions of Travel* (1965), and *Geography III* (1976).[43] Each volume intensifies qualities already manifest in the Florida poems of her first book: "her apparent lack of insistence on meanings beyond the surface of the poem, the poem's seeming randomness and disintegration." The words "apparent" and "seeming" make a critical point. Bishop finds a release or reprieve from dominating systems in the facts of disintegration and randomness, but she does not simply yield to those forces. She also resists the provisional and indeterminate. She does so in ways that affirm as well as oppose their ineluctable power. This is an essential aspect of Bishop's work. In a comment on the travel poems, Bonnie Costello defines it: The problem of Bishop's poems is "how to present moments of rest and coalescence which nonetheless preserve the sense that our condition is inherently restless. Bishop's solution is to create places, objects, figures representing a unity around which we collect ourselves, but at the same time symbolizing our transience." Kalstone makes the same point in different terms when he says that Bishop's poetry raises "questions common to much poetry after Wallace Stevens: [H]ow is meaning developed from individual and unamplified details? How does the observer's apparent lack of insistence, devoid of rhetorical pressure, rise to significance (if, indeed, that is the word for it)?" The absence of "pressure toward a 'beyond'" combined with an interest in—a need—for patterns of meaning, those are the factors that frame Bishop's frame-breaking work.[44]

Some of the finest poems in Bishop's last three books are landscape or nature pieces. They explore the relationship of seeing to significance in the contexts just described, while also considering implications for making art and for knowing. Those poems are central to present concerns. But before discussing some representative examples, there are two other matters of development I want to mention. One is implied by Lynn Keller's assertion that the "content and technique of Bishop's later works establish reconciliation and mediation as the artist's most significant activities."[45] The other, especially notable in *Questions of Travel* and *Geography III*, is Bishop's increasingly personal treatment of the disruptions of her childhood, her acknowledgment of their persistent power over her, and her interrogation of the ability of memory and art to contest or transform that power. Those personal issues are intimately related to Bishop's epistemological and esthetic assumptions.

In an interview, Bishop spoke about childhood: "You are fearfully observant then. You notice all kinds of things, but there's no way of putting them all together."[46] This inability to put things together remains for Bishop a matter of suffering and strength. In one sense, the child's inability to organize the anomalous experience she perceives is saving. Had Bishop configured her childhood experiences of loss and displacement as a definitive system, she might not have survived. In the same way, freedom from the determining authority of a single system of knowledge or the modes of a largely male poetic past liberated Bishop to find her own ways to apprehend the world and to write about it. This is part of the point of "Roosters," where the fact that roosters can carry many and contradictory meanings helps prevent dejection. As Bishop said in response to a questionnaire, "the poet's concern is not consistency."[47]

Such notions condition Bishop's sense of the self and the world as constantly in flux. But if fluidity provides protection from excessive and ensnaring codes of meaning, it also terrifies. Bishop's early loss of both her parents, and her childhood experiences of illness and dislocation, confirmed in her a distrust of supposedly stable systems. It also confirmed a strenuous desire to discover or create such systems for herself. The obverse of Bishop's pleasure in the flexibility of things to bear multiple and contradictory meanings is her rigorous precision in the handling of facts themselves. She once wrote to Lowell to correct an error he had made about raccoons: "My passion for accuracy may strike you as old-maidish—but since we do float on an unknown sea I think we should examine the other floating things that come our way very carefully; who knows what might depend on it?"[48] For Bishop, the effort to know and render the literal with precision is a way to steady the self, to stay afloat. This does not mean that she trusts to observation, art, or knowledge as vessels of salvation; they are leaky boats. But she does believe they can help us to survive. Bishop commits herself to the most accurate observation she can sustain, while insisting that no knowledge or form is objective or authorized. She makes meaningful works of art that threaten whatever meanings they imply.

Several poems in *A Cold Spring* express Bishop's "distrust of human readings of nature."[49] In the title poem, the convention of spring as the season of love and rebirth—including the resurrection—is both nervously ex-emplified and challenged, as if the (sexual?) happiness the poet felt were too provisional to be trusted or wholeheartedly expressed. The spring was "cold"; the violet, "flawed." The trees "hesitated"; the leaves "waited." When the leaves did come, they showed as "a grave green dust." Death and winter (the lilac blossoms fell like snow) intrude on spring. In much the same way, other details in the poem refuse to treat natural beauty as tran-scendent or sublime. Bishop includes factual details usually ignored in trib-utes to nature (the cow eating her after-birth) and allows human invention to invade the natural scene (the patterned dogwood petals—often read as a Christian emblem—are described as "apparently" having been burned "by a cigarette-butt"). At one point, the mating flight of fireflies is compared with bubbles in champagne. The toast to love and spring is real enough; so is the refusal to trust to correspondences, whether between human beings or between human and natural or natural and spiritual realms. Bishop takes her epigraph from Hopkins. His discovery that "[n]othing is so beautiful as spring" led him to glorify his resurrected God. Bishop modifies her source.

"The Bight" addresses the issue of correspondences more directly still. Now the model to be revised is symbolist rather than Christian (Baudelaire is mentioned), but the effect is the same (as it also is in "Cape Breton," where the amended pattern is romantic). "The bight is littered with old correspondences"; as a transcendentalist might, the poet attempts to read them. But the "sheer" water is more opaque than transparent; the air is rich with decay; reading turns out to be an act of inscription. Still, resemblances abound. Pelicans are like dredges; shark tails are like ploughshares; the tails of man-of-war birds are like wishbones or scissors; the sponge boats are like retrievers. Retrievers fetch ducks; perhaps that connects them to wishbones and therefore to the chicken wire fence along the dock. This is comically domestic and overdetermined. There is even some pseudotranscendentalist play with the union of things and words: pelicans, which are named from the Greek word for hatchet, are said to "crash . . . like pickaxes."

Most of those analogies are strained or accidental, not sublime. Like the pelicans, the poet is fishing, and "rarely coming up with anything to show for it." This is both funny and sad. The analogies that once connected the material to the spiritual now seem forced. The "old correspondences" that litter the beach "like torn-open, unanswered letters" are "little white boats . . . stove in, / and not yet salvaged, if they ever will be, from the last bad storm." Still, Bishop isn't sunk. The pleasure of resemblances is a kind of salvage, however incomplete, however provisional or "stove in" by anomaly. That is the way it is: "All the untidy activity continues, / awful but cheerful." Part of that activity is human effort, the awful but cheerful at-tempt of the poet and other dredgers to give these shallow, superficial waters depth, to keep them open to navigation, at least until the next bad storm comes in.

Helen Vendler defines Bishop's work as representing "one of the attempts made in our era to write a poetry no longer dependent on religious or nationalist feeling—a poetry purely human, refusing even Keats's mythological resources."[50] "At the Fishhouses" recalls and amends the romantic and transcendentalist myth in which natural supernaturalism replaces the supernatural. On a cold evening, an old man mends his nets in a silver landscape that is exquisitely beautiful but also a place of conventional commerce and labor, where the smell of codfish is so strong that it makes the nose and eyes run. This compromised setting is portentous with an incipient and dubious visionary power that Bishop's description both conveys and resists: "All is silver: the heavy surface of the sea, / swelling slowly as if considering spilling over." This blends visionary potential with threat; it gives the sea consciousness and takes it away with "as if"; it suggests a swelling to significance that may be nothing more than an indifferent tidal swing. If the sea did spill over, it might destroy all the lovely human dimensions of the scene. Or perhaps it would consecrate them in a sort of natural blessing. As elsewhere in Bishop, we anticipate the transparency sought and found in transcendentalist lyrics; we encounter an "opaque" sea, an "apparent translucence" that does not reveal but reflects and conceals. Something is manifest in this, but it is not revelation. The iridescence of flies and herring scales provides the setting's brilliance.

Nonetheless, the scene of "At the Fishhouses" does have a mystical dimension; it comes in part from the bond between the landscape and tradition. Everything here is silver with age, rich with ancient and stable patterns of recurrence. The old man "was a friend" of Bishop's grandfather; he represents contact with a safer and happier place and time, and he connects the human and natural spheres by means of skillful and dignified work. But the contentment this implies is challenged by other matters. The word "was" (in the phrase "was a friend") recalls Bishop's grandfather's death and a range of related losses. The old man's "black old knife, / the blade of which is almost worn away" suggests the eroding of his remaining life. His "almost invisible" net also signifies his imminent disappearance—but it indicates as well the sort of unassuming but orderly and useful art that Bishop admires. The poem has many such double effects. Bishop gives the old man a Lucky Strike. This may imply good fortune, especially in the context of fishing, but it is also comically self-deflating. It is one of several strategies by which the poet restrains her desire to transform the events she describes into a familiar poetic pattern, a transcendent moment discovering comforting truth; another such strategy occurs a little further on, when Bishop sings Baptist hymns to a seal who, like herself, is "a believer in total immersion." Those details suggest and undermine the possibility of sacramental communication with human and natural elements in the scene.

Like Wordsworth and the leech-gatherer, Bishop and the old man converse: "We talk of the decline in the population / and of codfish and herring." There is more of the tears of things in this than any clearly reparative wisdom. We do not hear of the old man again. Still, a transitional section describes a ramp that gently crosses the rugged rocks dividing the land from the sea. The ramp is made of silvered tree trunks laid "at intervals of four or five feet" (they are measured, yes, but not too "perfectly"). The ramp combines with the old man's netting and scaling to imply harmonious, although not innocent, intersections of the human and natural (the trees had to be cut down; the herring are caught, killed, and scaled of their "principal beauty"). The passage prepares for revelation *and* suggests that any vision is humanly imposed on the natural scene. Perhaps fortified by her contact with the past and with orderly if dissolving human actions, Bishop turns her attention back to the sea, which she now describes as "Cold dark deep and absolutely clear." Such modulations from the opaque to the transparent often attend the visionary moment in religious, transcendentalist, or symbolist poems, the moment when the superficial reveals its hidden depths. Here, the sea that had been a "heavy surface," "silver" and "opaque," has become "deep and absolutely clear." The absence of commas indicates a unity of experience exceeding the categories of syntactical convention. It suggests another kind of unity as well. The sea is as "dark" as it is "clear." "Cold" and "deep," it threatens human attempts to stay afloat.

Frank Bidart has written that the "great triumph" of Bishop's descriptions "is the drama of perception lying beneath them and enacted by them, her sense of the cost as well as the pleasures of . . . observing."[51] In "At the Fishhouses," this drama has to do in part with Bishop's shifting of her attention back and forth between the ocean and the land, between efforts to describe the sea so as to generalize about its meaning and retreats to the more familiar shore where human relationships with nature occur with greater ease and leave their mark in recognizable and restorative patterns— especially in this place, where use seems largely to avoid abuse. Bishop's description of the sea as "Cold dark deep and absolutely clear" has qualifications in addition to those already noticed: the sea is an "element bearable to no mortal, / to fish and seals. . . ." Taken purely on its own terms, stripped of any of the systems of meaning by which humans modify the world to ensure their own survival, elemental nature simply kills. But Bishop is no more willing to rest in naturalistic abstraction than she is to affirm the transcendentalist faith that nature harbors absolute truths that it sometimes reveals. The ellipsis is hers. She breaks off both excessively hopeful and despairing conclusions as "ill-fitting" this scene.

Ellipsis is also Bishop's way of exposing the seams of her own poetic process. The word "seals" distracts her from generalization, recalling a particular seal who seemed curious about her and her singing. This apparent (and comic) digression reveals the arbitrary nature of artistic orders, and Bishop typically refuses to repair or conceal the rupture. At the same time, though, the story of the seal suggests an amusing and comforting contact between human and natural realms. It modifies the alienness of the sea; like her conversation with the net-mender and her description of the ramp, it prepares Bishop for another attempt to describe the "veritable" ocean. Reflecting patterns in the scene, her terms involve both repetition and difference: "Cold dark deep and absolutely clear, / the clear gray icy water. . . ." This time Bishop manages to name her subject ("water"), but again the sentence is suspended by ellipsis. Again, she turns her attention to the land behind her—now, to think of the "dignified tall firs." Either they or their shadows look like Christmas trees "waiting for Christmas." This, too, is both visionary and deflating: the ascendancy of miracle cut down by suggestions of commerce and exploitation.

Once more, though, the thought of compromised but comforting human patterns encourages Bishop to return to the more difficult subject of the sea. It, too, is waiting: "The water seems suspended." Nature reveals a comforting, cyclical pattern, a kind of eternal return; it is also wholly indifferent, a blank repetition: "I have seen it over and over, the same sea, the same, / slightly, indifferently swinging above the stones." This time Bishop does not retreat from the task of description—or interpretation, its certain companion. She does not turn back to the land and traditional patterns of meaning (family, net-mending, ramp building, hymn singing, Christmas). Still, she retains contact with the communal. Describing the otherness of the sea, Bishop addresses the reader as "you." This companionable pronoun allows her finally to confront the alien, elemental sea without an elliptical retreat; she names its aching and bitter cold. The sea embodies clarity, but it is a clarity we can never possess or know; it would burn the hand and tongue. Even so, the poet can write and speak. Bishop's acknowledgment of the sea as an order indifferent to our needs destroys transcendentalist comfort, but it evokes another in its place. Again, she describes the sea:

> It is like what we imagine knowledge to be:
> dark, salt, clear, moving, utterly free,
> drawn from the cold hard mouth
> of the world, derived from the rocky breasts
> forever, flowing and drawn, and since
> our knowledge is historical, flowing, and flown.

Nature does not provide the truth we seek, but it might provide a language for it: it can be made to seem to speak. Bishop's measured eloquence is ripe with communal conventions. It recalls religious and transcendental poems in which reconciling and mediating truths are discovered in a natural world originally inscribed by God. But it denies the analogy on which such discoveries are based. The sea is not an equivalent for knowledge; it is not even "like" knowledge. Rather, the sea is like what we *imagine* knowledge to be. What we know and say are patterns that we make; whether moderating ramps or "almost invisible" nets, works of art or religious rites, they are not discoveries, but inventions, impositions, and subject to decay. For Bishop, insofar as nature is an equivalent for knowledge, the only knowledge is death. However, precisely because not all knowledge is pre-scribed by an authoritative hand, there is room for temporary deviation, for reconciliations and mediations in the course of life. Nature is a source: a mouth, a breast, but also rocky and hard. We can draw nurturing moments from it, but because those moments are invented within time, they are "historical," not timeless absolutes to be discovered and held to forever. They are metonymies, "flowing, and flown." Utterly free, our systems of order dissolve as they come, but by letting them go we can try to restore them as well.

None of this comes "from" nature; nature is context, origin and end, and finally beyond us. But human contact with indifferent nature can be mediated by human constructions, nets or ramps, poems or hymns. Taken as absolute or permanent, those constructions become destructive illusions. Taken as provisional products of a human need that can never be fully satisfied, they offer the contingent and temporary contentments of community and convention. This may seem cold comfort, but in Bishop's work that phrase encompasses whatever consolation she can trust. Although our "knowledge" and our art is a shifting inscription on a surface that erases all we write, the shared human activity of attempting such inscriptions is our only source of what imperfect and dissolving comforts we have. The clarifying commas in the line "dark, salt, clear, moving, utterly free" indicate that what we have for knowledge are versions of the sea; the rituals of language can lend the world a momentary shape but never constrain or comprehend it. There is some warmth in this, and still more in the progression of pronouns the poem discloses. That progression confirms a human community in search of patterns, patterns that, in their absence, we invent, and that we retain by letting them dissolve. "At the Fishhouses" begins in impersonal description. Then, the "he" and "my" of the old man and the speaker emerge. When the two converse, "he" and "my" become "we." Later, Bishop's "I" and the reader's "you" converge in "our"—and then, along with everything else, that moment of collective self-possession is also "flowing, and flown."

In her third book, *Questions of Travel*, Bishop "found the blend of description and self-presentation" toward which her work had been tending.[52] Several poems in the volume treat epistemological and esthetic issues in the context of descriptions of nature. Among them is "The Armadillo," in which the human presumption that we have access to absolute realms beyond the surfaces of earth becomes a threat to the natural world. Others are "Twelfth Morning; or What You Will," "First Death in Nova Scotia," "Filling Station," "Sandpiper," and the three Brazilian poems that open the book. As Kalstone has noted, those three, "Arrival at Santos," "Brazil, January 1, 1502," and "Questions of Travel," are "poems of method."[53] In them, Bishop extends her ideas about the limitations and powers of knowledge and art so as to include issues of history and culture. "Brazil, January 1, 1502" is the major poem of the group, a self-disrupting anatomy of imperial invasions.

The poem's title records the date of the Portuguese discovery and naming of Rio de Janeiro, the river of January, which is not a river but a bay. The name stuck, nonetheless. Such gaps between things and our versions of them, whether houses, poems, or paintings, histories or religions, have been Bishop's subject since "The Map." Sometimes, the rupture between the world and our representations of it is a source of distress in her work, an indication of essential homelessness, since our domesticating patterns are not discovered but imposed and always vulnerable to dissolution and loss. At other times, it is a source of liberation from structures that are confiningly rigid: the absence of absolutes can free us for expansive, if uneasy, exploration. Most often, Bishop sees the "untidy activity" of trying to know and shape the world as "awful but cheerful"; a human necessity, it results at best in uninsistent, self-decreating forms that "roughly but adequately . . . can shelter." This is especially so when we accept the limited power of culture to comprehend the world, allowing that every act of apprehension involves some partial set of mediating filters that obscure and oppress as well as release and reveal. "Brazil" exposes what occurs when those framing filters are assumed to be absolute truths, equivalent to reality, and then are reified by power.

Confident that their cultural assumptions were divinely warranted facts, the sixteenth-century Portuguese explorers found the wild and alien landscape of Brazil "not unfamiliar." Conventional descriptions of the earthly paradise in both high and popular culture helped to motivate the European discovery and colonization of the "new world." And although the actual Brazil differed dramatically from those descriptions ("no lovers' walks, no bowers / no cherries to be picked, no lute music"), the explorers found it "corresponding nevertheless, / to an old dream of wealth and luxury." Correspondences *were* "found," and dreams came true; there were "cherries to be picked," and bowers of a kind. The explorers' confidence in their cultural superiority was fortified by their religion. This permitted them to treat both nature and indigenous people, especially women (whose voices sounded like the calls of birds) as objects for consumption. For women and nature both, rape was the explorers' means of possession. "Directly after Mass . . . they ripped away into the hanging fabric" of the jungle, "each out to catch" an Indian woman "for himself." When the domesticating patterns of art and culture are founded on a theory of representation that figures them as absolute rather than provisional orders, the result is imperialistic appropriation and destruction.

Bishop's poem extends such judgments into the present. The conceptions driving the Portuguese explorers were "already out of style when they left home," yet continued to exercise power. They still do. The first word of "Brazil" is "Januaries." The unusual plural, like the poem's implied grammatical structure ("'As then, so now'"), connects 1502 with 1959, when Bishop sent her poem to Lowell for New Year's Day.[54] Her own description of Brazil, although largely empirical, in the style of *her* time, is also caught up in the human tendency to see the world in terms of the inherited signifying filters of art and culture—a tendency implied by the poem's epigraph, from Sir Kenneth Clark's *Landscape into Art*: ". . . embroidered nature . . . tapestried landscape." Herself an "invader" of Brazil, Bishop also embroiders and inscribes the scene she sees. Nature is personified as female, birds are seen as "symbolic," vines are called scaling-ladders, and mating lizards are arranged in an allegorical tableau of "Sin." The explorers saw the jungle wall as a "hanging fabric"; Bishop, too, sees it as a kind of tapestry "just finished / and taken off the frame." Her esthetic appropriation is suggested by these words as well: "satin," "relief," "web," "arcs," "wheel," "profile," and "worked."

There is a difference, however, between Bishop's view and that of her predecessors. Bishop does not attempt to take possession of the scene. As in "The Fish," she employs a domestic and domesticating vocabulary to achieve a certain knowledge, admits a final opacity, and then lets go. She deliberately exposes the limits as well as the power of her strategies for apprehension. Rather than excising errors in her description, she incorporates them in the text: "like giant water lilies / up in the air—up, rather, in the leaves." She includes contradictions: "solid but airy." She uses the word "or" several times to indicate that her terms are but some among many possible ones. And she insists that the "tapestried landscape" she creates is not a matter of discovered identity but of provisional and invented likeness: the jungle is "fresh *as if* just finished / and taken off the frame" (emphasis added). Bishop rips the fabric of her poem, not the jungle. Those strategies challenge the imperialisms of the eye and I, of art or church or state, by admitting that the other evades our construction of it by "always retreating . . . behind" the screens we embroider to contain it. This chastens epistemological, esthetic, and other modes of power without surrendering the attempt to proceed from seeing to significance and signification.

Bishop's attack on cultural imperialism in "Brazil" is the culmination of such early work as "Cootchie," "Jerónimo's House," and "Faustina." Multicultural perspectives inform other poems in *Questions of Travel*, too: "Squatter's Children," "Manuelzinho," "The Riverman," and "Manners"—and such poems from *Geography III* as "In the Waiting Room" (the details from *National Geographic*) and "Crusoe in England," as well as "Santarém," published the year before Bishop died. They define the social and political implications of her pluralistic approach to the world, an approach that accepts the epistemological and esthetic limitations of human attempts to know and create. The possibilities as well as the limits of those attempts are the subject of nature poems in Bishop's final book.

Many poems in *Geography III* "revisit" Bishop's earlier work.[55] For instance, the reflexively titled "Poem" is about another painting by Bishop's great-uncle, the artist of "Large Bad Picture" (the family connections are made explicit here). In an early letter to Marianne Moore, Bishop wrote, "I remember in the 5th or 6th grade, in *précis* writing, the teacher confounded me by saying that there actually were people to whom a description 'of a forest' meant more than the 'forest' itself."[56] Confounded or not, Bishop often created her poems in the gap between description and the thing described, in the ruptures of representation. "Poem" describes a painting that depicts a place in Nova Scotia, Bishop's own Great Village. Like other artwork Bishop admires, the painting is unprofessional and uninsistent, a "little . . . sketch," "About the size of an old-style dollar bill." The mention of cash recalls the word "commerce" from "Large Bad Picture," but this picture "has never earned any money in its life." "Useless and free," "a minor family relic," its owners "looked at it sometimes, or didn't bother to." The term "relic" captures Bishop's tone: the picture is a bit of family junk and a little sacred as well.

Bishop's description is unsentimental (only in Nova Scotia "does one see gabled wooden houses / painted that awful shade of brown"). And she emphasizes the gap between reality and art. She does this in part by exposing the conventions of perspective and scale we adopt in viewing pictures: the cows are "tiny"; the geese, "miniscule." She also challenges the convention by which the materials of mimetic art are treated as transparent: the cows are "two brushstrokes each"; a wild iris is "white and yellow, / fresh-squiggled from the tube." Bishop raises further doubts as well: "that gray-blue wisp" is "a thin church steeple . . . or is it?" She even blurs the principle of museum conservation that assumes that accidental changes to the surface of a work are separate from the work itself: "A specklike bird is flying to the left. / Or is it a flyspeck looking like a bird?" The weird chiasmus of "fly," "speck," "like," and "bird" insists (as the title does) that words in poems are as arbitrary and opaque as paint. As Helen McNeil points out, Bishop always enjoyed the unconscious foregrounding of the art and nature breach in amateurish work.[57] Her own conscious attention to that breach places her poems at the intersection of modernist and post-modernist esthetics.

For all that she sees through and deflates the conventions of representation, here—as in other later work—Bishop is also concerned with the power of art to reconcile and mediate. She remembers the scene the painting depicts: "Heavens, I recognize the place . . . !" To recognize is to know again, and art and memory can conjoin to provide such knowledge, a way of holding on to things that are "flowing, and flown" away. There is solace in this. The painting was handed down through family generations and creates a sense of continuity especially important to Bishop, not least because the great-uncle she "never knew" was an artist whose "specialty" ("a half inch of blue sky / below the steel-gray storm clouds") is very like her own. The picture also restores a connection with place, the landscape of Bishop's early youth. "Heavens" is colloquial, of course, mere exclamation, but it also recalls that the village of Bishop's childhood once seemed a kind of paradise. Those connections are powerful, and "strange." They produce a vision, or "look," in which both art's power over time and art's chronic limits are expressed at once. Bishop says about the village in the painting, "it's still loved, / or its memory is (it must have changed a lot)." Time is real: "Those particular geese and cows / are naturally before my time"; the word "are" suggests how an artist's fiction might tentatively keep the past alive.

Art's power is partial, and, like everything else, art is subject to loss and time. Still, its restorative power consoles, though it cannot redeem:

> Life and the memory of it cramped,
> dim, on a piece of Bristol board,
> dim, but how live, how touching in detail
> —the little that we get for free,
> the little of our earthly trust. Not much.
> About the size of our abidance
> along with theirs: the munching cows,
> the iris, crisp and shivering, the water
> still standing from spring freshets,
> the yet-to-be-dismantled elms, the geese.

This is an affecting memorial, keeping memory nourished and refreshed ("the munching cows"; "spring freshets"), but a memorial is what it is, a memento of what has gone. The elms are dismantled now, the water dried up, our abidance shrinkingly small.

Other poems in *Geography III*, "Crusoe in England," "The End of March," and "The Moose," work in similar ways. In "The Moose," intimate contact with a familiar place, the sounds of generational and neighborly connection (recorded in the oft-repeated stories that are everybody's art), and the intersection of human and natural realms all weave together to create a vision of community and peace. That vision is lovingly conveyed, and deliberately displaced. The countryside described with such intense and observant affection is being left behind. The affirming "Yes" recalled from lullaby-like grandparental stories is "half groan, half acceptance"; it means "'Life's like that. / We know *it* (also death).'" The moose, which appears from "the impenetrable wood" like a miraculous manifestation, is described in some of Bishop's most charged and ambiguous language: it is female, "high as a church, / homely as a house / (or, safe as houses)." In Bishop's world, houses were rarely safe. The appearance of the moose gives "all" on the bus a "sweet / sensation of joy," but when the moment is over what is left is "a dim / smell of moose, an acrid / smell of gasoline." Like that duplicitous smell, this image also condenses Bishop's provisional sense of what communities of place, remembered knowledge, and the constructions of art can do: heading west, the bus goes over a bridge; "a loose plank rattles / but doesn't give way."

Posed (it is not quite "poised") at the boundary of seeing and significance, Elizabeth Bishop's work is a caustic decreation of human presumptions about the ability of knowledge or art to discover or create meaning, permanence, and truth. Bishop often suspects that every appearance of meaning is a fraudulent trick of language or light. In the early story "In Prison," the narrator says of the sunset: "I refer to that fifteen minutes or half an hour of heavy gold in which any object can be made to look magically significant."[58] But Bishop also examines the "material" world in order to discover how the secular visions or "looks" she calls the "spiritual" might be seen to proceed from it. She does so while insisting that consoling human visions are invented impositions, unauthorized projections of our needs, but also structures that preserve for a while what they cannot keep or redeem. Bishop's poems deny revelation; they also "keep it living in surmise."[59]

AFTERWORD

THE PRECEDING CHAPTERS indicate many changes and continuities in American poets' attitudes toward epistemology, esthetics, and nature in the years between the publication of Frost's first book in 1913 and the appearance of Bishop's last in 1976. A comparison of Frost's "The Most of It" and Bishop's "The Moose" might exemplify some of those developments. For instance, both poems turn to nature in order to recall and revise traditional means of discovering or inventing the transcendent, and in order to redefine the possibilities of poetry, but "The Moose" goes even further than "The Most of It" in modifying an oracular voice and stance. Bishop's poem is more personal, more formally "relaxed," and more obviously provisional. It also offers more in the way of comfort. Bishop's poem addresses issues of gender, especially when set beside "The Most of It." And its "international" dimension suggests limitations in the very notion of a specifically "American" art. All of those matters might be pertinent here. Nonetheless, and in place of any conclusion, I want to focus on an aspect of "The Moose" and "The Most of It" that shows the two as fundamentally alike.

Frost's cliff and lake are wholly other; the powerful buck he describes is dramatically inhuman, whether he comes in response to human cries or not. Bishop's landscape is more ordinary, almost domestic; the moose cow is a gentler, homelier creature. But Bishop's woods are as "impenetrable" as any in Frost; the moose is as "grand" and "otherworldly" as the buck, her appearance as "accidental." The point is this: however confident or doubtful about transcendence and art they may have been, American poets from Frost to Bishop—from Bradstreet to Bishop—have conceived of nature as "the wild province," a world utterly independent and apart, under whose vast and changeless rules human beings live and die as they always have.

Whatever its differences, all the poetry I have discussed is based on that conception. More recent American poets—John Ashbery, A. R. Ammons, and Robert Hass among them—continue to turn to nature to frame epistemological and esthetic questions arising from "mixed" attitudes toward transcendence as truth or illusion and toward nature as text or inscription. But I suspect that in their work there are hints of an unprecedented change. The notion of nature as an independent other wholly separate from the human sphere may itself be dead or dying. This is not simply a matter of noticing that appropriations of nature can "redeem" or destroy some part of the natural world—all American nature poets have been aware of that. Something else is in the air. Bill McKibben suggests in *The End of Nature* that the very conception of nature as inhuman, inexhaustible, and independent soon may disappear; large-scale climatic changes brought on by human actions may make what we now call nature seem just one more human invention, another evasion of as. Whether we experience that development as a further freedom or as the ultimate loss, perhaps the weather itself will seem but another unwarranted inscription on a world we once believed had been given us to read.

NOTES

CHAPTER ONE: EVASIONS OF AS

1. Wallace Stevens, *The Collected Poems* (New York: Knopf, 1954) 486.

2. Hyatt H. Waggoner, *American Poets from the Puritans to the Present* (Boston: Houghton Mifflin, 1968) xvii.

3. Robert Daly, *God's Altar: The World and the Flesh in Puritan Poetry* (Berkeley: University of California Press, 1978); Mason I. Lowance, Jr., "Religion in Puritan Poetry: The Doctrine of Accommodation," *Puritan Poets and Poetics: Seventeenth-Century American Poetry in Theory and Practice*, ed. Peter White (University Park: Pennsylvania State University Press, 1985) 33–46; Mason I. Lowance, Jr., *The Language of Canaan: Metaphor and Symbol in New England from the Puritans to the Transcendentalists* (Cambridge: Harvard University Press, 1980); and Michael Clark, "The Honeyed Knot of Puritan Aesthetics," *Puritan Poets and Poetics* 67–83.

4. Daly, *God's Altar* 1–81.

5. Charles Feidelson, Jr., *Symbolism and American Literature* (Chicago: University of Chicago Press, 1953) 77–78, 77–92.

6. All lines are from Anne Bradstreet, "Contemplations," *Poems of Anne Bradstreet*, ed. Robert Hutchinson (New York: Dover, 1969) 79–87.

7. For a detailed discussion of this issue, see Thomas M. Davis, "The Traditions of Puritan Typology," *Typology and Early American Literature*, ed. Sacvan Bercovitch (Amherst: University of Massachusetts Press, 1972) 11–45.

8. The importance of typology to Puritan practice and to the development of American consciousness has been much discussed. See especially Lowance's *The Language of Canaan* and Bercovitch's *Typology and Early American Literature* and *The Puritan Origins of the American Self* (New Haven: Yale University Press, 1975).

9. This remarkable figure is noted by Donald E. Stanford, "Edward Taylor," *Major Writers of Early American Literature*, ed. Everett Emerson (Madison: University of Wisconsin Press, 1972) 68. The poem is in *The Poems of Edward Taylor*, ed. Donald E. Stanford, 2d ed. (New Haven: Yale University Press, 1963) 14–15.

10. Donald E. Stanford, "Introduction," *The Poems of Edward Taylor* xxvii.

11. *The Poems of Edward Taylor* 340–41.

12. Karl Keller, "'The World Slickt Up in Types': Edward Taylor as a Version of Emerson," *Typology and Early American Literature* 175, 183, 190.

13. Lawrence Buell, *New England Literary Culture: From Revolution through Renaissance* (Cambridge: Cambridge University Press, 1986) 193.

14. Perry Miller, "From Edwards to Emerson," *Errand into the Wilderness* (Cambridge: Harvard University Press, 1956) 184–204; Feidelson, *Symbolism and American Literature*. See also Lowance, *The Language of Canaan* and Bercovitch, *Typology and Early American Literature* and *The Puritan Origins of the American Self*.

15. Perry Miller, "The Marrow of Puritan Divinity," *Errand into the Wilderness* 48–98.

16. David Lawrence, "Jonathan Edwards as a Figure in Literary History," *Jonathan Edwards and the American Experience*, ed. Nathan O. Hatch and Harry S. Stout (New York: Oxford University Press, 1988) 244.

17. Buell, *New England Literary Culture* 40.

18. Mason I. Lowance, Jr., "'Images or Shadows of Divine Things' in the Thought of Jonathan Edwards," *Typology and Early American Literature* 210.

19. Perry Miller, "Introduction," *Images or Shadows of Divine Things*, by Jonathan Edwards (New Haven: Yale University Press, 1948) 1–41.

20. Lowance, *The Language of Canaan* 249–76. Quotations are from 252–53 and 258.

21. Lowance, *The Language of Canaan* 260–61, 275.

22. Perry Miller, "The Rhetoric of Sensation," *Errand into the Wilderness* 167–83.

23. James Turner, *Without God, Without Creed: The Origin of Unbelief in America* (Baltimore: Johns Hopkins University Press, 1985).

24. Miller, "Edwards to Emerson" 184–204. Quotations are from 185, 191, 195, and 195–96.

25. Lowance, *The Language of Canaan* 274.

26. Feidelson, *Symbolism and American Literature* 50–52.

27. M. H. Abrams, *Natural Supernaturalism: Tradition and Revolution in Romantic Literature* (New York: Norton, 1971) 12–52.

28. *Emerson in His Journals*, ed. Joel Porte (Cambridge: Harvard University Press, 1982) 190. (Entry for June 21, 1838.)

29. The standard work on these issues is Marjorie Hope Nicolson, *Mountain Gloom and Mountain Glory: The Development of the Aesthetics of the Infinite* (Ithaca: Cornell University Press, 1959). Abrams provides a summary in *Natural Supernaturalism* 98–102.

30. Ralph Waldo Emerson, *Nature*, A Facsimile of the First Edition; With an Introduction by Jaroslav Pelikan (Boston: Beacon, 1985) 20. All further citations of *Nature* (with one exception) are from this edition and are indicated by page numbers in the text.

31. Barbara Novak, *Nature and Culture: American Landscape and Painting, 1825–1875* (New York: Oxford University Press, 1980) 196.

32. Waggoner, *American Poets* 100.

33. Waggoner, *American Poets* 131.

34. Quoted in F. O. Matthiessen, *American Renaissance: Art and Experience in the Age of Emerson and Whitman* (New York: Oxford University Press, 1941) 9.

35. *Emerson's "Nature"—Origin, Growth, Meaning*, ed. Merton M. Sealts, Jr., and Alfred R. Ferguson (New York: Dodd, Mead, 1969) 15. (The first edition, and thus the facsimile, has errors in this passage.)

36. *The Complete Works of Ralph Waldo Emerson*, ed. Edward Waldo Emerson, The Centenary Edition, 14 vols. (Boston: Houghton Mifflin, 1903–4) 9:228.

37. Matthiessen, *American Renaissance* 63–64.

38. *The Complete Works of Ralph Waldo Emerson* 4:18.

39. Quoted in Matthiessen, *American Renaissance* 63.

40. Quoted in F. O. Matthiessen, *The James Family* (New York: Knopf, 1947) 43.

41. Quoted in Matthiessen, *American Renaissance* 3.

42. See Buell, *New England Literary Culture* 182–85.

43. Matthiessen, *American Renaissance* 52–53, 41.

44. Quoted in Roy Harvey Pearce, *The Continuity of American Poetry* (Princeton: Princeton University Press, 1961) 430.

45. Waggoner, *American Poets* 102. Significant expansions of this argument appear in Mutlu Konuk Blasing, *American Poetry: The Rhetoric of Its Forms* (New Haven: Yale University Press, 1987) 67–83, and in R. A. Yoder, *Emerson and the Orphic Poet in America* (Berkeley: University of California Press, 1978).

46. The best discussion is in Blasing, *American Poetry* 67–83.

47. For an efficient summary, see Buell, *New England Literary Culture* 74, 420n47.

48. David Van Leer, *Emerson's Epistemology: The Argument of the Essays* (Cambridge: Cambridge University Press, 1986).

49. Yoder, *Emerson and the Orphic Poet* xiv, 169, 204, 205.

50. Alicia Suskin Ostriker, *Stealing the Language: The Emergence of Women's Poetry in America* (Boston: Beacon, 1986) 3.

51. Blasing, *American Poetry* 1–2.

52. Feidelson, *Symbolism and American Literature* 158.

53. These issues are discussed in Naomi Schor, *Reading in Detail: Aesthetics and the Feminine* (New York: Methuen, 1987).

54. Novak, *Nature and Culture* 76, 125, 54, 62.

55. The formulation is Cynthia Griffin Wolff's. This section is indebted to her *Emily Dickinson* (New York: Knopf, 1987).

56. Wolff, *Emily Dickinson* 192–93.

57. Edward Hitchcock, *Religious Lectures on Peculiar Phenomena in the Four Seasons* (Amherst, 1850) 100, 112.

58. *The Complete Poems of Emily Dickinson*, ed. Thomas H. Johnson (Boston: Little, Brown, 1960) #185. Subsequent references are to this edition and are indicated by "Johnson numbers" in the text.

59. Wolff, *Emily Dickinson* 193.

60. Blasing, *American Poetry* 9.

61. Buell, *New England Literary Culture* 114.

62. Buell, *New England Literary Culture* 70.

63. Buell, *New England Literary Culture* 128–29; see also 105–36. I am indebted to Buell's reading of this poem, and to his discussion of nineteenth-century New England poetry, the best summary available.

64. Buell, *New England Literary Culture* 161; see also Wolff, *Emily Dickinson* 560–61n22.

65. See Wolff, *Emily Dickinson* 451–91. Quotations are from 476, 477, 482, and 457.

66. Leo Marx, *The Machine in the Garden: Technology and the Pastoral Ideal in America* (New York: Oxford University Press, 1964) 35–44. Quotations are from 42–43 and 43.

67. Roderick Nash, *Wilderness and the American Mind*, rev. ed. (New Haven: Yale University Press, 1973).

68. Henry Nash Smith, *Virgin Land: The American West as Symbol and Myth* (Cambridge: Harvard University Press, 1950) 55.

69. Marx, *Machine in the Garden* 141–226.

70. The phrase is apparently Miller's. It appears in "Nature and the National Ego," *Errand into the Wilderness* 209, and was borrowed as the title for the posthumous *Nature's Nation*.

71. Novak, *Nature and Culture* 20.

72. Smith, *Virgin Land* 52.

73. Novak, *Nature and Culture* 38.

74. Miller, "Nature and the National Ego" 206–8.

75. R. W. B. Lewis, *The American Adam: Innocence, Tragedy, and Tradition in the Nineteenth Century* (Chicago: University of Chicago Press, 1955) 1–7.

76. Marx, *Machine in the Garden* 141–249, 342–45, 353. Quotations are from 343 and 344–45.

77. Bernard Rosenthal, *City of Nature: Journeys to Nature in the Age of American Romanticism* (Newark: University of Delaware Press, 1980) 15–26, 98–99, 120–24.

78. Buell, *New England Literary Culture* 71–82, 101–2, 115–16, 132–34, 162.

79. Wolff, *Emily Dickinson* 174.

80. David Perkins, *A History of Modern Poetry: From the 1890s to the High Modernist Mode* (Cambridge: Harvard University Press, 1976) 84–99. Quotations are from 96, 102, 95.

CHAPTER TWO: ROBERT FROST

This chapter is especially indebted to works by Frank Lentricchia, Richard Poirier, and John Lynen, cited below, and to a series of essays by Darrel Abel ("Emerson's 'Apparition of God' and Frost's 'Apparition of Mind,'" *University of Toronto Quarterly* 68 [1978]:41–52; "Two Philosophical Poets: Frost, Emerson, and Pragmatism," *ESQ* 25 [1979]:119–36; "The Instinct of a Bard: Robert Frost on Science, Logic, and Poetic Truth," *Essays in Arts and Sciences* 9 [1980]:59–75; and "Robert Frost's 'Second-Highest Heaven,'" *Colby Library Quarterly* 16 [1980]:78–90).

1. Betty Flanders Thomson, *The Changing Face of New England* (Boston: Houghton Mifflin, 1958) 22–26.

2. Albert Gelpi, *A Coherent Splendor: The American Poetic Renaissance, 1910–1950* (Cambridge: Cambridge University Press, 1987) 31, 24.

3. William Pritchard, *Frost: A Literary Life Reconsidered* (New York: Oxford University Press, 1984) 97.

4. Frank Lentricchia, *Robert Frost: Modern Poetics and the Landscapes of Self* (Durham: Duke University Press, 1975) xii.

5. Edward Connery Lathem, ed., *Interviews with Robert Frost* (New York: Holt, Rinehart and Winston, 1966) 64.

6. Robert Frost, *Selected Prose of Robert Frost*, ed. Hyde Cox and Edward Connery Lathem (New York: Holt, Rinehart and Winston, 1966) 106–7.

7. *Selected Prose* 18.

8. *Selected Prose* 107.

9. Robert Frost, *Selected Letters of Robert Frost*, ed. Lawrance Thompson (New York: Holt, Rinehart and Winston, 1964) 98; Lathem, *Interviews* 242; *Selected Letters* 343; *Selected Letters* 482; William R. Evans, ed., *Robert Frost and Sidney Cox: Forty Years of Friendship* (Hanover, N.H.: University Press of New England, 1981) 224; Reginald Cook, *Robert Frost: A Living Voice* (Amherst: University of Massachusetts Press, 1974) 59.

10. *Selected Prose* 28; *Selected Prose* 116; Lathem, *Interviews* 64; Louis Untermeyer, *The Letters of Robert Frost to Louis Untermeyer* (New York: Holt, Rinehart and Winston, 1963) 47; *Selected Letters* 503.

11. *Selected Prose* 18, 20; *Selected Prose* 71; *Selected Prose* 97; Lathem, *Interviews* 283.

12. Richard Poirier, *Robert Frost: The Work of Knowing* (New York: Oxford University Press, 1977) xvi.

13. Lisa Steinman, *Made in America: Science, Technology, and American Modernist Poets* (New Haven: Yale University Press, 1987).

14. *Selected Prose* 105–6.

15. Cf. Albert J. Von Frank, "'Nothing That Is': A Study of Frost's 'Desert Places,'" *Frost: Centennial Essays*, vol. 1, ed. Committee on the Frost Centennial of the University of Southern Mississippi (Jackson: University Press of Mississippi, 1974) 129.

16. *Selected Prose* 24.

17. *Selected Prose* 37. (Further quotations from this essay are cited by parenthetical page references in the text.)

18. *Selected Prose* 24.

19. *Selected Letters* 466.

20. Untermeyer, *Letters* 285.

21. Untermeyer, *Letters* 285.

22. Cf. my "Comparing Conceptions: Frost and Eddington, Heisenberg, and Bohr," *American Literature* 59 (1987):167–89.

23. "Glossary," *Niels Bohr: A Centenary Volume*, ed. A. P. French and P. J. Kennedy (Cambridge: Harvard University Press, 1985) 371–72.

24. Cf. Max Jammer, *The Conceptual Development of Quantum Mechanics* (New

York: McGraw-Hill, 1966) 176n88 and 177–79, and R. V. Jones, "Complementarity as a Way of Life," *Niels Bohr: A Centenary Volume* 320.

25. Jones, "Complementarity" 320.

26. Untermeyer, *Letters* 47.

27. Lawrance Thompson, *Robert Frost: The Years of Triumph, 1915–1938* (New York: Holt, Rinehart and Winston, 1970) 290.

28. Aage Petersen, "The Philosophy of Niels Bohr," *Niels Bohr: A Centenary Volume* 301; Petersen, "Niels Bohr" 305; Petersen, "Niels Bohr" 301–3.

29. Ruth Moore, *Niels Bohr: The Man, His Science, and the World They Changed* (New York: Knopf, 1966) 127.

30. *The Writings of William James*, ed. John J. McDermott (New York: Modern Library, 1968) 489, 108.

31. Louis Mertins, *Robert Frost: Life and Talks-Walking* (Norman: University of Oklahoma Press, 1965) 287.

32. Untermeyer, *Letters* 34; Thompson, *The Years of Triumph* 414; *Selected Prose* 112; Untermeyer, *Letters* 58; Lathem, *Interviews* 108, 120; Cook, *Robert Frost* 13; *Selected Prose* 76.

33. Untermeyer, *Letters* 378; Lathem, *Interviews* 185; Lawrance Thompson and R. H. Winnick, *Robert Frost: The Later Years, 1938–1963* (New York: Holt, Rinehart and Winston, 1976) 150.

34. Cf. Linda Hutcheon, *A Poetics of Postmodernism: History, Theory, Fiction* (New York: Routledge, 1988).

35. Robert Langbaum, "Hardy, Frost, and the Question of Modernist Poetry," *Virginia Quarterly Review* 58 (1982):72.

36. *Selected Letters* 441.

37. *Selected Prose* 96.

38. *Selected Letters* 344.

39. Untermeyer, *Letters* 47.

40. Poirier, *Robert Frost* x.

41. Poirier, *Robert Frost* 136.

42. Lathem, *Interviews* 114.

43. Reuben Brower, *The Poetry of Robert Frost: Constellations of Intention* (New York: Oxford University Press, 1963) 242.

44. Lentricchia, *Robert Frost* 38.

45. Lentricchia, *Robert Frost* 123–31, 129.

46. Paul de Man, *Allegories of Reading* (New Haven: Yale University Press, 1979) 63n.

47. *Selected Prose* 25.

48. All quotations from Frost's poems are from *The Poetry of Robert Frost*, ed. Edward Connery Lathem (New York: Holt, Rinehart and Winston, 1969).

49. Poirier, *Robert Frost* 82.

50. Poirier, *Robert Frost* 15, xvi. (Poirier quotes the James passage; Fuller's memoir is in *Our Harvard*, ed. Jeffrey L. Lant [New York: Taplinger, 1982] 21–22.)

51. David Perkins, *A History of Modern Poetry: From the 1890s to the High Modernist Mode* (Cambridge: Harvard University Press, 1976) 244–46.

52. Anthony Hecht, "The Pathetic Fallacy," *Obbligati: Essays in Criticism* (New York: Atheneum, 1986) 21.

53. Lawrence Buell, *New England Literary Culture: From Revolution through Renaissance* (Cambridge: Cambridge University Press, 1986) 134.

54. "On Extravagance: A Talk," *Robert Frost: Poetry and Prose*, ed. Edward Connery Lathem and Lawrance Thompson (New York: Holt, Rinehart and Winston, 1972) 458.

55. *Selected Prose* 24.

56. Poirier, *Robert Frost* 174.

57. Cf. my "Metaphor in Frost's 'The Oven Bird,'" *Robert Frost: The Man and the Poet*, ed. Earl. J. Wilcox (Rock Hill, S. C.: Winthrop Studies on Major Modern Writers, 1981) 19–30.

58. Pritchard, *Frost: A Literary Life* 206ff.

59. Poirier, *Robert Frost* 252.

60. Harold Bloom, "Introduction," *Robert Frost*, Modern Critical Views (New York: Chelsea House, 1986) 5, 6.

61. Robert Pinsky, *The Situation of Poetry: Contemporary Poetry and Its Traditions* (Princeton: Princeton University Press, 1976) 67.

62. Cf. John F. Lynen, "Du Côté de Chez Frost," *Frost: Centennial Essays* 562–94.

63. Lawrance Thompson, *Robert Frost: The Early Years, 1874–1915* (New York: Holt, Rinehart and Winston, 1966) 550.

64. Poirier, *Robert Frost* 284–85.

CHAPTER THREE: WALLACE STEVENS

This chapter is especially indebted to works by Helen Vendler, Harold Bloom, George Lensing, Milton Bates, and Samuel French Morse, cited below, and to the Stevens chapter in Albert Gelpi's *A Coherent Splendor: The American Poetic Renaissance, 1910–1950* (Cambridge: Cambridge University Press, 1987), 49–90.

1. *Letters of Wallace Stevens*, ed. Holly Stevens (New York: Knopf, 1966) 247.

2. *Letters* 22.

3. Harold Bloom, *Wallace Stevens: The Poems of Our Climate* (Ithaca: Cornell University Press, 1977) 23.

4. Quoted in Holly Stevens, *Souvenirs and Prophecies: The Young Wallace Stevens* (New York: Knopf, 1977) 53–54, 54, 104.

5. George S. Lensing, *Wallace Stevens: A Poet's Growth* (Baton Rouge: Louisiana State University Press, 1986) 26. Lensing provides an extensive discussion of Stevens's religious and intellectual development.

6. The marking is mentioned in Lensing, *Wallace Stevens* 26.

7. *Letters* 50.

8. *Letters* 58–59.

9. *Letters* 96.

10. *Letters* 86.

11. *Letters* 348.

12. *Letters* 142.

13. *Letters* 29.

14. Quoted in H. Stevens, *Souvenirs and Prophecies* 215.

15. Bloom, *Wallace Stevens* 28.

16. Helen Vendler, *Wallace Stevens: Words Chosen Out of Desire* (Knoxville: University of Tennessee Press, 1984) 62.

17. Milton J. Bates, *Wallace Stevens: A Mythology of Self* (Berkeley: University of California Press, 1985) 111.

18. *Letters* 533.

19. *Letters* 289.

20. Wallace Stevens, *Opus Posthumous*, ed. Samuel French Morse (New York: Knopf, 1957) 170; *Letters* 294.

21. Denis Donoghue, "Nuances of a Theme by Stevens," *The Act of the Mind: Essays on the Poetry of Wallace Stevens*, ed. Roy Harvey Pearce and J. Hillis Miller (Baltimore: Johns Hopkins University Press, 1965) 227–29; Donoghue, "The Snow Man," *New York Review of Books* 3 Mar. 1977:22.

22. *Letters* 300, 293.

23. *Letters* 87.

24. Wallace Stevens, *The Necessary Angel: Essays on Reality and the Imagination* (New York: Knopf, 1951) 25; *Letters* 368.

25. All quotations from Stevens's poems are from *The Collected Poems of Wallace Stevens* (New York: Knopf, 1964) unless otherwise noted in the text.

26. Lisa M. Steinman, *Made in America: Science, Technology, and American Modernist Poets* (New Haven: Yale University Press, 1987) 138.

27. *Letters* 302; *Opus Posthumous* 267 (264 in the 1982 Vintage Books edition, which was repaginated when "On Poetic Truth," erroneously attributed to Stevens in the original edition, was removed).

28. *Letters* 820.

29. *Letters* 710, 864; *Opus Posthumous* 173.

30. Helen Hennessy Vendler, *On Extended Wings: Wallace Stevens' Longer Poems* (Cambridge: Harvard University Press, 1969) 21.

31. *Opus Posthumous* 167, 170.

32. *The Necessary Angel* 61, 72.

33. *The Necessary Angel* 72, 73.

34. Susan B. Weston, *Wallace Stevens: An Introduction to the Poetry* (New York: Columbia University Press, 1977) 141.

35. *Letters* 402.

36. *Letters* 369.

37. *The Necessary Angel* 165.

38. *Letters* 300.

39. *Letters* 370.

40. *Opus Posthumous* 163.

41. *Letters* 430.

42. The matter is discussed in Bates, *Wallace Stevens* 201–2.

43. *The Necessary Angel* 32.

44. *Opus Posthumous* 167.

45. *Letters* 402.

46. *Opus Posthumous* 162.

47. *The Necessary Angel* 35–36.

48. *Letters* 367.

49. Vendler, *Wallace Stevens* 29, 40–41.

50. *Letters* 444.

51. *Letters* 80.

52. Samuel French Morse, *Wallace Stevens: Poetry as Life* (New York: Pegasus, 1970) 92.

53. Quoted in H. Stevens, *Souvenirs and Prophecies* 177.

54. Quoted in H. Stevens, *Souvenirs and Prophecies* 166.

55. *The Necessary Angel* 27.

56. *The Necessary Angel* 29; *Letters* 402.

57. *Letters* 277.

58. Cf. Weston, *Wallace Stevens* 65–66. Especially interesting in this regard is Frank Lentricchia's discussion of Stevens from a revised feminist perspective in *Ariel and the Police: Michel Foucault, William James, Wallace Stevens* (Madison: University of Wisconsin Press, 1988).

59. Bloom, *Wallace Stevens* 104.

60. *The Necessary Angel* 40.

61. Vendler, *On Extended Wings* 13.

62. *The Necessary Angel* 58.

63. Vendler, *On Extended Wings* 13–37.

64. J. Hillis Miller, "Wallace Stevens' Poetry of Being," *The Act of the Mind* 151.

65. Weston, *Wallace Stevens* 85.

66. Frank Kermode describes the Canon Aspirin as an "expert in sedation"; Harold Bloom sees him as an aspirer, "an apocalyptic cure for our headache of unreality." The matter is discussed in Bloom, *Wallace Stevens* 204–5.

67. Charles Berger, *Forms of Farewell: The Late Poetry of Wallace Stevens* (Madison: University of Wisconsin Press, 1985) 9.

68. *Opus Posthumous* 218.

69. *Opus Posthumous* 117–18. A slightly different version of the poem appears in Wallace Stevens, *The Palm at the End of the Mind: Selected Poems and a Play*, ed. Holly Stevens (New York: Knopf, 1971) 398.

70. Bloom, *Wallace Stevens* 351.

71. *The Necessary Angel* 175.

CHAPTER FOUR: MARIANNE MOORE

This chapter is especially indebted to works by Bonnie Costello, Margaret Holley, John Slatin, and Laurence Stapleton, all cited below.

1. Robert Pinsky, "Marianne Moore: Idiom and Idiosyncrasy," *Poetry and the World* (New York: Ecco, 1988) 60.

2. Moore used the words "lucid" and "cryptic" in a comment on a student's manuscript. The comment is quoted in Laurence Stapleton, *Marianne Moore: The Poet's Advance* (Princeton: Princeton University Press, 1978) 225.

3. Margaret Holley, *The Poetry of Marianne Moore: A Study in Voice and Value* (Cambridge: Cambridge University Press, 1987) 1.

4. John Slatin, *The Savage's Romance: The Poetry of Marianne Moore* (University Park: Pennsylvania State University Press, 1986) 4.

5. Elizabeth Bishop, "Efforts of Affection: A Memoir of Marianne Moore," *The Collected Prose*, ed. Robert Giroux (New York: Farrar, Straus & Giroux, 1984) 129.

6. Holley, *Poetry of Marianne Moore* 1, 3.

7. Donald Hall, *Marianne Moore: The Cage and the Animal* (New York: Pegasus, 1970) 16.

8. *The Complete Prose of Marianne Moore*, ed. Patricia C. Willis (New York: Viking, 1986) 652.

9. "W. S. Landor," *The Complete Poems of Marianne Moore* (New York: Macmillan and Viking, 1981) 214; *Complete Prose* 585–86.

10. *Complete Prose* 653.

11. *Complete Prose* 284–85, 292–93, 514, 361, 492, 417, 471, 388, 101.

12. R. P. Blackmur, "The Method of Marianne Moore," *Marianne Moore: A Collection of Critical Essays*, ed. Charles Tomlinson (Englewood Cliffs: Prentice-Hall, 1969) 70; "He 'Digesteth Hard Yron,'" *Complete Poems* 100.

13. For instance, Hall, *Marianne Moore* 99–100.

14. Bishop, "Efforts of Affection" 130; *Complete Prose* 341–42.

15. Holley, *Poetry of Marianne Moore* 79–81.

16. "Interview with Donald Hall," *A Marianne Moore Reader* (New York: Viking, 1961) 253.

17. "Interview with Donald Hall" 273; "To a Giraffe," *Complete Poems* 215.

18. *Complete Prose* 284–85.

19. *Complete Prose* 170.

20. "Armor's Undermining Modesty," *Complete Poems* 151; "England," *Complete Poems* 46; "The Mind is an Enchanting Thing," *Complete Poems* 135.

21. Bonnie Costello, *Marianne Moore: Imaginary Possessions* (Cambridge: Harvard University Press, 1981) 26–28, 34, 133–37; Slatin 5, 94, 108, 163, 172–74.

22. I quote from the "longer version" of "Poetry," which Moore included in the notes to her incomplete *Complete Poems* 266–67. Quotations from Moore's poems are from this edition unless otherwise noted.

23. *Complete Prose* 256; Helen Vendler, "Marianne Moore," *Part of Nature, Part of Us: Modern American Poets* (Cambridge: Harvard University Press, 1980) 61; "Marriage," *Complete Poems* 69; *Complete Prose* 675, 54, 73, 74.

24. *Complete Prose* 420, 371, 504, 356.

25. Pamela White Hadas, *Marianne Moore: Poet of Affection* (Syracuse: Syracuse University Press, 1977) 22–24.

26. Costello, *Marianne Moore* 35.

27. *Complete Prose* 203.

28. *Complete Prose* 606.

29. *Complete Prose* 96.

30. *Complete Prose* 310.

31. H. W. Janson, *History of Art* (Englewood Cliffs and New York: Prentice-Hall and Abrams, 1962) 117.

32. *Complete Prose* 116.

33. *Complete Prose* 208.

34. Hadas, *Marianne Moore* 135.

35. Harold Rosenberg, quoted in Stapleton, *Marianne Moore* 34.

36. Holley, *Poetry of Marianne Moore* 38–39.

37. *Complete Prose* 31.

38. Blackmur, "Method of Marianne Moore" 67.

39. Slatin, *Savage's Romance* 93.

40. Costello, *Marianne Moore* 26.

41. *Complete Prose* 328.

42. Holley, *Poetry of Marianne Moore* 15.

43. *Complete Prose* 176.

44. *Complete Prose* 325; "Foreword," *A Marianne Moore Reader* xv; *Complete Prose* 351.

45. Hadas, *Marianne Moore* 44.

46. *Complete Prose* 265, 398, 266.

47. Costello, *Marianne Moore* 9.

48. Hugh Kenner, "Disliking It," *A Homemade World: The American Modernist Writers* (New York: Morrow, 1975) 92, 117; Charles Tomlinson, "Introduction: Marianne Moore, Her Poetry and Her Critics," *Marianne Moore: A Collection of Critical Essays* 3.

49. *Complete Prose* 383.

50. George W. Nitchie, *Marianne Moore: An Introduction to the Poetry* (New York: Columbia University Press, 1969) 81; Costello 16.

51. *Complete Prose* 325, 367, 396, 398, 397, 435, 398, 422, 396.

52. Vendler, "Marianne Moore" 61.

53. *Complete Prose* 422, 336, 376, 114; "Interview with Donald Hall" 273; *Complete Prose* 554, 153.

54. *Complete Prose* 314.

55. *Complete Prose* 663.

56. "Interview with Donald Hall" 254–55; *Complete Prose* 533.

57. *Complete Prose* 207, 286, 443, 184.

58. Marguerite Young reports Moore's recollection of this fact in "An Afternoon with Miss Moore," *Festschrift for Marianne Moore's Seventy-Seventh Birthday*, ed. M. J. Tambimuttu (London: Frank Case, 1966) 69; Nitchie makes the connection with "Injudicious Gardening" 185n12.

59. *Complete Prose* 249.

60. Quoted by Denis Donoghue, "The Proper Plenitude of Fact," *Marianne Moore: A Collection of Critical Essays* 169.

61. Holley, *Poetry of Marianne Moore* 37, 117–18.

62. "Masks," *Contemporary Verse* 1 (January 1916):6; "A Fool, A Foul Thing, A Distressful Lunatic," *Observations* (New York: Dial Press, 1924) 18.

63. *Complete Prose* 503.

64. *Observations* 16.

65. *Complete Prose* 169.

66. Holley 16.

67. *Complete Prose* 324.

68. *Complete Prose* 362–63, 384.

69. Jean Garrigue, *Marianne Moore* (Minneapolis: University of Minnesota Press, 1965) 32.

70. Both phrases are from the poem "Black Earth" (1918), later called "Melancthon," *Selected Poems* (New York: Macmillan, 1935) 43–45.

71. Hadas, *Marianne Moore* 8.

72. Blackmur, "Method of Marianne Moore" 72.

73. *Complete Prose* 151.

74. Slatin, *Savage's Romance* 69–77. "Reinforcements" is in *Observations* 42.

75. Kimon Friar and John Malcolm Brinnin, eds., *Modern Poetry: British and American* (New York: Appleton-Century-Croft, 1951) 523.

76. *Complete Prose* 690.

77. Patricia Willis documents Moore's journey to Mount Rainier and traces the compositional history of "An Octopus" in "The Road to Paradise: First Notes on Marianne Moore's 'An Octopus,'" *Twentieth Century Literature* 30 (1984): 242–66. Slatin discusses the poem and its postlapsarian and "Americanist" dimensions at length, 156–75. Holley, *Poetry of Marianne Moore* 56–58 and 64–67, and Costello, *Marianne Moore* 81–95 also provide helpful commentary.

78. *Complete Prose* 215.

79. Donoghue, "Proper Plenitude of Fact" 165.

80. *Complete Prose* 324.

81. *Complete Prose* 595.

82. Costello, *Marianne Moore* 144.

83. Holley, *Poetry of Marianne Moore* x.

84. *Complete Prose* 553, 209.

85. Holley, *Poetry of Marianne Moore* 121.

CHAPTER FIVE: ELIZABETH BISHOP

This chapter is especially indebted to works by David Kalstone, Thomas J. Travisano, David Bromwich, Anne Stevenson, Lynn Keller, Helen McNeil, John Unterecker, and Bonnie Costello, cited below.

1. David Kalstone, *Becoming a Poet: Elizabeth Bishop with Marianne Moore and Robert Lowell*, ed. Robert Hemenway (New York: Farrar, Straus & Giroux, 1989) 14, 15, 50.

2. Quoted in Anne Stevenson, "Letters from Elizabeth Bishop," *TLS* 7 Mar. 1980:261–62.

3. Richard Howard, "Comment on 'In the Waiting Room' and Herbert's 'Love Unknown,'" *Elizabeth Bishop and Her Art*, ed. Lloyd Schwartz and Sybil P. Estess (Ann Arbor: University of Michigan Press, 1983) 209; James Merrill, "Afterword," in Kalstone, *Becoming a Poet* 254; Richard Wilbur, "Elizabeth

Bishop," *Elizabeth Bishop and Her Art* 265; Anthony Hecht, "Elizabeth Bishop," *Obbligati: Essays in Criticism* (New York: Atheneum, 1986) 122; Ashley Brown, "An Interview with Elizabeth Bishop," *Elizabeth Bishop and Her Art* 295–96.

4. Stevenson, "Letters from Elizabeth Bishop" 261.

5. Lawrence Buell, *New England Literary Culture: From Revolution through Renaissance* (Cambridge: Cambridge University Press, 1986) 128–29.

6. Quoted in Anne Stevenson, *Elizabeth Bishop* (New York: Twayne, 1966) [21]; Thomas J. Travisano, *Elizabeth Bishop: Her Artistic Development* (Charlottesville: University Press of Virginia, 1988) 56.

7. Elizabeth Bishop, *The Collected Prose*, ed. Robert Giroux (New York: Farrar, Straus & Giroux, 1984) 46.

8. *The Collected Prose* 114.

9. *The Collected Prose* 144.

10. Buell, *New England Literary Culture* 128–34.

11. J. D. McClatchy, "'One Art': Some Notes," *Elizabeth Bishop*, Modern Critical Views, ed. Harold Bloom (New York: Chelsea House, 1985) 153.

12. *The Collected Prose* 273–74.

13. *The Collected Prose* 55.

14. *The Complete Prose of Marianne Moore*, ed. Patricia C. Willis (New York: Viking, 1986) 93.

15. *The Collected Prose* 172, 178–79, 179.

16. Helen McNeil, "Elizabeth Bishop," *Voices & Visions: The Poet in America*, ed. Helen Vendler (New York: Random House, 1987) 400.

17. David Bromwich, "Elizabeth Bishop's Dream-Houses," *Elizabeth Bishop*, ed. Bloom 170.

18. John Unterecker, "Elizabeth Bishop," *American Writers: A Collection of Literary Biographies*, ed. Leonard Unger, Supplement I, Part I (New York: Scribner's, 1979) 87; Robert Dale Parker, *The Unbeliever: The Poetry of Elizabeth Bishop* (Urbana: University of Illinois Press, 1988) 29.

19. Quoted in Travisano, *Elizabeth Bishop* 106.

20. In a letter to Stevenson, Bishop writes, "I don't care much for grand, all out efforts [in art]." "Letters from Elizabeth Bishop" 261.

21. All quotations from Bishop's poems are from *The Complete Poems, 1927–1979* (New York: Farrar, Straus & Giroux, 1983).

22. From a letter from Bishop to Elizabeth Spires, quoted in the headnote to Spires, "Elizabeth Bishop," *Poets at Work: The Paris Review Interviews*, ed. George Plimpton (New York: Viking Penguin, 1989) 366; Spires, "Elizabeth Bishop" 371.

23. Elizabeth Bishop, "As We Like It, Miss Moore and Edgar Allan Poe," *Quarterly Review of Literature* 4 (1948):132.

24. From a 1974 interview at the Academy of American Poets, quoted by Robert Giroux in his "Introduction" to *The Collected Prose* xii.

25. Stevenson, *Elizabeth Bishop* 27. The words "idyllic" and "backward" are hers.

26. *The Collected Prose* 10–11.

27. *The Collected Prose* 180.

28. *The Collected Prose* 253, 257, 259, 272.

29. Kalstone, *Becoming a Poet* 73.

30. Stevenson, *Elizabeth Bishop* 34.

31. *The Collected Prose* 14, 30, 31, 21, 19–20, 31–32.

32. Penelope Laurens, "'Old Correspondences': Prosodic Transformations in Elizabeth Bishop," *Elizabeth Bishop and Her Art* 90; Helen Vendler, "Elizabeth Bishop," *The Music of What Happens: Poems, Poets, Critics* (Cambridge: Harvard University Press, 1988) 292.

33. *The Collected Prose* 31.

34. Kalstone, *Becoming a Poet* 3–106; Lynn Keller, "Words Worth a Thousand Postcards: The Bishop/Moore Correspondence," *American Literature* 55 (1983):405–29; Lynn Keller, *Re-Making It New: Contemporary American Poetry and the Modernist Tradition* (Cambridge: Cambridge University Press, 1987) 79–136; Susan Schultz, "A Literary Friendship: Marianne Moore and Elizabeth Bishop," *The Wilson Quarterly* 13 (1989):128–38; Bonnie Costello, "Marianne Moore and Elizabeth Bishop: Friendship and Influence," *Marianne Moore*, ed. Harold Bloom (New York: Chelsea House, 1987) 119–37.

35. Kalstone, *Becoming a Poet* 29.

36. Details of the arrangement of *North & South* and dates of magazine publication are given in Travisano, *Elizabeth Bishop* 17–20.

37. The Roquefort story is in Keller, *Re-Making It New* 114; the phrase "the always-more-successful surrealism of everyday life" is from the so-called Darwin letter, quoted in Stevenson, "Letters from Elizabeth Bishop" 261; the phrase "the formula of the normal as the 'strangest thing there is'" is from Robert Pinsky, "The Idiom of a Self: Elizabeth Bishop and Wordsworth," *Elizabeth Bishop and Her Art* 58. A number of critics comment on Bishop's modified surrealism: for instance, Stevenson, *Elizabeth Bishop* 38, 60; McNeil, "Elizabeth Bishop" 406–7; Travisano, *Elizabeth Bishop* 42–46; Keller, *Re-Making It New* 114–15.

38. McNeil, "Elizabeth Bishop" 400.

39. Merrill, "Afterword" 253.

40. Quoted in Kalstone, *Becoming a Poet* 115.

41. Keller, "Words Worth a Thousand Postcards" 425.

42. McNeil, "Elizabeth Bishop" 425.

43. Bishop also published *The Complete Poems* (1969); it includes a section of new and uncollected work.

44. Kalstone, "Elizabeth Bishop: Questions of Memory, Questions of Travel," *Five Temperaments* (New York: Oxford University Press, 1977) 14; Costello, "The Impersonal and the Interrogative in the Poetry of Elizabeth Bishop," *Elizabeth Bishop and Her Art* 129; Kalstone, *Five Temperaments* 15; the phrase "lack of pressure toward a 'beyond'" is from McNeil, "Elizabeth Bishop" 425.

45. Keller, *Re-Making It New* 135.

46. Spires, "Elizabeth Bishop" 378.

47. *Mid-Century American Poets*, ed. John Ciardi (New York: Twayne, 1950) 267.

48. Quoted in Kalstone, *Becoming a Poet* 213.

49. Alan Williamson, "*A Cold Spring*: The Poet of Feeling," *Elizabeth Bishop and Her Art* 101.

50. Vendler, "Elizabeth Bishop" 295.

51. Frank Bidart, "On Elizabeth Bishop," *Elizabeth Bishop and Her Art* 214.

52. Kalstone, *Becoming a Poet* 222.

53. Kalstone, *Becoming a Poet* 214.

54. Bromwich, "Elizabeth Bishop's Dream-Houses" 169; Kalstone, *Becoming a Poet* 194.

55. Kalstone, *Five Temperaments* 34.

56. Quoted in Keller, "Words Worth a Thousand Postcards" 412.

57. McNeil, "Elizabeth Bishop" 404.

58. *The Collected Prose* 187.

59. Bromwich, "Elizabeth Bishop's Dream-Houses" 173.

INDEX